···· AND HE WILL BE
YET WISER *Proverbs 9:9*

TEACH YOURSELF

TO COOK

By
EVELYNE WHITE
and
JESSIE R. WATSON

THE ENGLISH UNIVERSITIES PRESS
LONDON

First printed in 1938. In 1952 a foreword and a new chapter entitled 'Adventure in Cookery' were added. This commemorative edition includes these two 1952 updates.

This edition first published in UK 2008 by Hodder Education, part of Hachette Livre UK, 338 Euston Road, London NW1 3BH.

This edition first published in US 2008 by The McGraw-Hill Companies, Inc.

The **teach yourself** name is a registered trademark of Hodder Headline.
Copyright © 1938 Evelyne White and Jessie R. Watson

British Library Cataloguing in Publication Data: a catalogue record for this title is available from the British Library.
Library of Congress Catalog Card Number: on file.

Printed in Great Britain for Hodder Education, an Hachette Livre UK Company, 338 Euston Road, London NW1 3BH, by Gutenberg Press Ltd, Malta.

Impression number   10 9 8 7 6 5 4 3 2 1
Year   2012 2011 2010 2009 2008

FOREWORD BY MARGUERITE PATTEN, OBE

Teach Yourself to Cook was first published in 1938: a troubled year in Britain, with the very real possibility of war. Although rationing would soon affect the whole of Britain, at the time of publication there were improvements on the domestic front – new cookers were appearing on the market as well as refrigerators, so many kitchens were being modernized and children were taught cooking at school in domestic science lessons (soon to be renamed home economics). At home, women cooked family meals (in those days men rarely did any home cooking).

Why was *Teach Yourself to Cook* hailed with delight? Because it provided an imaginative and practical range of recipes which encouraged readers to produce new dishes to vary the somewhat restrictive and repetitive meals that were typical in the majority of British homes. Also, many women and young people longed to know more about imaginative cooking to entertain their friends and show off their culinary skills.

A new edition of *Teach Yourself to Cook* was published in 1952. As well as the original material, there were recipes dealing with dried eggs, which had been so valuable during the years of food rationing, plus a section on 'Adventure in Cookery'.

Today, in 2008, this book is a wonderful historical record. There are no exotic foreign recipes. The lists of essential flavourings for successful cooking show just how tastes have changed; they remind us what a huge range of flavouring ingredients plus ready-made sauces are on sale today. Many of the ingredients we use today come from all around the world and need costly transport to bring them to this country. The lengthy list of equipment deemed essential in this book makes one thankful for modern liquidizers (blenders) and food processors that make today's food preparation both speedy and easier.

Though the original book was written 70 years ago its message is still very important today. Choose whatever type of menu you prefer and, if you cannot cook at the present time, it is possible to teach yourself to do so. Follow reliable recipes carefully and you and your family will benefit from delicious home-cooked meals.

I am delighted to write the foreword to this commemorative edition of *Teach Yourself to Cook*. It gives a message for today, as well as an authentic reminder of times past.

Marguerite Patten

FOREWORD

IT is generally accepted that when English cooking is really good it cannot be excelled. A well-made veal-and-ham pie, a tasty steak-and-kidney pudding, succulent roast beef with a light Yorkshire pudding, an apple pie with thick Devonshire cream can all be perfect. Unfortunately, however, the average household cookery is poor when compared with that of France and other continental countries. There are several reasons for this. First, because too little trouble is taken to produce appetising meals, instead, reliance is placed on what is described as good plain cookery, but which actually is certainly plain, but rarely good. Other reasons for our culinary failure are non-understanding of the possibilities of our home-produced vegetables and fruit; a restriction to pepper and salt in the use of seasonings, with the result that dishes lack flavour and interest; and a deadly similarity in the methods of cooking employed. For instance, potatoes dry and broken, or badly mashed, and greens pressed into flavourless masses or in a too-wet condition, are frequently served. There are over one hundred ways in which potatoes alone can be prepared; therefore there is no reason why they should never appear other than as boiled, mashed, roasted or chipped. Good cooking requires both time and effort, and many of our housewives are apparently unable or unwilling to give either to this all-important work.

This book has been planned so that the least culinary-minded housewife can produce food which is well cooked and appetising, and thus obtain such a knowledge of the art of cooking that she is spared much worry, and, may be, her family and herself a good deal of indigestion. The recipes are simple and easy to follow, and lay a sound foundation for more advanced work. Later, there is a chapter entitled " Adventure in Cookery," so that, having mastered the earlier work, the housewife can read this carefully and then try some experiments for herself. It has often been said that variety is the spice of life, and equally true it is that monotony destroys appetite. Consequently, to make home-cooked meals interesting to the family, the cook should endeavour to put something of her own personality into her work and produce results intriguing to herself and enjoyable and exciting to those who partake of them.

v

Throughout this book it will be observed that oven temperatures are given in terms of Regulo numbers. To accommodate those readers who cook by electricity or on gas stoves which do not bear these numbers, we give the equivalent temperatures. Thus:

Type of Food	Gas Mark	Approx. Temperature Centre Oven	Heat of Oven	Approx. Temp. Electric Cooker Oven Therm. Setting
Fruit bottling	¼	240°	Very Slow	250°–275°
Stews	½	265°	or	
Custards, milk puddings, egg dishes	1	290°	Very Cool	
Rich fruit cake	2	310°	Slow or Cool	275°–300°
Slow roasting, shortbread	3	335°	Very Moderate or Cool	300°–350°
Madeira and plain fruit cake, biscuits	4	355°	Moderate	350°–375°
Queen cakes, sponges	5	380°	Moderately Hot or Fairly Hot	400°–425°
Plain buns, plate tarts, short pastry	6	400°		
Quick roasting, scones	7	425°	Hot	450°
Flaky pastry	8	445°	Very Hot	475°
Puff pastry	9	470°		

If a recipe gives a temperature in degrees rather than a gas thermostat number, this chart will act as a quick "ready reckoner".

Remember that there are three heat zones in a gas oven; hottest at the top, hot in the middle, and cooler at the bottom. Thermostat settings refer to the centre of the oven. It is these three heat zones that allow you to cook different foods—even a complete dinner—in a gas oven at the same time without changing the dishes round.

In an electric cooker the heat at the top and bottom of the oven does not differ greatly. This enables you to cook, for example, two batches of scones, small cakes, sponges or plate tarts without having to alter their position.

The middle zone of the oven is coolest.

CONTENTS

Illustrations

I. THE HOUSEWIFE'S WORKSHOP

IF cooking is to be the efficient process it should be, then the kitchen, which is the workshop of the housewife, must be arranged with the care given to any other type of work-place. Every housewife cannot have a new kitchen built, but it is possible that, knowing what will make for ease in cooking, she may adapt some of the ideas enumerated here, and so make her cooking more pleasant, easy and proficient, saving alike her energy and time.

Labour-saving and efficiency are not, however, entirely a matter of equipment. Kitchens differ, and it is well worth the time of every housewife to consider whether her arrangements are such as to make for the saving of movements, and so to arrange the furniture and equipment that it is most convenient and ensures the minimum amount of walking and physical strain.

Before discussing the actual equipping of the kitchen, there are two points to note. First, ventilation must be satisfactory if cooking fumes are not to spread all over the house. When cooking is being done, the window should be open at the top. A ventilator above the kitchen window is also useful for carrying away odours. Secondly, comes lighting. It must be possible to see clearly at table, sink and stove.

Furnishing of the Kitchen

Walls and Ceiling. The best form of decoration is a dado of glazed white tiles, with above a painted surface. Since brightly-coloured paint is not more expensive than dark paint, it is an advantage to use yellow, beige or primrose for the walls, with a paler tint of the same colour for the ceiling. Doors and other woodwork may be finished in a darker glossy paint. Ordinary wallpaper and distemper are not good for kitchen use, therefore if tiles are too expensive, a light-coloured paint should be used for the walls.

Floors. These are best tiled or made of one of the modern composition materials. Wooden floors should be covered with linoleum, which will give the best results if it is sealed down. If polished and not scrubbed, it remains easy to clean and wears well. Brightly-coloured rush mats complete the floor covering.

Curtains. Squared gingham or the gaily-coloured oilcloths now obtainable are suitable.

Sink. Where there is no scullery, as in most modern houses and flats, the sink will be in the kitchen. It should be deep, and made of porcelain, with a draining-board on each side and a plate-rack fixed above one draining board. A cupboard below the sink can be used to store pails and other cleaning equipment. Draining-boards of white porcelain enamel are now obtainable, and are pleasant to look upon and easy to clean.

Cooking-Stove. The cooking-stove is extremely important. Although there are excellent kitchen ranges which combine arrangements for cooking and for heating water, most housewives will need, in addition, an electric or gas cooker. In the country, where electricity or gas is not available, an oil-range can be used satisfactorily. A further note on cooking-stoves is given on page 27.

Kitchen Cabinet. This may be considered another essential of the up-to-date kitchen. In the usual type the top portion is arranged for the storage of dry cooking ingredients, and the lower cupboard for baking utensils. A porcelain-covered table is placed between, and can be drawn out to afford additional space for the preparation of food.

Cupboards. One for the holding of china and glass is necessary, and space in it may be economised if hooks for cups are fixed under the shelves or at the sides of the cupboard. China, etc., not in general use should be placed on the upper shelves. If tea-services, early-morning tea-sets, etc., are grouped together, and after washing invariably returned to these places, much economy of effort is achieved. If brooms, brushes and dust-pans are kept in the kitchen, they should be placed in a narrow cupboard with a shelf above for dusters, cleaning materials, etc.

Shelves. These are essential for holding saucepans, and should be placed above or near the cooking-stove; if covered with linoleum or oilcloth, they can be readily sponged.

Table. The best type of kitchen table is one covered with a porcelain-enamelled top. Where space is extremely limited a combined table-cabinet is a useful piece of equipment. A wooden table should be covered with oilcloth, and triangular pot-stands used for hot pans.

Other Equipment. It is important to have nothing in the kitchen that is not necessary. One or two wooden chairs with rush or wooden seats; a fender, either tiled or of untarnishable metal; a clock; a roller-towel fitting, and a fitment on which tea-towels can be dried complete the furnishing. If the kitchen is also a maid's sitting-room, then there should be a comfortable chair for her use.

Kitchen Equipment

The following lists suggest all that is necessary in materials for cooking and for cleaning processes:

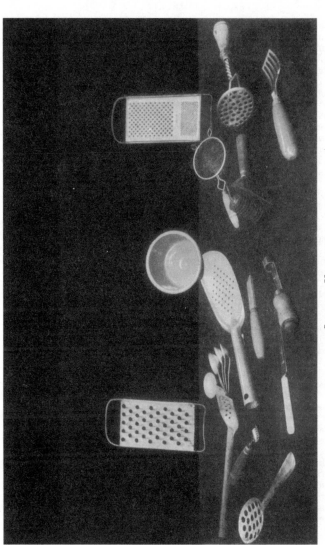

[*To face p.* 10.

COOKING UTENSILS.

VALUABLE ADJUNCTS TO THE STORE CUPBOARD.

I. Cooking Utensils.

Apple Corer.
Baking Board.
Basting Ladle.
Bread Board.
Bread Knife.
Bread Tins (3).
Butter Dish.
Butter Patters.
Cake Tins.
Casseroles (different sizes).
Chopper.
Chopping Board.
Clock.
Colander (aluminium).
Condiment Set (kitchen use).
Cook's Fork.
Cook's Knife.
Cook's Spoon.
Corkscrew.
Cups and Saucers (2).
Dessert Spoon.
Dish-covers (wire or gauze).
Egg Brushes.
Egg Slicer.
Egg Whisk.
Enamel Plates (3).
Fancy Jelly-moulds.
Fireproof Dishes.
Fish Kettle.
Fish Slice.
Flan Tin.
Flour Dredger.
Flour Sifter.
Frying-pans (2 of different sizes and 1 for deep frying).
Funnel.
Girdle.
Grater.
Icing Bag and Tubes.
Jelly Bag.
Jelly Mould.
Jugs (1 set).
Kettles (2).
Kitchen Paper.
Ladle.
Lemon Squeezer.
Measuring Spoons.

Milk Pan (double).
Mincing Machine.
Mixing-bowls (2).
Nutmeg Grater.
Omelet Pan.
Oven Tins.
Pastry Board.
Pastry Brush.
Pastry Cutters (fluted and plain).
Pastry Tins (1 dozen on a sheet).
Perforated Spoon.
Pie Dishes (2 or 3).
Pint Measure.
Plates (6 for cooking).
Potato Knife.
Potato Slicer.
Preserving Pan.
Pudding Basins (1 set).
Ramekin Cases (fireproof).
Rolling-pin.
Salt Canister (enamelled).
Sandwich Tins.
Saucepans (6 aluminium pans of various sizes; 2 lipped pans; 1 small brass pan).
Scales.
Scissors.
Sieves (wire and hair).
Skewers.
Soufflé Dish.
Soup Ladle.
Steamer (3-tier).
Strainers (2; 1 pointed).
Sugar Sifter.
Table Knives (2 or 3).
Tablespoon.
Tart Tins.
Teaspoons.
Tin Opener.
Trays (1 set).
Vegetable Presser (wood).
Vegetable Rack.
Wire Cake-tray.
Wooden Spoons (2 or 3).
Yorkshire-pudding Tin.

II. Food Service Equipment

Dish Papers (oval and round of various sizes).

Greaseproof Paper.
Pie-dish Frills.

III. Cleaning Equipment

(a) Bass Broom.
Carpet Sweeper.
Dish-cloths.
Dish Mop.
Dustpan.
Floor Mop.
House Flannels (3).
Kitchen-aid with rubber handle.
Long-handled Sweeping Broom.
Metal Pan Scrubber.
Pails (2 galvanised).
Plate Brush.

Scrubbing Brushes (2).
Short Soft Banister Brush.
Sink Brush.
Sink Tidy.
Soap Dish.
Vacuum Cleaner.
Washing-up Bowl.
Wash-leather.
Wire Stove-brush.
(b) Glass Cloths (6).
Oven Cloths (2).
Pudding Cloths (2).
Roller Towels (3).
Tea Towels (6).

2. STORAGE OF FOOD

A larder for the storage of perishable foods and a cupboard to hold dry goods are necessary.   A refrigerator is an additional help.

Larder. This room should face north or north-east, and should be cool, light and well ventilated.   The ideal is to have a window on each of two adjoining walls so that a cross-current of air is obtainable.   In summer-time the windows may be open at the bottom, and covered with a screen of very fine muslin so that flies and other insects are excluded.   Walls, ceiling and floor should have smooth, non-absorbent, easily cleaned surfaces.   Tiled walls and floor and painted ceiling are admirable.   If this is not possible, then the walls should be painted white, yellow or beige.   Linoleum sealed to the floor is the best substitute for tiles.   There should be one or two tiled shelves or, failing tiles, shelves may be covered with porcelain-enamelled tin or with oil-cloth tacked down firmly and closely to the shelves.

Equipment.

Wide bowls for milk.
Wire gauze meat covers.
Muslin or muslin covers.
Bread pan.
Vegetable rack, preferably of wire.
Refrigerator, if possible.
Notebook to enter requirements.

Care. Absolute cleanliness is essential. It is advisable to wipe the shelves and floors daily with a damp cloth, and periodically they should be washed. Each morning the larder should be examined, so that adequate use can be made of left-overs, and the menu for the day adjusted if necessary.

Hints as to Keeping of Food in Summer. Meat, fish and milk should be kept in a refrigerator, if possible. Cheese will keep moist in summer if wrapped in a piece of muslin that has been wrung out of vinegar, and stored in a shady place. Lettuce and cress left over from a meal should be wrapped in damp muslin. Lettuce which has wilted can be freshened by being placed in cold water to which has been added a little vinegar. Apples, tomatoes and oranges, well separated from each other, should rest on a shelf. Lemons will be kept fresh and juicy if put in a bowl of cold water.

Sauces, stocks and soups should be poured into basins and covered with muslin, and boiled up each day. Stew and meat dishes should be put in clean dishes and covered with muslin, or gauze covers, after being removed from the table.

Jellies and similar dishes set to cool should be covered to keep out the dust.

Larder Economies

(a) Sour milk is good for baking.

(b) Sour cream can be used in making fruit fools.

(c) Small scraps of cheese should be grated and kept in a tightly-corked bottle for use in sauces, etc.

(d) **Eggs.** Yolks not required for immediate use should be put in a basin and covered with a little water; this will stop them from hardening. Whites should be covered with grease-proof paper.

(e) Lemons, if cut, should be placed on a plate and covered with a tumbler.

(f) **Suet.** Sprinkle chopped suet with flour and cover with muslin, and it will keep for several days.

Refrigerator. This enables the housekeeper to keep perishable foodstuffs in perfect condition, and allows of salads and cold foods to be served quite cold. Ice-cream is readily made, and ice cubes for the cooling of summer drinks are always obtainable. Moreover, the preparation of sandwiches for picnics can be done the evening before, or at any time when the housewife has some spare time, and put in the refrigerator, and they are in excellent condition when wanted.

When choosing a refrigerator several factors must be considered: (a) the size of the family; (b) the amount of entertaining done; (c) the larder accommodation; (d) whether it is to be run on electricity, gas or oil; (e) the upright shape is generally considered most convenient; (*f*) the door should open and shut easily; (*g*) the refrigerator should be readily and easily cleaned; the best type requires only to be wiped out and dried; (*h*) the lighting should be automatic.

Hints on Using the Refrigerator. (1) Hot foods and soups should not be put into the refrigerator until they are cool. (2) Doors should not be opened unnecessarily. (3) Strongly smelling foods should be kept together and away from milk, etc.

Hints on Keeping Food Fresh in Summer without a Refrigerator

(*a*) **Milk.** Place the bottle or jug of milk in a bowl of cold water in a cool place and cover with muslin the ends of which dip into the water.

To keep milk overnight, scald by bringing it to boiling point.

(*b*) **Butter.** Place on a large plate, and cover with a clean earthenware flower-pot which rests on the plate and is covered with muslin, the ends of which dip into water.

(*c*) **Cream.** Keep in the container in which it is bought and place in a basin of cold water, until it is to be used.

(*d*) **Meat.** Wipe over with vinegar and water and cover with a gauze meat cover.

Note.—In summer the larder should be particularly well ventilated and kept as cool as possible.

3. THE STORE CUPBOARD

A well-aired cupboard should be available for the storage of foodstuffs in constant use. This should be examined daily and cleaned out at frequent intervals.

It adds to the interest of this cupboard if a definite colour scheme is decided upon, and if the inside is painted in accord with the colours of the containers and jars. Ordinary screw-top jars are excellent, or ordinary jam jars can be used and metal lids bought to fit.

Hints.

(1) It is a good plan occasionally to wash and dry jars thoroughly before refilling. If, after washing, they are placed in a warm oven, the drying is completed.

(2) With modern methods for quick delivery and transport there is little point in keeping large stores of any food.

(3) Soap and candles improve with keeping.

(4) Tea, flour, sugar, meal, rice and other dry grains may be bought in comparatively large quantities if desired.

(5) Coffee, spices, coconut, cheese, suet and bread should be bought in small quantities.

(6) Empty biscuit tins, bottles and jars should be collected by the grocer as they are finished with. The modern housewife has little room for storage of such empties.

Stores

The following are common household necessities:

Baking-powder.
Barley (pearl).
Blanc-mange Powders.
Butter.
Castor Sugar.
Chocolate Powder.
Cocoa.
Coffee.
Cornflour.
Currants.
Custard Powder.
Eggs.
Flour.
Granulated Sugar.
Grated Parmesan Cheese.
Gravy Browning.
Haricot Beans.
Jam.
Lard.
Lentils.
Lump Sugar.
Macaroni.
Margarine.
Marmalade.

Mayonnaise.
Meat Cubes or Extract.
Meat Jelly.
Mint (dried for winter use).
Mixed Spices.
Mustard.
Parsley (dried).
Peas (dried or tinned).
Pepper.
Pickles (piccalilli, ketchup, onions and mixed pickles).
Rennet.
Rice.
Sage.
Sago.
Salad Oil.
Salt.
Sardines.
Sauces: Yorkshire Relish, Tomato Ketchup.
Sultanas.
Tapioca.
Tea.
Vinegar.

Additional Items for the Store Cupboard

Almonds, ground and whole.
Anchovy Essence.
Anchovy Fillets.
Angelica.
Aspic Jelly.
Biscuits (sweet, and water or cheese biscuits).
Bottled or Tinned Fruits.
Bottled or Tinned Vegetables.
Candied Peel.
Capers.
Cayenne Pepper.
Celery Salt.

Cherries (glacé).
Chillies.
Coralline Pepper.
Curry Paste.
Curry Powder.
Dried Herbs (sage, bay leaves, mace, pepper-corns, mint, thyme, marjoram).
French Mustard.
Garlic.
Gelatine.
Gherkins.
Ground Ginger.
Horse-radish (dry).
Horse-radish Cream.

Icing Sugar.
Olives.
Onion Salt (most useful).
Paprika.
Parmesan Cheese.

Peppercorns.
Pistachio Nuts.
Powdered Cinnamon.
Tinned Tomatoes and other vegetables.

Essences for Flavouring: Anchovy, Almond, Cinnamon, Clove, Coffee, Lemon, Orange Flower Water, Pineapple, Raspberry, Ratafia, Vanilla, Violet.

Colourings: Carmine, Chocolate, Coffee, Orange, Tomato.

Spices: Allspice, Cinnamon, Cloves, Ground Ginger, Mixed Spices.

4. CHOICE OF FOOD

It is advisable to shop only at reliable stores; the cheapest food is not necessarily the best.

The menu should be studied for the day, so that left-overs may be utilised.

Bills should be sent with all food, and these and the goods should be examined immediately.

Short accounts are best. They should rarely be allowed to run longer than a week.

Nothing perishable should be ordered unless it is definitely required.

Fish

The most important point about fish is that it should be quite fresh. Oily and fresh-water fish should be cooked as soon as possible after purchase.

General points that indicate freshness: Bright, prominent eyes; bright red gills; bright scales; firm flesh with no blue tinge, and a fresh odour. *Signs of staleness:* Sunken, grey-looking eyes, brown or yellow gills, limp, soft flesh, any unpleasant smell.

Points to Look for in Particular Fish:

Mackerel. Underside white and pearl-like in appearance.

Plaice. Spots bright orange red.

Turbot. Thick; underside cream colour.

Salmon. Bright red flesh with bright scales.

Oysters. When these are fresh, the shell will close tightly on the knife when they are being opened. If the shell gapes, the oyster is losing its freshness.

Crabs and Lobsters. Should be heavy and stiff. Any limpness is a sign of staleness.

Meat

General signs of freshness: The flesh is slightly elastic when touched, no moisture being left on the finger; the fat is firm and quite free from blood streaks and kernels. *Signs of staleness:* Flesh wet and sodden.

Beef. Should smell fresh, the flesh be dark red in colour and the fat firm and creamy white. *Inferior beef* is dark in colour, with deep yellow-coloured fat.

Veal is pale pink in colour and should be finely grained, with white fat: the kidney should be well covered with fat. *Stale Veal* shows a bluish tinge in the lean parts and the fat is moist and soft.

Mutton is not so red as beef and the fat is whiter.

Pork. Pale pink flesh, firm, fine-grained; smooth, thin rind. If the flesh is clammy, then the pork is unfit for food. Pork should not be eaten out of season.

Internal Parts. Liver, kidneys, sweet-breads, and tripe must be absolutely fresh.

Hams. To test if a ham is wholesome, stick a knife in it up to the knuckle; if when withdrawn it is pleasant to smell, the ham is good; if a bad smell is noticed, then the ham is tainted.

Bacon. The lean should adhere to the bone, the fat be firm and inclined to pink in colour; and the rind thin.

Poultry

Young Poultry should have legs that are smooth and pliant; the scales should be fine, the feet soft and supple; the comb pliant, the skin white and unwrinkled, the breast plump and white. The breastbone of a fowl for roasting should be soft and the legs smooth; in one for boiling the breastbone will be firm and legs smooth.

Game

A young bird has legs that are smooth and pliable, feet are supple and moist, and the beak is pliable.

Signs of staleness: Sunken eyes and a greenish tint on the skin.

Venison. To test for freshness, run a sharp knife into the joint; if there is no unpleasant smell from the tip when withdrawn, the meat is fresh.

Rabbits and Hares should have soft ears, and smooth, sharp claws.

Vegetables

Stale vegetables are distinctly unwholesome; therefore freshness is extremely important; moreover the flavour is best when vegetables are young.

Carrots, turnips, parsnips, should be firm and crisp and with smooth skins quite free from decay and discoloration.

Shrivelled skins are a sign of staleness. Uniformity in size ensures even cooking.

Cabbages, cauliflowers and other greens should be bright in colour, crisp, and not wilted. Slimy, faded leaves are a sign of staleness. Cabbages should have close-growing leaves; sprouts should be compact, firm and round; cauliflower should have a firm white head and a closely-grown flower.

Beans and peas should be bright in colour, and crisp, with well-filled pods.

Celery, sea-kale, etc., should have crisp firm white stems.

Fruit

Strawberries, raspberries and other soft fruits should be quite dry.

Apples, oranges, grape-fruit, etc., should be heavy.

5. JOINTS FOR COOKING

Beef: *Roasting and Baking:* Ribs, sirloin and topside.

Grilling and Frying: Undercut steak, fillet, rump steak.

Boiling: Aitchbone, silverside, brisket (if salted), thick flank, thin flank, ox tongue.

Stewing and Braising: Shoulder steak, ox tail, skirt, flank, silverside, kidney, top and back ribs.

Salting and Boiling: Round, aitchbone, silverside and brisket.

Entrées: Fillet is the most tender part.

Meat Pies and Puddings: Steak, skirt, thick brisket.

Cheap Cuts for Stock and Soups: Shin, leg, neck, clod, cheek, thin brisket.

Veal: *Roasting and Baking:* Fillet, shoulder and blade bone, loin, breast, heart.

Grilling and Frying: Loin cutlets, and chops from neck or fillet.

Stewing and Braising: Breast, shoulder and blade bone, heart, knuckle (for stock).

Mutton and Lamb: *Roasting and Baking:* Leg, loin, shoulder, breast (if boned, stuffed and rolled), best end of neck.

Grilling and Frying: Fillet of leg, loin chops, best end neck chops.

Boiling: Leg, neck, middle and best ends, head, shoulder.

Stewing and Braising: Neck, breast, leg, head, trotters, shoulder.

Pork: *Roasting and Baking:* Leg, loin, fore end and spare ribs.

Grilling and Frying: Loin chops, liver and fry.

Boiling and Salting: Leg, head and cheek, spring.

Stewing and Boiling: Feet.

Internal Parts: *Kidneys.* Sheep's kidney is best for grilling, frying and braising. Bullock's kidney is stronger and not very tender, therefore it must be soaked for some hours before using, and then cooked very slowly.

Liver. Calves' liver is best and most expensive. Sheep's liver is cheaper. Both can be used for frying, stewing and braising. Bullock's liver is nutritious and cheap, but, since it is coarse in fibre, it requires prolonged cooking.

Hearts. These may be stewed or braised. Stuffed and baked ox heart is an economical dish.

Sweetbreads. These are stewed, fried or braised, and are of special value for entrées and invalid dishes.

Tongue. This is boiled, braised or stewed.

Lambs' Fry and Pigs' Fry. These make cheap economical dishes.

Tripe. This is nourishing and easily digested.

Note.—New Zealand lamb and mutton are good and inexpensive. Legs and shoulders prove economical joints.

6. TIMES REQUIRED FOR COOKING MEAT

Roasting and Baking in the Oven

It is difficult to give any exact rule for the time required for roasting meat, for obviously the type of joint and its thickness must be taken into account. A thin piece of meat will take less time than a thick piece of equal size. If, however, the following approximate times are followed and some allowance is made for the type of joint, the results should be good.

Beef—topside, sirloin and rolled ribs: 15–20 minutes to the lb. and 20 minutes over.

Veal—breast and chump: 25 minutes to the lb. and 25 minutes over.

Mutton—leg, loin and shoulder: 20 minutes to the lb. and 20 minutes over.

Breast, boned and stuffed: 25 minutes to the lb. and 25 minutes over.

Lamb—leg, loin and shoulder: 20 minutes to the lb. and 20 minutes over.

Pork—leg, loin and spare rib: 25 minutes to the lb. and 25 minutes over.

Grilling

Steak—rump or fillet: 5–7 minutes each side, about 15 minutes altogether.

Liver: 7–10 minutes.

Kidneys: 10 minutes.

Beef Sausages: 12 minutes.

Pork Sausages: 15 minutes.

Mutton Chops: 5–7 minutes for each side.

Pork Chops: 15–20 minutes.

Veal Cutlets: 20 minutes.

Bacon: 3 minutes.

Braising

Beef or Veal: 1½–2 hours.

Sweetbreads: ¾ hour.

Boiling

Ham (large): 15 minutes to the lb. and 15 minutes over.

Ham (small): 25 minutes to the lb. and 25 minutes over.

Mutton: 25 minutes to the lb. and 25 minutes over.

Beef: 25 minutes to the lb. and 25 minutes over.

Salt Beef: 30 minutes to the lb. and 30 minutes over.

Tongue: 20 minutes to the lb. and 20 minutes over.

POULTRY AND GAME

Roasting

Chicken: 10 minutes in a quick oven and 35–50 minutes in a reduced heat.

Fowl: 30 minutes in a quick oven and ½–1 hour in a reduced heat according to size.

Game (grouse, partridge, ptarmigan, pheasant, etc.): 30–50 minutes according to size.

Goose: 15 minutes to the lb. and 15 minutes over.

Pigeon: 20–30 minutes.

Rabbit or Hare: 1 hour 15 minutes.

Turkey: 15 minutes to the lb. and 15 minutes over.

Grilling

Pigeon: 20–30 minutes.

Boiling

Fowl: 1–2 hours according to size.

Stewing

Chicken (in casserole): 1 hour.

Pigeons (in casserole): 1 hour 30 minutes to 2 hours.

Rabbit: 30 minutes to 1 hour.

Steaming

Fowl: 2 hours.

FISH

Boiling

Cod, fresh haddock, hake, salmon, turbot:
(*a*) For pieces under 1 lb. in weight, allow 10 minutes.
(*b*) For pieces over 1 lb. in weight, allow 8–10 minutes to the lb. and 8–10 minutes over according to the thickness of the piece.

Frying

Cod and hake steaks: 10–15 minutes depending upon the thickness.
Haddock fillets: 5 minutes.
Herrings: 8 minutes when whole; 5 minutes when boned.
Plaice and sole fillets: 4 minutes.
Sole (whole): 8 minutes in deep fat; 10 minutes in shallow fat.
Smelts: 3 minutes.
Trout: 20 minutes.
Whitebait: 1 minute in deep fat.
Whiting (whole): 5–7 minutes.

Steaming

Steaks or fillets: 15–35 minutes according to the thickness.

Baking

Cuts of cod, hake, halibut, etc.: 30 minutes.

Baking Stuffed Fish

Cod Steaks: 25–30 minutes according to thickness.
Fresh Haddock: 25–30 minutes.
Herrings: 30 minutes.
Sole: 25–30 minutes.

VEGETABLES

Boiling

Artichokes (Globe): 30–40 minutes.
Artichokes: 30 minutes.
Asparagus: 15–20 minutes.
Beetroot: 1½–2 hours.
Broad Beans: 40 minutes.
Brussels Sprouts: 20–30 minutes.
Butter Beans: Soak overnight in boiling water containing bicarbonate of soda (1 teaspoonful to 2 quarts of water). Then cook from 45 minutes to 1 hour.

Cabbage: 20–30 minutes.
Carrots: 30–40 minutes.
Cauliflower: 20–25 minutes.
Celery: 30–45 minutes.
French Beans: 20 minutes.
Green Peas: 15–30 minutes.
Haricot Beans: as for Butter Beans (see page 21).
Leeks : 30 minutes.
Onions: 40–50 minutes.
Parsnips: 30–40 minutes.
Potatoes (new): 25–30 minutes.
      (old): 30–40 minutes.
Salsify: 1 hour.
Sea-kale: 25–30 minutes.
Spinach: 15 minutes.
Turnips and Swedes: 30 minutes.
Turnip Tops: 15–25 minutes.
Vegetable Marrow: 10 minutes.

Baking

Potatoes (in jackets): 1 hour.
Tomatoes (stuffed): 10–15 minutes.

Roasting

Potatoes (with joint): 40–50 minutes.

Braising

Celery: 1½ hours.
Onions (stuffed): 1 hour.

Grilling

Mushrooms: 5 minutes on each side.

7. FOODS IN SEASON

A. Foods Seasonable all the Year Round

Fish: Brill, cod, dory, eels, flounders, haddocks (smoked and fresh), halibut, mackerel, mullet, plaice, prawns, shrimps, soles, turbot, whiting.
Meat: Beef, mutton, veal (best in spring and early summer).
Game and Poultry: Capons, chickens, fowls, pigeons.
Vegetables: Beetroot, cabbage, carrots, cucumbers, leeks, mushrooms, onions, potatoes, shallots, tomatoes (English or imported), turnips.
Fruit: Apples, bananas, grapefruit, grapes, lemons, oranges, pineapples.
Note.—These foods are not mentioned in the monthly lists that follow.

B. Seasonal Foods

(Names of foods are printed in italics when they appear for the
first time.)

Fish

January: Bloaters, dabs, herrings, skate, smelts, sprats,
whitebait.

Also Oysters, scallops.

February: Bloaters, dabs, herrings, *salmon*, skate, smelts,
sprats, whitebait.

Also Oysters, scallops.

March: Bloaters, dabs, salmon, skate, smelts, whitebait.

Also Oysters, scallops.

April: Bloaters, dabs, *hake*, salmon, skate, smelts, *trout*,
whitebait.

Also Oysters, scallops.

May: Hake, salmon, trout, whitebait.

Also *Crabs, lobster.*

June: Hake, salmon, trout, whitebait.

Also Crabs, lobster.

July: Hake, *herrings*, salmon, trout, whitebait.

Also Crabs, lobster.

August: Hake, herrings, salmon, trout.

Also Crabs, lobster.

September: *Bloaters*, *dabs*, herrings, salmon, trout.

Also Crabs, lobster, *mussels, oysters.*

October: Bloaters, dabs, herrings, *skate, smelts, sprats, whitebait.*

Also Oysters, *scallops.*

November: Bloaters, dabs, herrings, skate, smelts, sprats,
whitebait.

Also Oysters, scallops.

December: Bloaters, dabs, herrings, skate, smelts, sprats,
whitebait.

Also Oysters, scallops.

Meat

January: Pork.	**July:** Lamb.
February: Pork.	**August:** —
March: Pork.	**September:** *Pork.*
April: *Lamb*, pork.	**October:** Pork.
May: Lamb.	**November:** Pork.
June: Lamb.	**December:** Pork.

Game and Poultry

January: Ducks, geese, *guinea-fowl*, hares, partridges,
pheasants, plovers, quails, rabbits, snipe, teal, turkeys,
widgeon, wild duck, woodcock.

February: Guinea-fowl, hares, plovers, quails, rabbits, snipe,
teal, widgeon, wild duck, woodcock.

March: *Ducklings*, guinea-fowl, plovers, rabbits, snipe, wood-cock.

April: Ducklings, *quails*.

May: Ducklings, *goslings*, quails.

June: *Ducks*, goslings, quails.

July: Ducks, goslings, quails.

August: *Blackcock, ducks, geese, grouse, hares, plovers, ptarmigan, snipe, teal, turkey poults, venison, widgeon, wild duck, woodcock.*

September: Blackcock, ducks, geese, grouse, hares, *partridges*, plovers, ptarmigan, *rabbits*, snipe, teal, turkey poults, *turkeys*, venison, widgeon, wild duck, woodcock.

October: Blackcock, ducks, geese, grouse, hares, partridges, *pheasants*, plovers, ptarmigan, rabbits, snipe, teal, turkeys, venison, widgeon, wild duck, woodcock.

November: Blackcock, ducks, geese, grouse, hares, partridges, pheasants, plovers, ptarmigan, rabbits, snipe, teal, turkeys, venison, widgeon, wild duck, woodcock.

December: Ducks, geese, grouse, hares, partridges, pheasants, plovers, ptarmigan, rabbits, snipe, teal, turkeys, widgeon, wild duck, woodcock.

Vegetables

January: *Broccoli*, Brussels sprouts, celery, *cress*, curly kale, endive, Jerusalem artichokes, parsnips, red cabbage, salsify, savoys, sea-kale, Spanish onions, swedes, *turnip tops*.

February: Broccoli, Brussels sprouts, celery, cress, curly kale, endive, Jerusalem artichokes, parsnips, salsify, savoys, sea-kale, Spanish onions, swedes, turnip tops.

March: Broccoli, *cauliflower*, cress, curly kale, endive, Jerusalem artichokes, *new Jersey potatoes*, parsnips, *radishes*, salsify, savoys, sea-kale, Spanish onions, swedes, turnip tops.

April: Broccoli, cress, curly kale, *dwarf beans*, Jerusalem artichokes, new potatoes, parsnips, radishes, sea-kale, *spinach*, swedes, turnip tops.

May: *Asparagus, cauliflower*, cress, dwarf beans, horse-radish, Jerusalem artichokes, *new carrots*, curly kale, *lettuce*, new potatoes, *new turnips*, parsnips, *peas*, radishes, sea-kale, spinach, *spring onions, tomatoes* (English).

June: Asparagus, cauliflower, cress, dwarf beans, horse-radish, lettuce, new potatoes, peas, radishes, sea-kale, spinach, spring onions, tomatoes.

July: Asparagus, *broad beans*, cauliflower, cress, dwarf beans, endive, horse-radish, leeks, lettuce, new potatoes, peas, radishes, *runner beans*, spinach, spring onions, tomatoes, *vegetable marrow*.

August: Broad beans, cauliflower, cress, dwarf beans, *globe artichokes*, lettuce, new potatoes, peas, radishes, runner beans, spring onions, spinach, tomatoes, vegetable marrow.

September: *Brussels sprouts*, cauliflower, *celery*, cress, dwarf beans, globe artichokes, *Jerusalem artichokes*, lettuce, *parsnips*, peas, radishes, *red cabbage*, runner beans, spinach, spring onions, *swedes*, tomatoes, vegetable marrow.

October: Brussels sprouts, cauliflower, celery, cress, dwarf beans, Jerusalem artichokes, globe artichokes, *horse-radish*, lettuce, parsnips, peas, radishes, red cabbage, runner beans, *salsify*, spinach, swedes, tomatoes, vegetable marrow.

November: Brussels sprouts, cauliflower, celery, cress, dwarf beans, endive, horse-radish, lettuce, Jerusalem artichokes, parsnips, red cabbage, runner beans, salsify, *savoys*, Spanish onions, spinach, swedes, tomatoes, vegetable marrow.

December: Brussels sprouts, celeriac, celery, *curly kale*, endive, horse-radish, Jerusalem artichokes, parsnips, red cabbage, salsify, savoys, *sea-kale*, Spanish onions, spinach, swedes, tomatoes.

Fruit

January: Cranberries, pears, rhubarb (forced).
February: Cranberries, pears, rhubarb (forced).
March: Rhubarb (forced).
April: Rhubarb (forced).
May: *Green gooseberries, melons, rhubarb.*
June: *Apricots, cherries,* green gooseberries, melons, *peaches, raspberries,* rhubarb, *strawberries.*
July: Apricots, cherries, *currants,* gooseberries, melons, peaches, *plums,* raspberries, rhubarb, strawberries.
August: Apricots, cherries, currants, gooseberries, *greengages, loganberries,* melons, *mulberries,* peaches, plums, raspberries, rhubarb, strawberries.
September: Apricots, *blackberries, bilberries,* currants, *damsons,* gooseberries, greengages, loganberries, medlars, melons, mulberries, peaches, *pears,* plums, raspberries, rhubarb, *sloes.*
October: Apricots, bilberries, blackberries, *cranberries,* damsons, medlars, melons, peaches, pears, plums, *quinces,* rhubarb, sloes.
November: Apricots, cranberries, medlars, melons, peaches, pears, quinces, sloes.
December: Apricots, cranberries, peaches, pears, *rhubarb* (forced).

8. SELECTION OF MENUS

The Body Requires each Day foods containing protein, fats, carbohydrates, mineral salts and vitamins, and water.

Protein Foods: lean meat, ham, game, poultry, liver, kidney, cheese, fish, eggs, milk, wheaten bread, oatmeal, peas, beans, lentils, nuts.

Fats: butter, cream, cheese, suet, lard, margarine, the fat of meat, olive oil.

Carbohydrates: flour, potatoes, root vegetables, cereals.

Mineral Salts: fruit, vegetables, milk.

Vitamins: These substances have been found essential to the maintenance of health. Detailed discussion of them is, however, unnecessary because they are found in ample proportions in a diet which is well-balanced.

While the actual quantities of the foodstuffs required by the body have been worked out by scientists, it is not practicable for the housewife to attempt any such distribution in her catering. If the diet is balanced and representative of the foods given above, it will be right. Any dietary should be based on an adequate supply of meat, fish, eggs, milk, butter, cheese, green vegetables, salads and fruits. In short, every day's menus should include some of the foods in each of the following five classes:

1. Vegetables, fresh fruits.
2. Meat, fish, cheese, eggs, beans, peas.
3. Fats.
4. Cereals.
5. Sugars, jams, jellies.

Other Points for Consideration in Menu-making:

1. The type of meal and the number to partake of it.

2. The seasons: in cold weather more hot dishes will be included; in hot weather cold dishes and salads.

3. If the housewife is single-handed, it is important to choose a few dishes that can be cooked and served perfectly.

4. It is worth while considering colour, garnish and flavour for the whole meal. No dishes succeeding each other should be alike in appearance, flavour or garnish.

5. Variety in menus is important.

6. Materials should be ordered in good time so that preparations need not be unduly hurried.

9. DISHING-UP AND SERVICE OF FOOD

1. In dishing-up it must be remembered that food should be presented in such a way that it looks appetising.

2. A dish of suitable size should be used; those either too large or too small spoil the appearance of the food.

3. There should be no splashes of gravy on the edges of the dish.

Hors d'œuvres: Oysters, smoked salmon, grapefruit, and melon are as a rule served on individual dishes and placed at each cover. Hors d'œuvres may be offered in a sectional dish, or may be served in individual plates.

Soups: These may be served in individual cups or in soup plates, or may be served from a tureen at table or from a side-table. There should be no trace of fat in a soup.

Fish: (a) Portions of fried fish are garnished and served in plates, and sauces are handed. Fried fish should be well drained before serving. If it is to be served at table, it should be placed on a dish covered with a paper d'oyley, having been first well drained on kitchen paper.

(b) Salmon, turbot, and other boiled fish are served on a dish covered with a folded napkin, and portions are served from it.

(c) Whitebait may be served individually or given out at table.

Meat: These dishes are garnished according to their kind. String and skewers are removed before they are presented at table.

Hot meat must be served on a really hot dish.

Cold Dishes, like pressed beef, ham, pies, etc., should be garnished and made to look as attractive as possible.

Casseroles. Unless glass casseroles are used, a folded napkin should be put round the dish before it is presented at table.

Sweet Dishes. These are served whole or in portions, according to kind. Individual glasses for creams, jellies, fruit salads can be made to look very attractive if, after being daintily garnished, each is placed on a plate covered with a paper d'oyley.

Savouries. These are served on individual plates, and if hot, should be very hot.

10. COOKING STOVES

Whatever the type of cooker—gas, electric or oil—the fullest information about its working is obtainable from the Company supplying it, and demonstrations are arranged for the purchaser or hirer.

Gas-stoves are now obtainable in all-white porcelain enamel with flat surfaces which are easy to clean.

All modern gas-stoves are fitted with a heat-regulating arrangement for the oven. The best known is the Regulo-Automatic Control.

To Use the Regulo. Turn the Regulo head to the number required, turn the oven tap on full and light the gas. Allow 15 minutes heating for Regulo settings up to Mark 7 and 20–25 minutes for higher marks. When the oven is hot, insert the food and close the door. There is no need to alter the gas nor to open the oven door for testing or examination of the food during the cooking. The table below gives the required details:

Food.	Regulo Number.	Time.
Meat	7 or 6	See note A, page 29.
Poultry or Game	7 or 6	See note B, page 29.
Cakes :		
Tea Cakes	6	20–25 mins.
Rock Cakes	6	20 mins.
Sponge Sandwich	5	15–20 mins.
Queen Cakes	5	15–20 mins.
Macaroons	3	25 mins.
Ginger Cake	4	Varies according to size.
Large Cakes, *e.g.* :		
Madeira, 1 lb. size	4	1 hr.
Fruit	4 or 3	1 hr. per lb.
Christmas	1	1 hr. per lb.
Pastry, Rough Puff and Flaky	8	10–15 mins. Use middle shelves, and do not place too near the back of the oven.
Tarts	7 or 6	30–45 mins.
Jam tartlets	7	15–20 mins.
Meat Pies (uncooked meat)	4	About 2 hrs.
(cooked meat) puff or flaky pastry	8	Half an hour.
Short crust (cooked meat)	6	30–40 mins.
Yorkshire Pudding	7	25–45 mins., according to size (on shelf under joint).
Hot Pot (in closed casserole)	4	About 2–3 hrs.
Lancashire Hot Pot (closed dish)	4	About 2–3 hrs.
Baked Custard	1	30–45 mins. or longer, according to method and size.
Milk Puddings, contents of pies, etc.	1	2 hrs. or longer, according to size.
Stews (closed vessel)	¼ or ½	2–4 hrs.

Notes.

A. Meat (English).

For Beef   allow 15 minutes to the lb.

Beef without bone	,,	20	,, ,, ,,
Mutton	,,	20	,, ,, ,,
Veal			
Pork	,,	25	,, ,, ,,
Stuffed meat			

For Joints up to 6 lb. weight allow 15 minutes extra.

For Joints over 10 lb. weight deduct 15–30 minutes from cooking time.

These times serve as a guide, but the shape of the joint and proportion of bone should be taken into consideration, *e.g.*, a thick cut of beef weighing 3 lb. will require as long as a thin cut of beef weighing 4 lb.

Chilled Meat.

Chilled Meat should be properly thawed by the butcher before delivery. If this has not been done and there is not time to leave the joint in a warm place for several hours, then it can be put in the oven with the " Regulo " at Mark 1 for ½ to ¾ hour. Remove the joint and heat the oven at Mark 6 before roasting.

B. Poultry and Game.

The following times will serve as a guide :—

Chicken	. . .	¾ to 1 hour.
Fowl	. . . .	1 to 1½ hours.
Duck	. . . .	1¼ to 2 hours.
Goose or Turkey	. .	1½ to 3 hours (according to size).

Information about the Regulo automatic oven heat control device is given by kind permission of Radiation, Limited.

Pressure Cooking

During the past two or three years Pressure Cookery has become increasingly popular. There is sound reason for this, for in those departments of cookery for which it is most suitable there is considerable saving in time and fuel, and a pleasing preservation of vitamins and flavour.

Pressure cooking is cooking in carefully controlled steam heat, that is, it depends on the sealing-in of the steam which normally escapes from a saucepan. There are several types of these cookers now available, and if the manufacturer's instructions are exactly followed, complete satisfaction is obtained. Indeed, for cooking by boiling, steaming, stewing, and braising, methods of cooking which usually take a long time, the pressure cooker is ideal. Moreover, it forms a most convenient method of bottling fruit and vegetables at home.

Precautions.

(a) Begin cooking by putting the amount of water given in the recipe into the cooker. (b) Then place the food in. (c) Put on the heat indicated in the recipe and follow the instructions precisely until the required pressure is registered. (d) From this moment begin to reckon the cooking time. Accuracy in timing is all-important. There can be no guess-work, for a minute either way will make all the difference between perfectly cooked food and that which is under- or over-cooked. (e) Never leave the cooker when it is on high heat for some other duty, in such cases remove it from the heat. (f) The cooker is not opened until the pressure has been reduced. (g) If several different foods are to be cooked together, then they should require the same cooking times, since none can be removed until all are cooked. (h) When cooking foods of different flavours at the same time, place each in a separate container, or wrap each in greaseproof paper, otherwise the flavours are apt to spread from one to the other. Some pressure cookers are supplied with dividers for this purpose. (i) Vegetables cook most satisfactorily if sliced, diced, or shredded. (j) The time for cooking fish depends on the thickness and size of the fish. (k) Similarly, cooking times for meat vary with size, thickness, and toughness. Meat dishes such as beef stew, haricot mutton, Hungarian goulash, and those prepared in casseroles are best for pressure cooking.

11. HOW TO PREPARE A TWO-COURSE DINNER

(*A*.) *All cooking to be done in the oven.*
Roast Stuffed Breast of Veal.
Baked Potatoes in Jackets.
Brussels Sprouts.   Gravy.
Apple Amber.

Order of Preparations

1. Prepare the veal.   A joint of about 3–4 lb. should take slightly less than 2 hours to cook.
Prepare the stuffing: 4 oz. breadcrumbs, 2 oz. suet, a little parsley, and 1 egg are sufficient for a joint of the size indicated above (see page 65).
Stuff the veal.   Place it in a tin with 2 oz. dripping ready for the oven.
2. Prepare the sprouts and let them soak in water (see page 100).   Afterwards lay them in a pie-dish or casserole.
3. Scrub the potatoes.
4. Prepare the apple amber (see page 140).

5. Place the meat on the second shelf of the oven.

6. Place the potatoes just underneath.

7. Cook all for half an hour.

9. Place the sprouts in the oven and put the apple amber at the bottom.

10. Put the Regulo at No. 6 and leave for the required time.

11. Cover the meat with a tin if it seems to be getting too brown.

Serving

1. Reduce the heat to No. $\frac{1}{4}$ about 15 minutes before the meal is to be served.

2. Take out the meat and place it on a dish and keep it hot.

3. Make the gravy (see page 122).

4. Lift the potatoes on to a dish and lift out the sprouts.

5. Take all the first course to table, together with the required number of hot plates.

6. Keep the apple amber hot in the oven at No. $\frac{1}{4}$. Take hot plates to table with it.

(*B*.) *Cooking to be done partly by boiling and partly in the oven*.

> Brown Stew.
> Boiled Cauliflower with White Sauce.
> Steamed Potatoes.
> Apple Tart.
> Custard Sauce.

Allow $2\frac{1}{2}$ to 3 hours for the cooking of the stew (see page 66).

1. Prepare the meat and start the stew to cook.

2. Pare the potatoes and leave in cold water.

3. Trim the cauliflower and soak in cold water with salt added.

4. Prepare the Apple Tart (see page 140). This can be eaten hot or cold. If to be served hot, cook after the meat has been stewing for 2 hours. Then keep hot with the oven at No. $\frac{1}{4}$.

5. After the meat has had 2 hours, put on water to boil for the vegetables.

6. Put the potatoes in a steamer and steam for half an hour.

7. Now put the cauliflower on to boil in the water over which the potatoes are steaming.

8. Prepare custard sauce (see page 121), cover with a plate and keep hot with the tart.

9. Put the plates to heat.

10. Serve the brown stew, potatoes, cauliflower and sauce. Take in the hot plates to table at the same time.

11. Remove the dishes and serve the apple tart and custard sauce.

12. HOMELY MEASURES

When scales and weights are not available, homely measures may be used. It is advisable, however, since cups are not all of the same size, to try out a tea-cup and breakfast cup which will hold 4 oz. and 7 oz. of dry materials respectively and a quarter pint and half pint of water and then keep these for the purpose.

Liquids

1 teacupful = $\frac{1}{4}$ pint.
1 breakfastcupful = $\frac{1}{2}$ pint.
1 tumblerful = $\frac{1}{2}$ pint.

Note.—For the cups the measure should be taken level with the top of the handle.

Dry Materials

1 tablespoonful = 1 oz.
1 dessertspoonful = $\frac{1}{2}$ oz.
1 teaspoonful = $\frac{1}{4}$ oz.

Note.—In the case of suet, rice, sugar, and similar materials, the measure should be taken level with the rim of the spoon. For flour and similar soft materials the measure should be heaped as high above the rim as the depth of the spoon below it.

1 level teacupful = $\frac{1}{4}$ lb.
1 breakfastcupful = 7 oz.
2 tablespoonfuls breadcrumbs = 1 oz.
1 tablespoonful jam or treacle = 2 oz.
Piece of butter size of small hen egg = $1\frac{1}{4}$ oz.
Piece of butter size of walnut = $\frac{1}{2}$ oz.
6 ordinary-sized lumps of sugar = 1 oz.

13. HOW TO WASH UP

When a table is cleared after a meal the procedure is as follows:

1. All cooked foods are removed from the dishes on which they were served, put on clean plates and placed in the larder, as are all other foodstuffs.

2. Scraps are removed from plates, and grease may be wiped off with newspaper.

3. Milk-jugs, basins and dishes used for the preparation of milky puddings, etc., are filled with cold water as soon as emptied.

4. Dishes are best stacked according to kind before beginning the washing-up.

5. Fill a bowl with boiling water, add soap or soap powder.

6. Wash silver first.

7. Wash china next, leaving the dirtiest and greasiest to the last.

8. Rinse china and put in a cup-and-plate-rack to dry. Rinsing must be thorough if a rack is used for drying, and the china should be rubbed with a dry cloth before being used.

9. Washing utensils used in cooking are dealt with next. (Water should be changed when dirty.)

10. Pans are washed last.

11. Pie-dishes when burnt should be rubbed with a mild powder.

Glass. Wash this in warm soap suds, rinse in cold water and dry with a linen glass-cloth kept for the purpose. A few drops of ammonia in the rinsing water helps to brighten the glass.

Saucepans. Fill these with cold water after use. Never use soda in the cleaning of aluminium. Dry all saucepans thoroughly before putting them on the shelf.

Omelet Pans, Cake- and Bread-Tins and Patty-Tins. If these must be washed instead of being wiped out with a cloth while hot, they should be placed before the fire to finish drying.

Sieves. These should be brushed clean as soon as possible after use, rinsed and dried.

Mincing Machine. This must be taken to pieces after use, the scraps of meat being removed, and then washed in hot water, rinsed and dried first with a cloth and then before the fire.

Stew-Pans and Kettles. When new, before using these fill them with cold water and bring it to the boil. Then empty, wash, rinse and dry.

Note: (a) Dish-cloths should be made of open material which does not readily retain grease. The use of a mop is a pleasant way of washing dishes.

(b) Mops and dish-cloths should be washed out in soapy water after the washing-up is completed.

(c) Towels should be washed out after the heaviest meal of the day.

(d) Sink basket and sink bowl must be kept clean, otherwise they quickly become unpleasant to use.

(e) The sink should be scrubbed out with hot water, soda and soap, at least once a day.

B

RECIPES

14. STOCKS AND SOUPS

Soup-Making

The chief art in making good stock for soups lies in blending the flavours so that nothing predominates. There are five kinds of soups:

1. Broths.
2. Thickened Soups.
3. Purées.
4. Clear Soups.
5. Fish Soups or Bisques.

Broths

Broths are made from unclarified stock and flavoured with vegetables cut up very small. The best known are Scotch Broth and Sheep's Head Broth.

Thickened Soups

These include all soups in which thickening is added—*e.g.*, Onion Soup, Kidney Soup, Fish Soup and many others.

The thickening is usually some farinaceous foodstuff, such as flour, cornflour, sago, or eggs, and cream.

The usual proportion is 2 oz. of thickening to 2 pints of liquid.

Purées

These soups are thickened by boiling until very soft and then sieving. If starchy vegetables—*e.g.*, potatoes—are used, the proportion is 1 lb. vegetables to 2 pints liquid. If watery vegetables—*e.g.*, tomato, cabbage, and onions—allow 2 lb. vegetables to 2 pints liquid. If dried vegetables—*e.g.*, peas, beans, lentils—allow ½ lb. vegetables to 4 pints liquid.

Clear Soup

This may be either very light brown or very dark brown in colour. The clear stock is purified by using egg-whites and shells. To 2 pints of stock use the whites and shells of three eggs. The addition of various garnishes gives the soup its name.

Fish Soups

These soups are very suitable for invalids, and are also served during Lent.

Note.—For making soups choose a strong pan with a tight-fitting lid.

Making of Stocks

1. Stock is used as a basis for soups, stews, gravies, etc.
2. The meat used in its preparation can either be fresh or cooked.
3. Bones are chopped up very finely.
4. Trimmings of vegetables may be added.
5. Left-over cooked meat, bacon rind, and gristle may be used.
6. Eggshells help to clear the soup.

Some of the Things which are Unsuitable:

1. Cooked vegetables.
2. Any food left on individual plates.
3. Food that has been in a sickroom.
4. Food left over which contains milk or cream.
5. Fat or marrow.

To Keep Stock Fresh:

1. Keep it in a strong earthenware jar.
2. Always have a layer of fat on top, until the stock is to be used, when it must be removed.
3. Boil up stock each day.
4. When not in use keep in a cool place.
5. Never leave the stock in the stock-pot over-night.

Bone Stock

1. Choose a very strong iron pan with a tight-fitting lid.
2. Aim at extracting all the nourishment from the bones.
3. Fresh bones or cooked bones may be used, or even a mixture of both.
4. Second stock may be made by re-boiling the bones.
5. Break the bones into small pieces and wash well.
6. Place in a pan of cold water and add a little salt.
7. Bring slowly to the boil, skim, and simmer very slowly for about 8 hours.
8. Flavourings of vegetables may be added, but omit cauliflower, as it sours very quickly.
9. Strain well and use as required.
10. If to be kept for several days, the stock must be boiled up each day.

BROWN STOCK

Ingredients

1½ lb. hough or shin of beef.	1 stick of celery.	1 onion.
4 pennyworth of bones.	1 or 2 carrots.	Seasoning.
Small piece of turnip.	6 pints of water.	1 oz. dripping.

Method

1. Wash the bones and divide into small pieces.
2. Remove all fat from meat and cut up small.
3. Prepare the vegetables and cut up into pieces.
4. Melt the dripping and fry the pieces of meat to a nice brown.
5. Place bones and fried meat on to boil in the cold water in the stock-pot.
6. Lightly fry the vegetables.
7. Cook the meat and bones for 2 hours very slowly.
8. Add the vegetables and seasoning and cook for 3 hours longer.
9. Strain and skim off any fat.
10. Leave in a basin till required for use.

CLEAR STOCK

Ingredients

2 *lb. veal.*	2 *lb. shin of beef.*	1 *onion.*
1 *carrot.*	½ *small turnip.*	*Celery (if liked).*
6 *pints of water.*	*Bunch of herbs.*	*Seasoning.*

Method

1. Remove all fat or marrow from the meat and lay aside to be used later.
2. Cut up the meat and chop the bones.
3. Place the cold water in the stock-pot and add the meat and bones. Leave to soak for 1 hour.
4. Add salt and bring slowly to boil.
5. Skim very carefully.
6. Simmer very gently for 3 hours.
7. Add the prepared vegetables and seasonings and boil very gently for 2 hours.
8. Strain through a white cloth or bag and lay aside till required.

FISH STOCK

Ingredients

Fish trimmings and 1 *cod's head.*	1 *onion.*
Shells of fish may be used.	4 *pints of water.*
4 *peppercorns.* *Salt.*	1 *slice of bread.*

Method

1. Wash and clean all the trimmings.
2. Scrub the shells.
3. Pare and slice the onion.
4. Put trimmings, etc., and sliced onion on to boil in cold water with salt.

5. Cook slowly and add the slice of bread after ½ hour. This absorbs some of the strong, fishy flavour.

6. Cook for 1 hour only.   Do not cook for longer than 1 hour, as the stock becomes very bitter in flavour.

7. Strain.

8. Use for fish soup or for sauces to be served with fish.

HOUSEHOLD STOCK

Ingredients

½ *lb. lentils, beans or peas.*   4 *pints water.*   *Seasoning.*

Method

1. Wash the lentils, beans or peas.
2. Put on to boil with cold water and seasoning.
3. Simmer slowly for 2½ hours.
4. Strain and use as for meat or bone stock.

WHITE STOCK

Ingredients

2 *lb. veal (knuckle is best) or* 1 *lb. lean mutton and* 1 *rabbit.*
6 *pints water.*   1 *onion.*   1 *piece of celery.*
Herbs.   2 *cloves.*   6 *white peppercorns.*

Method

1. Wash the rabbit and cut into joints.
2. Remove meat from bones of veal or mutton and chop the bones.
3. Cook as for clear stock.

BARLEY SOUP

Ingredients

1 *tablespoonful barley.*   1½ *pints stock.*   *Seasoning.*
Small piece of butter.   1 *gill milk.*   1 *egg.*
1 *onion (small).*

Method

1. Scald the barley by putting it into a pointed strainer and pouring through boiling water until it runs clear.
2. Put the stock into the pan and add the scalded barley.
3. Cook for 1 hour.
4. Pare and cut up the onion and add to the soup.
5. Cook gently for ½ hour longer.
6. Strain and add the butter and milk and seasoning.
7. Whisk the egg till very light, and add just before serving.

Note.—Do not flavour this soup too highly if it is to be served to invalids.

(Sufficient for 4 persons.)

CARROT SOUP

Ingredients

2 *carrots (large)*.	1½ *pints stock*.	1 *onion*.
1 *teacupful milk*.	*Seasoning*.	1 *oz. flour*.

Method

1. Wash, scrape, and grate the carrots.
2. Peel and slice the onion.
3. Place prepared carrots and onion on to cook in the stock and cook till tender.
4. Sieve the soup and return to the saucepan.
5. Blend the flour and add the milk.
6. Stir into the soup and stir till boiling.
7. Season and serve with small diced fried bread.

(Sufficient for 4 persons.)

CAULIFLOWER SOUP

Ingredients

1 *cauliflower*.	1½ *pints stock*.	1 *oz. flour*.
1 *oz. butter*.	½ *gill milk*.	*Seasoning*.
1 *tablespoonful chopped parsley*.		

Method

1. Wash the cauliflower and remove the outer leaves. Cut stalk across and soak in cold salted water.
2. Divide into sprigs.
3. Put stock on to boil and add the cauliflower sprigs.
4. Cook gently till tender.
5. Melt the butter in a small pan, add the flour, and cook for 1 minute.
6. Add the milk and stir till boiling.
7. Add this to the soup and stir till well blended.
8. Cook for 20 minutes longer.
9. Add seasoning and chopped parsley, and serve with small diced fried bread.

(Sufficient for 4 persons.)

CELERY SOUP

Ingredients

1 *head of celery*.	2 *pints stock*.	1 *gill milk*.
Seasoning.	1 *oz. flour*.	1 *oz. butter*.
½ *small onion*.	½ *gill cream*.	

Method

1. Melt the butter.
2. Wash and scrub the celery and cut it into lengths.
3. Cook in the melted butter very slowly for about 30 minutes.

4. Add the boiling stock and cook until the celery is soft. Add the chopped onion and cook for 20 minutes longer.

5. Rub through a sieve and return to the pan.

6. Blend the flour and milk and stir into the soup.

7. Season, and just before serving add the cream, and hand small diced fried bread.   (Sufficient for 4 persons.)

FISH SOUP

Ingredients

1½ pints fish stock.	½ pint milk.	1 tablespoonful parsley.
1 small fresh haddock.	Seasoning.	1 tablespoonful flour.
1 onion.		

Method

1. Skin the fish and remove all fish from the bones.   Lay aside.

2. Place the stock in the pan and put on to boil.

3. Prepare the onion and add to stock and cook for ½ hour.

4. Strain off the onion and add the pieces of fish to the stock. Cook for 15 minutes.

5. Blend the flour and milk and stir this into the soup. Simmer for 5 minutes.

6. Add seasoning and chopped parsley.

7. Serve very hot with water biscuits handed separately.
                    (Sufficient for 4 persons.)

GRAVY SOUP

Ingredients

2 pints brown stock.	Seasoning.
1 oz. cornflour.	2 oz. macaroni.

Method

1. Cook the macaroni in boiling salted water till quite tender.

2. Cut into rings.

3. Put stock into the pan and boil slowly.

4. Cook slowly for 15–20 minutes.

5. Blend the cornflour and add.

6. Stir till boiling.

7. A little parsley may be added if liked.

8. Season and serve with small diced fried bread.
                    (Sufficient for 4 persons.)

HARICOT-BEAN SOUP

Ingredients

¼ lb. beans.	½ pint milk.	1 onion (small).
A piece of turnip.	Seasoning.	Chopped parsley.
1½ pints liquid, either stock or water.	1 carrot.	1 tomato.

Method

1. Soak the beans over-night.
2. Boil them gently in the liquid for about ½ hour.
3. Prepare the vegetables and add them to the beans and cook for 2 hours.
4. Rub through a sieve and return all to the pan.
5. Add the milk and seasoning.
6. Add chopped parsley and cook for 5 minutes longer.
7. Serve very hot with toast fingers handed separately.

(Sufficient for 4 persons.)

HOLLANDAISE SOUP

Ingredients

2 *pints of stock.*	6 *potatoes.*	1 *oz. cornflour.*
2 *sticks of celery.*	1 *onion.*	*Seasoning.*
Juice of a lemon.		

Method

1. Put the stock on to heat.
2. Prepare the potatoes, celery and onion, and cut up very fine.
3. Add to the stock and cook for 1¼ hours.
4. Strain and return to the pan.
5. Blend the cornflour and stir it into the soup.
6. Add seasoning and lemon juice.
7. Boil for 5 minutes longer.
8. Serve very hot with small diced fried bread.

(Sufficient for 4 persons.)

KIDNEY SOUP

Ingredients

½ *lb. ox kidney.*	2 *pints stock.*	1 *oz. butter.*
Seasoning.	1 *oz. flour.*	½ *oz. sugar.*

Method

1. Wipe the kidney, cut away all fat and cut it into neat pieces.
2. Heat the sugar in the pan and brown it slowly, and then add the butter.
3. Add the kidney and fry gently for a few minutes.
4. Add a little of the flour and fry all again.
5. Add 1 pint of the stock and stir till boiling. Simmer slowly for 2½ hours.
6. Add the other pint of stock and cook for ½ hour.
7. Blend the remainder of the flour and add.
8. Season well and serve hot.

(Sufficient for 4 persons.)

LAST-MINUTE SOUP

Ingredients

2 *dessertspoonfuls cornflour.*
2 *tablespoonfuls chopped onion.*
2 *dessertspoonfuls chopped parsley.*

2 *pints milk.*
1 *oz. butter.*
Seasoning.

Method

1. Pare and chop the onion.
2. Warm the milk and add the chopped onion.
3. Simmer for 30 minutes.
4. Add the butter.
5. Blend the cornflour and add.
6. Stir till boiling.
7. Season and add the parsley.
8. Serve hot.

(Sufficient for 4 persons.)

LENTIL SOUP

Ingredients

¼ *lb. lentils.*
Seasoning.
1 *tablespoonful chopped parsley.*

1 *oz. dripping.*
A piece of turnip.
1 *onion.*

2 *pints stock.*
3 *potatoes.*
2 *carrots.*

Method

1. Wash the lentils and soak for 12 hours.
2. Melt the dripping.
3. Prepare the vegetables and cut them up into small pieces.
4. Add the vegetables to the melted dripping.
5. Strain the lentils and add them to the dripping.
6. Cook very slowly with the lid on for ½ hour.
7. Add the stock and cook for 2 hours.
8. Rub through a sieve.
9. Return to the pan and add seasoning and chopped parsley.
10. Serve very hot.

(Sufficient for 4 persons.)

MULLIGATAWNY SOUP

Ingredients

1 *oz. bacon.*
½ *carrot.*
2 *pints stock.*
½ *teaspoonful curry paste.*

1 *oz. butter.*
Seasoning.
Juice of ½ lemon.

1 *onion (small).*
1 *tablespoonful flour.*
Boiled rice.
½ *teaspoonful curry powder.*

Method

1. Melt the butter in a pan.
2. Prepare the vegetables and cut them up into small pieces.
3. Add to the melted butter.

4. Cut up the bacon and add.
5. Cook all together for a few minutes.
6. Add curry paste, curry powder and flour and mix well.
7. Add stock and simmer for ½ hour.
8. Strain the soup.
9. Add lemon juice and seasoning.
10. Serve with boiled rice, handed separately.

(Sufficient for 4 persons.)

MUTTON SOUP

Ingredients

1 lb. lean mutton.	1 small carrot.	1 small onion.
Seasoning.	2 pints water.	1½ oz. rice.
A small piece of turnip.		

Method

1. Remove all fat and cut the meat into small pieces.
2. Add some salt to the water in the pan, and then add the pieces of mutton.
3. Soak for 1 hour.
4. Bring slowly to boiling point, skim and simmer slowly.
5. Prepare vegetables and add them tied in muslin.
6. Cook for 3 hours.
7. Remove the vegetables and strain the soup.
8. Return the soup to the pan and add the rice, which has been well washed.
9. Cook for ½ hour.
10. Season and serve.

(Sufficient for 4 persons.)

ONION SOUP

Ingredients

4 Spanish onions.	½ pint milk.	1 oz. dripping.
2 pints stock.	2 oz. flour.	Seasoning.

Method

1. Pare the onions, and cut in thin rings.
2. Melt the dripping and fry the onions in it for a few minutes.   Do not brown.
3. Add the stock and cook all for about 1½ hours.
4. Blend the flour with the milk and stir into the soup.
5. Stir till boiling.
6. Season and serve.

Note.—Chopped parsley may be added if liked.

(Sufficient for 4 persons.)

OX-TAIL SOUP

Ingredients

1 ox-tail.	1 carrot.
2 tablespoonfuls flour.	1 onion.
2 oz. butter.	Seasoning.
½ lb. hough or shin of beef.	A small piece of turnip.
2 cloves and 4 or 5 peppercorns.	2 pints water or stock.

Method

1. Wipe the ox-tail and divide it into joints.
2. Cut the meat into small pieces.
3. Prepare the vegetables and cut up into small dice.
4. Melt the butter and lightly fry the meat in it.
5. Add the sliced onion and fry till a golden brown.
6. Add the other vegetables and then add the stock or water.
7. Cook slowly for 3 hours.
8. Strain the soup.
9. Blend the flour with a little water and stir it into the soup. Stir till boiling.
10. Season well and add a little of the meat cut up very small and a few diced vegetables.
11. Serve the remainder of meat and vegetables separately.

(Sufficient for 4 persons.)

PEA SOUP

Ingredients

¼ lb. peas.	2 pints water.	1 carrot (small).
½ leek.	¼ turnip.	Seasoning.
1 oz. flour.	½ gill milk.	½ oz. dripping.

Method

1. Soak the peas over-night.
2. Prepare and cut up the vegetables.
3. Melt the dripping and add the soaked peas.
4. Fry lightly and add the vegetables. Fry for a few minutes without browning.
5. Add the water and bring to the boil.
6. Simmer slowly for 2½ hours.
7. Rub through a sieve and return to the pan.
8. Blend the flour and milk and stir into the soup.
9. Stir till boiling.
10. Season and serve. (Sufficient for 4 persons.)

POTATO SOUP

Ingredients

6 potatoes.	1 onion.	½ carrot.
Seasoning.	½ oz. flour.	½ oz. dripping.
2 pints good stock.	½ tablespoonful chopped parsley.	

Method

1. Prepare the vegetables and cut them up into small pieces.
2. Melt the dripping and lightly fry the vegetables in it.
3. Add the stock and bring slowly to boiling point.
4. Boil with the lid on for 2 hours.
5. Sieve the soup and return it to the pan.
6. Blend the flour and stir into the soup, and stir all till boiling.
7. Season and add chopped parsley.
8. Serve at once.

Note.—Remains of chicken, turkey or other fowl, if boiled slowly and for several hours in water, and then carefully strained to remove all small bones, make delicious stock for this soup. (Sufficient for 4 persons.)

SCOTCH BROTH

Ingredients

½ lb. neck of mutton.	A piece of turnip.	1 small parsnip.
½ lb. flat ribs of beef.	1½ oz. pearl barley.	1 carrot (small).
½ gill fresh peas.	A piece of celery.	2 pints water.
½ tablespoonful chopped parsley.	½ leek.	Seasoning.

Method

1. Boil the water and then add the meat.
2. Scald the barley and then add it to the soup.
3. Prepare the vegetables and pass the turnip, celery, leek, parsnip and carrot through the mincer.
4. Add the minced vegetables to the boiling soup and cook for 2½ hours.
5. Shell the peas.
6. Add to the soup and cook for ½ hour longer.
7. Add seasoning and chopped parsley.
8. Serve very hot.
9. The meat is served separately with Parsley Sauce (see page 125) and vegetables.
10. Chopped cabbage may be added if liked.

Note.—A mixture of peas, beans, lentils, barley and rice (which can be bought ready mixed) may be used in place of barley: only in this case soak the mixture over-night.

(Sufficient for 4 persons.)

SPRING VEGETABLE SOUP

Ingredients

2 small turnips.	1 bunch carrots.	Seasoning.
½ gill milk or cream.	2 pints stock.	2 oz. barley.
1 bunch spring onions.	1 oz. butter.	

Method

1. Scald the barley and drain off the water.
2. Measure the stock into the pan and add the barley.
3. Put on to boil.
4. Prepare the vegetables and fry lightly in butter.
5. Add to the soup and cook for 2 hours.
6. Sieve and add the seasoning.
7. Just before serving, add the milk or cream.
8. Re-heat and serve at once.

(Sufficient for 4 persons.)

TAPIOCA CREAM

Ingredients

1 *quart white stock.*	*Seasoning.*	2 *egg-yolks.*
2 *oz. fine tapioca.*	½ *gill cream or milk.*	

Method

1. Wash the tapioca and drain off the water.
2. Soak in the stock for ½ hour.
3. Put on to boil and cook slowly for ½ hour.
4. Whisk the egg-yolks lightly and pour the milk or cream over them.
5. Whisk the soup carefully into this and mix well.
6. Return to the pan and add the seasoning.
7. Re-heat, but do not boil.
8. Serve very hot with small diced fried bread.

(Sufficient for 4 persons.)

TOMATO SOUP

Ingredients

1 *lb. fresh tomatoes or a small tin of tomatoes.*

1 *dessertspoonful corn-*	1 *Spanish onion.*	1 *oz. butter.*
flour.	2 *pints water.*	1 *carrot.*
½ *gill cream or milk.*	*A piece of celery.*	*Seasoning.*

Method

1. Pare and slice the onion.
2. Melt the butter and lightly fry the onion in it.
3. Prepare the vegetables and cut them up into small pieces.
4. Lightly fry the vegetables with the onion.
5. Add the water and the tomatoes.
6. Cook for 2 hours.
7. Rub through a hair sieve, and return to the pan, which has been washed to remove all seeds.
8. Blend the cornflour and milk or cream.
9. Season the soup.

10. Just before serving, add blended cornflour and cream and re-heat, but do not boil.

11. Serve at once with small diced fried bread.

(Sufficient for 4 persons.)

15. FISH

PREPARATION OF FISH FOR COOKING

1. Fish is best washed under cold running water.

2. When cleaning haddocks, whiting, cod, etc., a thin black skin is often found adhering to the inside flap of the fish. This is easily removed with salt.

3. Take off the scales with the blunt edge of the knife.

4. For filleting fish use a filleting-knife which has a thin, short, sharp blade.

5. Skin whitings and haddock from the head downwards.

6. Skin plaice and sole from the tail upwards.

7. Lemon juice helps to preserve the white colour in fish.

8. Vinegar also helps to keep the colour good.

9. When cooking salmon leave the scales on the fish, as they make a very effective silver garnish.

10. Fish should be completely gutted, but the roe retained. Well wash the roe in salt and water and replace it in the fish or cook it separately.

11. To egg and crumb fish for frying: Wash the fish and wipe on a clean cloth and sprinkle with flour. Pour a well-beaten egg on to a plate and lay the fish in it. See that both sides are brushed with the egg. On a sheet of kitchen paper have ready about ¼ lb. of crumbs. Lift each piece of fish on to the paper and shake the crumbs all over it. Take out with the fingers and shake lightly to remove all loose crumbs.

Boiling

1. Salt fish are put into cold water; salmon into boiling water; all others into hot water.

2. Water in which fish is boiled should be allowed to simmer, not to boil vigorously; this prevents the fish from breaking.

3. Fish should be removed with a fish slice and well drained.

Steaming

1. This may be done in a steamer or, if a small piece of fish, in a plate covered by another plate over a pan of boiling water. The water should be kept boiling vigorously.

Baking

1. Small fish are best covered with buttered paper to keep them moist.

2. The oven should be moderately hot. (Regulo 5.)

BAKED FISH

Ingredients

Tail piece of cod about 1½ lb.
1½ oz. butter.

½ lemon.
Seasoning.

Method

1. Skin the top side of the fish.
2. Butter a long casserole and lay the fish in it.
3. Place some small pats of butter on the top and sprinkle with lemon-juice and seasoning.
4. Cover with buttered paper.
5. Bake in a moderate oven for ½ hour. (Regulo 5.)
6. Serve with sauce, garnished with cut lemon and parsley, and accompanied by tomatoes and baked onions.

(Sufficient for 4 persons.)

Fish Suitable for Baking

1. Cuts of cod, hake, turbot or halibut.
2. Whole haddocks or whitings.
3. Whole plaice or sole.
4. Herrings or mackerel.
5. Fillets of fish.
6. Kippers.
7. Oysters may be baked in their shells.

BAKED STUFFED FISH

Ingredients

1 large fresh haddock (2 lb.).
1 tablespoonful chopped parsley.
2 oz. bread-crumbs.

2 oz. dripping.
1 oz. suet.
Seasoning.

Method

1. Mix together the bread-crumbs, parsley, suet and seasoning.
2. Clean the fish and dry well.
3. Fill with the prepared stuffing.
4. Sew up to keep firm.
5. Pass the tail through the eye.
6. Melt the dripping, and put in the fish.
7. Cook slowly and baste very frequently.
8. Cook in a moderate oven for ½ hour. (Regulo 5.)
9. Sprinkle with bread raspings before serving.
10. Serve with sauce. (Sufficient for 4 persons.)

Fish Suitable for Stuffing

1. Haddocks or whiting.
2. Sole, plaice or flounders.
3. Herrings or mackerel, whole or boned.
4. Fillets of fish.

BOILED FISH

Ingredients

1½ lb. middle cut of cod.　　　Seasoning.　　　Lemon juice.

Method

1. Wash the fish.
2. Put on water to boil and add salt and lemon juice.
3. Place in the fish and cook slowly for about 30 minutes.
4. To determine if the fish is cooked, push a wooden skewer into it near the bone; if cooked, the bone should separate from the flesh easily.
5. Drain well, garnish with parsley and cut lemon, and serve with a suitable sauce.

(Sufficient for 4 persons.)

Fish for Boiling

1. Haddocks or whitings.
2. Herrings.
3. Cuts of cod, turbot, halibut or hake.
4. Trout.
5. Salmon, whole or in cuts.
6. Salt fish.
7. Red herrings.

DRESSED CRAB

Ingredients

1 crab (medium size).　　　　A little vinegar.
A little melted butter.　　　　1 lettuce.
1 teaspoonful made mustard.　　2 oz. bread-crumbs.
1 teaspoonful chopped parsley.　Seasoning.

Method

1. Wash the crab well and leave it soaking in salt water for about ½ hour.
2. Put on water to boil, sufficient to cover the crab.
3. Place the crab in fast-boiling water and cook, according to size, for about 30–45 minutes.
4. Lay aside till cold.
5. Remove the small claws and break off the large ones. Lay aside the little ones for garnish.
6. Remove the fish from the large claws and keep only the white flesh. Throw away the dark-grey flesh.
7. Remove all fish from the shell and mix with the other fish from the claws.
8. Add bread-crumbs, vinegar, mustard, melted butter and seasoning.
9. Clean the shell and rub it with olive oil.

10. Pile in the mixture and garnish with parsley and small claws.

11. Wash the lettuce and serve the crab on a pile of leaves.

(Sufficient for 4 persons.)

DRESSED LOBSTER

Ingredients

1 *lobster* (*small*).	1 *gill Mayonnaise.*	*Seasoning.*
Juice of 1 *lemon.*	*Lettuce and water-cress.*	

Method

1. Put on a large pan of water to boil.

2. Tie the feelers and place the lobster into fast-boiling water.

3. Boil for about 40 minutes.

4. Lay aside till cold.

5. Remove claws and feelers and remove the flesh.

6. Slit down the underside of the lobster and remove all the flesh.

7. Form into flakes with a fork.

8. Add lemon juice, seasoning and Mayonnaise (see page 228).

9. Wash and scrub the shell and feelers, and rub over with oil to polish.

10. Serve in the shell or on a bed of lettuce leaves and watercress garnished with the legs and lemon butterflies.

(Sufficient for 4 persons.)

FILLETS OF SOLE À LA COLBERT

Ingredients

1 *sole* (*large*).	*Chopped parsley.*	*Fat to fry.*
1 *oz. butter.*	*Lemon juice.*	*Seasoning.*
Cut lemon.	*Egg and bread-crumbs.*	

Method

1. Wash the fish and remove the black skin.

2. Slit down the centre of the fish and raise up the fillets.

3. Do not remove, but trim the fins.

4. Egg and crumb the fillets.

5. Fry in deep fat.

6. Melt the butter and add lemon juice, seasoning and chopped parsley.

7. Pour this mixture into the opening made by raising the fillets.

8. Decorate with chopped parsley and cut lemon.

9. Serve very hot.

(Sufficient for 4 persons.)

SOLE À LA MAÎTRE D'HÔTEL

Ingredients

2 soles.
Salt and pepper.

Maître d'hôtel Butter (see page 123).
Lemon juice.

Method

1. Clean and fillet the soles.
2. Season and sprinkle over some lemon juice.
3. Roll the fillets and place on a buttered tin.
4. Bake in a moderate oven for 15 minutes.　(Regulo 5.)
5. Prepare the sauce and pour it over the fish.
6. Garnish with lemon and parsley.

(Sufficient for 4 persons.)

FINNAN HADDOCK

Ingredients

1 *Finnan Haddock* (1½ *lb.*).　　　　1½ *oz. butter.*

Method

1. Trim the ear parts and cut off the tail and fins.
2. Place on a grill with skin side up.
3. Grill for 6 minutes very slowly.
4. Turn the fish and cover with little pats of butter.
5. Grill for 10 minutes slowly, and baste frequently with the butter which will have melted.
6. Serve at once.　Use parsley as a garnish.

(Sufficient for 4 persons.)

FISH BAKED IN MILK

Ingredients

4 *whitings.*
4 *tablespoonfuls chopped parsley.*

1 *pint milk.*
2 *oz. butter.*

Seasoning.
2 *oz. flour.*

Method

1. Clean each fish and skin it.　Turn the tail round and fix with a small skewer to the head part.
2. Place on a roasting tin and pour the milk round.
3. Season and place a piece of butter on the top.
4. Cook in a moderate oven.　(Regulo 5.)
5. Baste frequently.
6. Time for cooking is about 10–15 minutes.
7. Serve on a hot dish.
8. Thicken the milk with the flour blended in a little cold milk or water.　Add the chopped parsley.
9. Pour sauce over the fish and serve at once.

Note.—Haddock or fillets of fish may be baked in the same manner.　　　　　(Sufficient for 4 persons.)

FRIED FILLETS OF FISH

Ingredients

1 *lb. filleted haddock.*	*Seasoning.*	*Lemon.*
Egg and bread-crumbs.	*Fat to fry.*	*Parsley.*

Method

1. Cut the fish into neat pieces, season, and dip each piece in beaten egg.
2. Roll in bread-crumbs.
3. Put on a bath of fat to heat.
4. When smoking hot the fat is ready for use.
5. Cook the fillets till a nice golden brown.
6. Drain off the fat and wrap in kitchen paper.
7. Serve on a plain paper on a hot dish.
8. Garnish with parsley and lemon.

Note.—If shallow fat is used, dip each piece of fish in flour and fry first on one side, then on the other. Serve as before.

(Sufficient for 4 persons.)

Suitable Fish for Frying

1. Fillets of haddocks, whiting, sole or plaice.
2. Small cod steaks.
3. Red mullet.
4. Trout.
5. Herrings or mackerel.
6. Slices of halibut.
7. Kippers.

FRIED FISH IN BATTER

Ingredients

1 *lb. of fish, filleted.*	*Lemon juice.*
Seasoning.	*Bath of fat.*

Batter

¼ *lb. flour.*	¼ *teaspoonful salt.*	1 *gill milk.*

Method

1. Mix the salt into the flour.
2. Stir in the milk very gradually, and beat steadily till quite smooth. Then lay aside till required.
3. Cut the fish into neat pieces.
4. Season each part and sprinkle on a little lemon juice.
5. Put fat on to heat; when smoking hot it is ready for use.
6. Dip each piece of fish into the prepared batter and fry till it is a nice golden brown.
7. Drain well and serve at once to preserve crispness.
8. Garnish with parsley and cut lemon.

(Sufficient for 4 persons.)

Fish Suitable for Using in Batter

1. Filleted fish of all kinds.
2. Cod steaks or hake steaks.
3. Small flounders or plaice, fried whole.
4. Cod's roe or small roes.

FRIED SOLE OR PLAICE (Whole)

Ingredients

1 *sole or plaice.*	3 oz. *dripping.*	*Seasoning.*
1 *lemon.*	1 *egg.*	*Bread-crumbs.*

Method

1. Wash the fish and remove the head.
2. Clean the fish and skin the dark side.
3. Season well and sprinkle with juice of a lemon.
4. Put on the dripping to melt.
5. Dip the fish in beaten egg.
6. Toss the fish in fine bread-crumbs till well coated.   Shake off any loose bread-crumbs.
7. Place the coated fish in smoking hot fat and cook on first side.
8. Turn the fish and brown the second side, basting the first side occasionally with hot fat.
9. Drain on kitchen paper and serve on a plain d'oyley.
10. Garnish with parsley and cut lemon, and serve at once.
            (Allow 1 small sole for each person.)

Other Fish that may be Cooked Similarly

1. Whole flounders.
2. Haddocks and whitings.

FRIED WHITING (Whole)

Ingredients

Whitings.	*Seasoning.*	1 *lemon.*
Parsley.	*Egg and bread-crumbs.*	*Fat to fry.*

Method

1. Clean the fish well.   Leave on the head, but remove the eyes.
2. Skin the fish on both sides.
3. Turn the fish round and put the tail through the head.
4. Put on a deep frying-pan with fat to get smoking hot.
5. Dip each fish in beaten egg.
6. Toss in bread-crumbs and shake off any loose crumbs.
7. Fry in smoking hot fat till a golden brown.
8. Drain well and serve at once on a hot dish.
9. Garnish with parsley and lemon.
                  (Allow 1 small fish for each person.)

GRILLED HERRINGS OR MACKEREL

Ingredients

1 lb. of herrings or mackerel (not too large).   *Parsley.*
1 oz. butter.   *Seasoning.*

Method

1. Clean the herrings or mackerel and remove the heads.
2. Scrape off the scales and make a cut or two on each side of the fish to allow fat to run out.
3. Season the fish well, add a little butter and then place on a tin.
4. Place under a hot grill and cook till brown on the first side.
5. Turn and cook the second side.
6. Decorate with parsley and serve very hot and crisp.

Note.—Herrings may be served with lemon, tomato sauce or mustard sauce as desired. Fried small roes and fried parsley also may be served with them. Mackerel may be served in a similar manner.   (Sufficient for 4 persons.)

GRILLED WHITE FISH

Ingredients

4 *cod Steaks.*   1 *lemon.*   *Seasoning.*   *Dripping.*

Method

1. Wash the steaks and dry on a clean towel.
2. Sprinkle with seasoning and lemon juice.
3. Melt a little dripping and brush over the fish.
4. Place the fish on a tin or enamel plate and cook under a hot grill.
5. When brown on one side, turn and brown the second side.
6. Serve very hot, garnished with parsley and lemon.
7. Any suitable sauce may be served.
     (Sufficient for 4 persons.)

Fish that may be Grilled Similarly

1. Steaks of hake, turbot and small halibut.
2. Herrings.
3. Mackerel.
4. Kippers.

LOBSTER SALAD

Ingredients

1 *tin lobster.*   *A piece of cucumber.*   6 *new potatoes,*
Mayonnaise.   *Small head of celery.*   *lightly boiled.*
1 *lettuce.*   1 *gill fresh peas (cooked).*   *Seasoning.*

Method

1. Wash the lettuce and leave in cold salted water till required.
2. Cut the cucumber, celery and potatoes into very small dice.
3. Remove the fish from the tin and drain well.
4. Using a fork, divide it into pieces.
5. Mix in all the other ingredients and season well.
6. Serve in a glass dish on a bed of lettuce leaves.
7. This dish is best if laid on ice for an hour before serving. Serve with Mayonnaise.

Crab and salmon may be treated similarly.

(Sufficient for 4 persons.)

SOLE AU GRATIN

Ingredients

2 *soles* (*medium*).
4 *oz. bread-crumbs.*
2 *oz. grated cheese.*
2 *oz. butter.*

1   *dessertspoonful chopped parsley.*
A little anchovy essence.

1 *lemon.*
1 *egg.*
Seasoning.

Method

1. Clean the fish and remove the head.
2. Skin it, starting from the tail upwards.
3. Raise the fillets on the thickest side, but do not remove.
4. Mix together the bread-crumbs, cheese, essence, parsley and melted butter.
5. Moisten with the beaten egg and season well.
6. Stuff the fish and place it on a buttered dish, and sprinkle over a little grated cheese.
7. Bake in a moderate oven for about 25–30 minutes. (Regulo 5.)
8. Decorate with lemon and parsley and serve at once.

Flounders and plaice may be treated similarly.

(Sufficient for 4 persons.)

SOUSED HERRINGS

Ingredients

1 *lb. herrings.*
1 *teacupful water.*
2 *small pickled onions.*

½ *pint vinegar.*
½ *teaspoonful salt.*

6 *peppercorns.*
Seasoning.

Method

1. Clean the fish and remove the heads.
2. Fillet the fish carefully to remove all small bones.
3. Slice the onions and place a slice on each fillet.
4. Sprinkle on some seasoning and roll up each fillet.
5. Place in an earthenware pie-dish and add the peppercorns and the remainder of the onions.

6. Mix the vinegar and water and pour over the fish.

7. Bake in a moderate oven for ½ hour.   (Regulo 5.)

Note.—Sour cream may be used instead of vinegar and water.   This is most common in the North.   The fish can be eaten either hot or cold.   (Sufficient for 4 persons.)

STEAMED FISH

Ingredients

Fillets of haddock.	*Lemon juice.*
Seasoning.	1 *oz. butter.*

Method

1. Wash and dry the fish.

2. Season and sprinkle with lemon juice.

3. Roll up the fillets and fasten each with a spent-match skewer.

4. Place on a buttered plate and put a piece of butter on top of each fillet.

5. Cover with another plate and steam over a pan of boiling water for 35 minutes.

6. Serve at once.

(Allow 1 fillet for each person.)

Other Fish Suitable for Steaming

1. Small cod steaks.

2. Small hake or turbot steaks.

3. Salmon.

4. Halibut steak, cut thin.

5. Brill.

6. Fillets of sole, plaice or flounder.

STEWED FISH

Ingredients

1 *or* 2 *cod steaks.*	1 *oz. butter.*
1 *teaspoonful chopped parsley.*	1 *oz. flour.*
½ *pint milk.*	*Seasoning.*

Method

1. Wash the fish well.

2. Sprinkle with seasoning.

3. Place in a pan and pour on the milk.

4. Simmer very slowly till tender.

5. Lift out the fish and add the butter to the milk.

6. Blend the flour and stir in, and then stir till boiling.

7. Add the chopped parsley.

8. Pour the sauce over the fish and serve at once.

(Sufficient for 4 persons.)

Other Fish Suitable for Stewing

1. Fillets of fish.
2. Small turbot, halibut or hake steaks.
3. Small whole plaice, sole or flounder.

STUFFED FRIED FILLETS OF FISH

Ingredients

4 *fillets of fish.*	1 *oz. bread-crumbs.*	*Bath of fat.*
1 *oz. butter.*	*A few small roes.*	*Seasoning.*
Egg and bread-crumbs.		

Method

1. Dry the fillets and sprinkle with seasoning.
2. Chop the roe and add it to the 1 oz. of bread-crumbs.
3. Melt the butter and add, and sprinkle in a little seasoning.
4. Spread a little of the mixture on each fillet, and roll up and fasten with a small skewer.
5. Dip each rolled fillet in beaten egg and toss in bread-crumbs.
6. When the bath of fat is smoking hot, put in the fillets to fry.
7. Cook till a golden brown.
8. Drain well, decorate with lemon and parsley and serve at once.

(Sufficient for 4 persons.)

STUFFED HERRINGS

Ingredients

4 *herrings.*	*Seasoning.*
4 *small roes.*	1 *oz. dripping.*

Method

1. Wash the fish and remove heads and scales.
2. Take out the bones.
3. Spread a roe on each fish, add a little seasoning and roll up.
4. Melt the dripping in a tin and place the fish in it.
5. Cook in a moderate oven for 30 minutes. (Regulo 5.) Baste occasionally.
6. It is not a good plan to fry these herrings in deep fat, as they have such a strong flavour that it is difficult to clear the fat again.

(Sufficient for 4 persons.)

FISH LEFT-OVERS

FISH AND SPAGHETTI ROLLS

Ingredients

¼ *lb. cooked spaghetti.*	½ *lb. cooked fish.*	*Seasoning*
A little sauce.	1 *oz. butter.*	1 *egg.*
Some Potato Pastry (see page 229).		

Method

  1. Flake the fish, and make sure there are no bones left in it.

  2. Add spaghetti and seasoning and stir in a little sauce.

  3. Roll out the pastry and spread on the fish mixture.

  4. Place a few pats of butter on top and roll up firmly.

  5. Place on a buttered tin, brush with beaten egg, and bake till a nice brown.   (Regulo 6.)

  6. Serve with tomato sauce or other suitable sauce.

(Sufficient for 4 persons.)

FISH CAKES

Ingredients

½ lb. cooked fish, free from skin and bone.   5 oz. potatoes.
Egg and bread-crumbs for coating.   1 egg.
Bath of fat for frying.   Seasoning.

Method

  1. Flake the fish and sieve the potatoes.

  2. Mix both together and add seasonings.

  3. Bind with some beaten egg.

  4. Form into round or oval cakes and leave on a board to firm up.

  5. Re-shape.

  6. Dip each cake in beaten egg.

  7. Toss in bread-crumbs, shaking off the loose crumbs.

  8. When the fat is smoking hot, fry the cakes till a golden brown.

  9. Drain on a paper.   Garnish with parsley.

  10. Serve at once to preserve crispness.

Note.—Tinned salmon well drained can be used for Fish Cakes.   (Sufficient for 12 cakes.)

FISH PIE

Ingredients

  1 lb. cooked fish.   Seasoning.
  1 pint White Sauce (see page 127).   Bread raspings.

Method

  1. Flake the fish and remove any skin or bones.

  2. Prepare the sauce and season well.

  3. Add the flaked fish and pour all into a buttered pie-dish.

  4. Sprinkle the top with bread raspings and re-heat in the oven.   (Regulo 7.)

  5. A little cheese may also be grated on the top if liked.

(Sufficient for 4 persons.)

FISH PUDDING

Ingredients

1 *lb. cooked fish.*
Grated cheese.
6 *oz. bread-crumbs.*

½ *pint White or Parsley*
Sauce (see pages 127
and 125).

1 *oz. butter.*
Seasoning.

Method

1. Flake the fish as for Fish Pie (see page 57).
2. Butter a pie-dish and put in a layer of fish.
3. Sprinkle with seasoning.
4. Pour over a little sauce and then put in a layer of bread-crumbs.
5. Now put in further layers of fish, sauce and bread-crumbs. Continue till all is used up.
6. Grate a little cheese on top and add a few pats of butter.
7. Re-heat in the oven, but do not over-cook. (Regulo 7.)

(Sufficient for 4 persons.)

FISH SCALLOPS

Ingredients

1 *lb. cooked fish.*
1 *small onion.*
Bread raspings.

2 *oz. flour.*
2 *oz. butter.*

1 *pint milk.*
Seasoning.

Method

1. Flake the fish.
2. Simmer the onion in the milk for ½ hour and then remove.
3. Make the sauce with the milk, butter, flour and seasoning.
4. Put the flaked fish in a buttered pie-dish and pour over the sauce.
5. Sprinkle with bread raspings and re-heat in the oven. (Regulo 7.)
6. Serve very hot. (Sufficient for 4 persons.)

FISH SOUFFLÉ

Ingredients

8 *oz. cold salmon or other fish.*
1 *teaspoonful anchovy essence.*
1 *teacupful milk.*

1½ *oz. butter.*
1½ *oz. flour.*

3 *eggs.*
Seasoning.

Method

1. Make a very thick white sauce with the milk, butter and flour. This is called a panada.
2. Add anchovy essence and seasoning.
3. Rub the fish through a sieve and mix with the sauce.
4. Stir in the egg-yolks.
5. Whisk the whites till stiff and fold in.

6. Turn into a buttered-and-papered soufflé tin.
7. Cover with buttered paper.
8. Steam very gently for 1 hour.
9. Do not allow to boil.
10. Serve with Anchovy Sauce (see page 118) or other sauce.

Note.—White fish may be used for the soufflé if desired.

(Sufficient for 4 persons.)

KEDGEREE

Ingredients

¾ lb. flaked fish.	1 egg.	Seasoning.
2 hard-boiled eggs.	2½ oz. rice.	

Method

1. Wash the rice in cold water.
2. Boil it till quite tender, and then pour on to a sieve. Allow cold water to rush through it. Drain it well.
3. Chop one egg.
4. Flake the fish and mix in the chopped egg and boiled rice and seasoning.
5. Bind the mixture with beaten egg.
6. Re-heat in a double saucepan.
7. Pile on a dish.
8. Decorate with the white of the second egg cut in rings and the yolk sieved over the top.
9. Serve hot or cold.

(Sufficient for 4 persons.)

16. MEAT DISHES

Roasting and Baking

1. The oven is heated for 15 minutes, then the meat is put in and the Regulo turned to 6 or 7. (See page 19.)
2. Baste frequently.

Grilling

Light the gas in the grill and turn it on full; when the grill is red-hot, place the meat under it on the grid with a tin below to catch the gravy. Turn the meat every two minutes, and cook till tender, generally from about 8 minutes to ¼ hour. (See page 20.)

Boiling

1. To boil a large piece of meat, put it in boiling water and allow it to boil for 15 minutes, then add a cupful of cold water and allow it to simmer till tender; allow 25 minutes to the pound after the simmering begins.

2. *Salt meat.*—Put this into cold water to extract some of the salt. Allow 30 minutes to the pound from the time it begins to simmer. It should not boil.

3. *Ham, bacon and tongue.*—Soak for several hours in cold water then scrape well before cooking. (See page 20.)

Stewing

This is an economical method of treating meat, because the nourishing juices which are extracted from the meat are served in the gravy. Further, coarser and cheaper joints can be used and little heat is required in cooking.

The meat is put into boiling water, closely covered and allowed to simmer until tender.

Frying

Deep Frying.—A large quantity of fat is used, so that the food is entirely covered with it in cooking. The fat is ready for use when a faint blue smoke rises from it. To test the heat throw a bread-crumb in; if it browns at once the fat is right.

Shallow Frying.—Just sufficient fat is used to prevent the food from burning. Cutlets, chops, steaks, bacon and vegetables are cooked in this way.

Cold-Meat Cookery

Cold-meat dishes require careful seasoning and flavouring to make them attractive. They should be served with thickened sauces. The meat should never be allowed to boil; simmering is quite enough, for it has already been cooked.

Flavourings

Sauces, such as Worcester Sauce, Ketchup, and Chutney, may be added to made-up meat dishes to improve the flavour and give just that added piquancy which makes re-heated foods palatable. They are so often insipid if care is not taken. In their use, however, it is well to remember that all people do not like highly flavoured foods, and in such cases flavouring should be used sparingly.

Mushrooms and tomatoes can be used successfully to give the extra flavour that makes food enjoyable.

Onion.—This is a most useful addition to stews and soups. It is obtainable all the year round.

Celery.—Used to flavour soup and stock. Useful if chopped with cheese in savoury dishes.

Curry.—The addition of curry gives a good flavour if it is liked. A very little can be added, and while giving the dish a distinctive flavour, does not make it too hot.

BAKED OR ROAST MEAT

Ingredients

4 lb. chine of beef.   2 oz. dripping.

Method

1. The meat may be boned and the bones used for stock or simmered for the gravy.
2. Melt the dripping in a roasting tin.
3. Place in the meat and baste with the hot fat.
4. Have the oven very hot and cook rather quickly. (Regulo 7.)
5. Allow 15–20 minutes to the lb. and 20 minutes over.
6. Baste very frequently.
7. When tender, lift out the meat and keep it hot.
8. Strain off the fat into a jar.
9. Pour boiling water or water from boiling potatoes into the tin and stir carefully, gathering all the brown sediment into the water. Season and strain into a sauce-boat and serve with the meat.

BEEF OLIVES

Ingredients

1 lb. steak cut off the round.	1 pint stock. 1 oz. dripping.	1 oz. flour. Seasoning.

Stuffing

¼ lb. bread-crumbs. 1 tablespoonful chopped parsley.	1 oz. finely chopped suet.	1 egg. Seasoning.

Method

1. Prepare the stuffing.
2. Mix all the dry ingredients together and bind with beaten egg.
3. Lay aside on a plate till required.
4. Lay the meat on a board and beat well with a wooden spoon to break the fibres and make the beef tender.
5. Trim off any excess fat and cut into neat pieces about 2½–3 ins. square.
6. Season each part, then spread with stuffing and roll up and tie into shape.
7. Melt the dripping and fry the meat rolls quickly till brown. Lift out.
8. Sprinkle in the flour and stir till well browned.
9. Slowly add the stock and stir till boiling.
10. Place the meat rolls in this mixture and cook for 2–2½ hrs. Remove the string from the rolls and serve on a dish with the sauce poured over. (Sufficient for 4 persons.)

BEEF-STEAK PIE

Ingredients

1 *lb. shoulder steak or skirt of beef.*   1 *oz. flour.*

2 *sheep's kidneys.*   1 *gill water or stock.*

½ *lb. Flaky Pastry* (see page 144).   *Seasoning.*

Method

1. Trim the meat and cut it into neat pieces.
2. Mix some seasoning into the flour and dip each part of meat into seasoned flour.
3. Cut up the kidney and flour it too.
4. Pile in a pie dish and pour in a little water or stock.
5. Lay aside till required.
6. Make the pastry and roll it out on a floured board till it is a size bigger than the pie dish.
7. Cut off a strip of the pastry all round, wet the edge of the pie dish and lay on the strip.
8. Wet the edge of the strip.
9. Roll out the pastry a little and place on top.
10. Make a hole in the centre and fold back the edges.
11. Trim off the outside edge and raise with a knife.
12. Roll out the trimmings and cut into leaves to decorate the pie. Brush over with beaten egg.
13. Cook quickly for 10 minutes and then reduce the heat. Cook for 1½–2 hours. (Regulo 4.)
14. Place a greased paper on the top if it is getting too brown.

(Sufficient for 4 persons.)

BEEF STEW

Ingredients

1 *lb. skirt of beef.*   1 *oz. flour.*   1 *oz. dripping.*

Seasoning.   1 *pint stock.*   1 *onion.*

Method

1. Skin the meat and cut it into neat pieces.
2. Pare and slice the onion.
3. Melt the dripping and fry the onion and pieces of meat till a nice brown.
4. Lift out and keep hot.
5. Add the flour to the dripping and stir till brown.
6. Slowly add the stock and stir till boiling. Season.
7. Place the meat and onion in the boiling stock and cook very slowly for 1½–2 hours.
8. Serve on a hot dish.

(Sufficient for 4 persons.)

BEEF-STEAK PUDDING

Ingredients

¾ *lb. stewing beef.*	½ *pint stock.*	1 *oz. flour.*
½ *lb. Suet Pastry*	2 *sheep's kidneys.*	*Seasoning.*
(see page 135).		

Method

1. Prepare a basin by slightly greasing it.   Grease a paper to cover it and lay aside.

2. Prepare the pastry and turn out on a floured board.

3. Cut off a piece for a lid, and line the greased basin with the part left.

4. Trim the meat and cut up in pieces.

5. Mix the seasoning and the flour, and in it dip each part of meat.

6. Cut up the kidneys and flour the parts.

7. Place all in the lined dish and add a little stock.

8. Roll out the remainder of the pastry to form a lid and put it on.

9. Cover with greased paper and steam in a pan of water for 3 hours.

10. Serve very hot. 　　　　　(Sufficient for 4 persons.)

BLANQUETTE OF VEAL

Ingredients

1 *lb. fillet of veal.*	*Seasoning.*	1 *egg.*
1 *oz. flour.*	1 *gill stock.*	2 *oz. butter.*

Method

1. Season the flour.

2. Cut up the veal and dip each part in the seasoned flour.

3. Fry lightly in the butter, but do not brown.

4. Add the stock and simmer slowly till tender.

5. Thicken with a little blended flour.

6. Just before serving add a well-beaten egg.

7. The sauce must not be allowed to boil after adding the egg.

8. Serve on a dish with the sauce poured over.

　　　　　　　　　　　(Sufficient for 4 persons.)

BOILED HAM

Ingredients

　　　　1 *ham or piece of ham.* 　　　　*Bread raspings.*

Method

1. Soak the ham and scrape it well.

2. Cover with cold water and bring slowly to the boil.

3. If the ham is inclined to be salt, pour off that water and refill the pan with cold water.

4. Cook very slowly and steadily.

5. Large hams take 15 minutes to the lb. and 15 minutes over. For small pieces of about 6 lb. allow 25 minutes to the lb. and 25 minutes over.

6. When cooked, the ham should leave the bone easily and the rind pare off readily.

7. Leave the ham to cool in the water in which it has been boiled.

8. When cool, remove the rind and sprinkle over with bread-raspings.

9. It can either be pressed with a weight on top of a second plate or left in its natural shape.

BOILED MUTTON WITH CAPER SAUCE

Ingredients

1 *leg of mutton.*	*Seasoning.*	1 *carrot.*
½ *pint Caper Sauce* (see page 119).	1 *turnip.* *Water.*	1 *onion.*

Method

Boiling is cooking by immersion in boiling salted water. There must be sufficient boiling water to cover the joint to be cooked.

1. Wipe the meat, and put on a pan of water. Add a little salt.

2. When the water is boiling, place in the meat.

3. Boil quickly for 10 minutes and then reduce the heat.

4. Simmer very slowly till tender.

5. After the meat has cooked for 1 hour, prepare and cut up the vegetables and add. Continue the cooking.

6. A leg weighing about 4 lb. takes about 2 hours to cook. The general time is about 25 minutes to the lb. and 25 minutes over.

7. Serve on a dish, using the vegetables as a garnish.

8. Caper Sauce can be poured over or handed separately.

BOILED SALT BEEF

Ingredients

3 *or* 4 *lb. salt beef.*	1 *carrot.*	1 *turnip.*
1 *lb. brussels sprouts.*	1 *onion.*	

Method

1. Wash the meat in cold water and tie it into a good shape.

2. Put on to boil in cold water, and if very salt pour off the water when it boils and put on in fresh water.

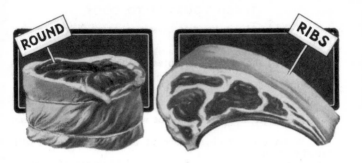

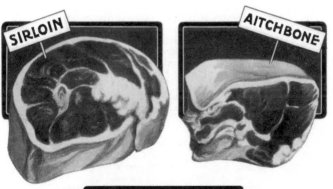

CUTS OF BEEF

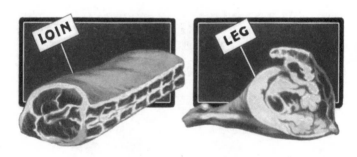

CUTS OF MUTTON

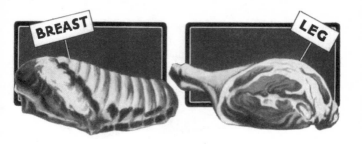
BREAST

LEG

NECK

SHOULDER

LOIN

CUTS OF VEAL

CUTS OF PORK

3. Skim frequently.

4. After an hour put in the prepared carrot, turnip, and onion and cook for 1 hour longer.

5. Pick over the sprouts and soak in cold salt water.

6. Add them to the pan about ½ hour before serving.

7. Allow about 30 minutes to the lb. and 30 minutes over.

8. Lift out the meat and serve on a hot dish, using the vegetables as a garnish and serving with a suitable sauce.

Note.—Suet dumplings may be cooked with the beef and served with it.

BOILED TONGUE

Ingredients

1 *ox tongue, either pickled or fresh.*   *Water to boil.*

Method

1. Soak the tongue for several hours and wash well before cooking.

2. If the tongue is pickled, put it on to boil in cold water. If fresh, put it into boiling water.

3. Time allowed for cooking is usually 20 minutes to the lb. and 20 minutes over.

4. The tip of the tongue can be skewered to the root to make the tongue a good shape when cooked.   Skin, beginning at the tip of the tongue, and trim the root.

5. Reheat if it is to be served hot.

6. If it is to be served whole, glaze it and decorate with aspic and savoury butter.

BONED AND STUFFED SHOULDER OF MUTTON

Ingredients

1 *shoulder of mutton* (can be bought boned).   *Dripping.*

Stuffing

1 *teaspoonful chopped parsley.*	1 *oz. suet.*	1 *lemon,*
2 *oz. bread-crumbs.*	*Seasoning.*	1 *egg.*

Method

1. Either get your butcher to bone the shoulder or do so yourself.

2. Put the bones in the stock-pot.

3. Prepare the stuffing.

4. Mix all the ingredients together and bind with beaten egg.

5. Stuff the shoulder with the mixture and tie with string.

6. Melt the dripping in a tin, and when hot put in the stuffed meat.

7. Baste with hot fat.

C

8. Cook briskly for 10 minutes and then reduce the heat.

9. Cook for about 1½–2 hours, according to size, using Regulo 7, and reduce to Regulo 6 after ½ hour.

10. Untie the string and serve the meat on a hot dish.

11. Strain off the fat and stir 1 tablespoonful of flour into the sediment. Stir over a gentle heat till brown. Add 1 pint of stock. Stir till boiling. Season and pour into a sauce-boat.

BRAIN CUTLETS

Ingredients
Calf's brain.   Egg and bread-crumbs.   Fat to fry.

Method

1. Wash the brain well in salt water.

2. Remove the skin.

3. Put on to boil in cold water, and bring slowly to the boil.

4. Allow to cool.

5. Cut into slices and, if liked, put a piece of macaroni at the end of each slice to form a cutlet bone.

6. Egg and bread-crumb each slice.

7. Fry in smoking hot fat till nicely browned.

8. Serve crisp and hot.   (Sufficient for 4 persons.)

BRAISED MEAT

Ingredients
1 lb. silverside.	1 carrot (small).	1 onion.
½ turnip.	A piece of celery.	Seasoning.
1 oz. dripping.	A little stock.	

Method

1. Prepare the vegetables and cut up small.

2. Wipe the meat and cut into neat strips.

3. Melt the dripping, and in it lightly fry the vegetables.

4. Put them into a casserole.

5. Fry the meat and place on top of the vegetables.

6. Pour in a little seasoned stock and put on the lid.

7. Cook very slowly for 2 hours, using Regulo 2 or 3.

8. Use the vegetables as a garnish when serving.

(Sufficient for 4 persons.)

BROWN STEW

Ingredients
1 lb. shin of beef or stewing steak.	1 oz. dripping.	Water.
	A piece of turnip.	1 onion.
1 carrot.	1 oz. flour.	Seasoning.

Method

1. Trim the meat and cut it into pieces.
2. Melt the dripping and lightly fry the meat. Lift the meat on to a plate.
3. Prepare and cut up the vegetables and fry them.
4. When nicely browned put them beside the meat.
5. Stir in the flour, and continue to stir over a gentle heat till brown. Pour in 1 pint of water or stock and stir till boiling.
6. Add the meat and vegetables. Season the stew.
7. Put on the lid and simmer slowly for 1½–2 hours.
8. Serve, using the vegetables as a garnish.

(Sufficient for 4 persons.)

CURRIED VEAL AND RICE

Ingredients

1 lb. veal.	½ pint stock.	1 oz. flour.
Juice of ½ lemon.	½ apple.	Seasoning.
½ teaspoonful curry paste.	½ oz. butter.	2 oz. rice.
1 oz. coconut or milk from a fresh coconut.		½ onion.

Method

1. Prepare the rice as described on page 227.
2. Keep it steaming slowly in a buttered paper in a pan drawn to the side of the fire.
3. Prepare the veal and cut in neat pieces.
4. Soak the coconut in the stock for ½ hour.
5. Pare and chop the onion.
6. Pare, core and chop the apple.
7. Melt the butter in a pan and lightly fry the apple and onion.
8. Add the curry paste and stir well.
9. Add the flour and mix well with the other ingredients.
10. Strain in the stock and stir till boiling. Season.
11. Add the veal and cook till tender.
12. Add a little milk or cream before serving.
13. Make a border of rice in an entrée dish and serve the curry in the centre.

(Sufficient for 4 persons.)

DRESSED TRIPE

Ingredients

1½ lb. Tripe.	2 onions (finely sliced).
Seasoning.	1½ pints White Sauce (see page 127).

Method

1. Wash the tripe well in cold salt water.
2. Blanch and put on to boil in sufficient cold water to cover the tripe.

3. Bring to the boil, and then scrape well and cut in neat pieces.

4. Fill up the pan again with cold water and place in the tripe.

5. Simmer gently for about 7–8 hours.

6. Skim frequently during the cooking.

7. Prepare the sauce.

8. The onions are simmered in the milk with which the sauce is made.

9. Season well and add the pieces of tripe.

10. Serve using the onion and some parsley sprigs as a garnish.

Note.—Tripe can be bought cooked ready for adding to the sauce. It is usually very good, as it is prepared by experienced tripe-dressers whose premises are generally under strict supervision with regard to cleanliness, etc. The cost is not more expensive, when the cost of the long, slow cooking is taken into consideration. (Sufficient for 4 persons.)

FRICASSÉE OF VEAL

Ingredients

1 *lb. of veal.*	1 *egg.*	*Seasoning.*
1 *oz. butter.*	1 *oz. flour.*	2 *gills milk.*

Method

1. Wipe the meat and cut into pieces.

2. Melt the butter and add the flour.

3. Cook for a few minutes without browning.

4. Slowly add the milk and stir till boiling.

5. Add the pieces of veal and simmer slowly till tender.

6. Season lightly.

7. Whisk up the egg, and just before serving stir it into the sauce.

8. Serve at once. (Sufficient for 4 persons.)

FRIED BACON AND EGGS

Ingredients

4 *slices of bacon.* 4 *eggs.*

Method

1. Trim off the rind and smooth out the bacon.

2. Warm the pan and place in the slices.

3. Prick the fat with a fork so that it will cook easily.

4. When brown, turn and cook the second side.

5. When the bacon is cooked and the fat is nice and crisp, place it on a hot dish to keep warm.

6. Break the eggs separately into a saucer to make sure they are fresh.

7. Pour one at a time into the hot fat.

8. Tilt the pan to the side so that the fat gets well over the egg.

9. Baste with a spoon.

10. When cooked lift on to the top of the bacon and cook the others.

11. Serve very hot.   (Sufficient for 4 persons.)

Note.—When cooking for children, fry some pieces of bread in the fat after the eggs are cooked, as this gives them a quantity of fat in an easily digested form.

FRIED CUTLETS
(Coated)

Ingredients

1 *lb. neck of mutton.*	*Fat to fry.*
2 *oz. batter.*	*Seasoning.*

Method

1. Prepare the chops.   Chop each one near the bone.
2. Trim off the fat and trim the bone.
3. Beat with a wooden spoon and shape well.
4. Coat each in batter.
5. Have the fat very hot, and fry the cutlets till a nice golden brown.
6. Serve very hot, using a few vegetables to be served with it as a garnish.   (Sufficient for 4 persons.)

FRIED CHOPS

Ingredients

4 *loin chops, either mutton or pork.*	1 *oz. flour.*
Fat to fry.	*Seasoning.*

Method

1. Trim the chops and cut off any excess fat.
2. Mix the flour and seasoning.
3. Dip each chop in the flour, coating both sides.
4. Heat the fat and fry the chop on one side till nicely browned.
5. Turn and cook on the second side.
6. Baste the first side while the second side is cooking.
7. Serve very hot.   (Sufficient for 4 persons.)

FRIED LIVER AND BACON

Ingredients

½ *lb. lamb's liver.*	¼ *lb. streaky bacon.*	*Seasoning.*
1 *oz. flour.*	1 *oz. dripping.*	

Method

1. Wash the liver and cut it into slices.
2. Mix the seasoning in the flour and dip each slice of liver in the mixture.
3. Melt the fat and fry the liver till it is a nice brown and very tender.
4. Lift out and keep hot.
5. Fry the bacon and serve as a garnish to the liver.

(Sufficient for 4 persons.)

FRIED OXTAIL

Ingredients

1 *oxtail.*	1 *oz. flour.*	1 *oz. butter.*

Method

1. Chop the tail into joints.
2. Boil slowly in water, with a little salt, added, for 1½–2 hours.
3. Remove pieces and drain well.
4. Melt the butter and fry the pieces of meat till a nice brown.
5. Lift on to a dish and keep hot.
6. Add the flour to the fat in the pan and stir till brown.
7. Gradually add about ½ pint of stock in which the tail was boiled, stir till boiling and pour into a sauce-boat.
8. A little may be poured round the meat if liked.

(Sufficient for 4 persons.)

FRIED SAUSAGES

Ingredients

1 *lb. pork or beef sausages.*   *A little parsley.*

Method

1. Separate the sausages, and prick each well with a fork.
2. Warm the pan and put in the sausages.
3. Cook slowly, so that the sausages will not burst.
4. When browned, turn and cook the second side.
5. Garnish with parsley.

(Sufficient for 4 persons.)

GALANTINE OF BEEF

Ingredients

¾ *lb. meat cut off the round.*	¼ *pint milk.*	1 *egg.*
¼ *lb. bacon (chopped finely).*	1½ *oz. flour.*	½ *oz. butter.*
½ *breakfastcupful bread-crumbs.*	1 *small cooked onion.*	*Seasoning.*

Method

1. Pass the meat through the mincer.
2. Mix with the chopped bacon and bread-crumbs.
3. Chop the onion and add.
4. Season well.
5. Whisk the egg and stir into the mixture.
6. Turn out on a floured board and form into a roll.
7. Tie in a buttered cloth and boil for 3 hours.
8. Make a sauce, using the flour, butter and milk.
9. Hard-boiled eggs may be placed in the centre of the roll. This makes a nice effect when the roll is sliced.
10. When cooked, drain and remove the cloth and place between two plates with a weight on top.
11. Serve cold with salad.   (Sufficient for 4 persons.)

GALANTINE OF VEAL

Ingredients

1 *lb. veal.*	¼ *lb. ham.*	*Seasoning.*
½ *teacupful bread-crumbs.*	2 *eggs.*	

Method

Make as for Galantine of Beef (see above), but cook for 1½–2 hours only.   (Sufficient for 4 persons.)

GRILLED CHOPS

Ingredients

4 *loin chops.*	*Seasoning.*	1½ *oz. butter.*

Method

1. Trim the chops and remove any excess fat.
2. Beat with a wooden spoon for 10 minutes.
3. Heat the grill.
4. Place the chops in a tin and put a pat of butter on each.
5. Place under the hot grill and cook till nicely browned.
6. Turn and cook the second side.
7. The time required is usually about 5–7 minutes per side.
8. Serve with Maître d'hôtel Butter (see page 123).
                    (Sufficient for 4 persons.)

GRILLED STEAK

Ingredients

1 *lb. undercut steak or* 1 *lb. top or first steak.*	*Butter.*

Method

1. Beat the meat well with a spoon to break the fibres.
2. Place on a tin and put a few pats of butter on the top.

3. Heat the grill, and when red hot put the tin under it.
4. Cook for about 5–7 minutes till nicely browned, and turn.
5. Cook the second side and baste occasionally.
6. Serve with Maître d'hôtel Butter (see page 123).

(Sufficient for 4 persons.)

HARICOT MUTTON

Ingredients

1 *lb. neck of mutton, best-end.*	1 *onion.*	2 *carrots.*
1 *pint water or stock.*	1 *small turnip.*	1 *oz. flour.*
	1 *oz. dripping.*	*Seasoning.*

Method

1. Wipe the meat and remove the spinal cord.
2. The meat can either be left whole or chopped into pieces.
3. Melt the dripping and lightly fry the meat. Lift on to a plate to keep hot.
4. Prepare the vegetables and cut up neatly.
5. Fry in the dripping for a few minutes.
6. Add the meat, and then pour over 1 pint of water or stock. Season.
7. Cook slowly for 1½–2 hours.
8. Blend 1 oz. of flour with water and stir into the sauce. Stir till boiling.
9. Serve using the vegetables as garnish.

(Sufficient for 4 persons.)

HOT POT

Ingredients

1 *lb. neck of mutton.*	2 *Spanish onions.*
1½–2 *lb. potatoes.*	*Seasoning.*

Method

1. Trim the meat as for haricot mutton, but divide into chops.
2. Place in a pie-dish.
3. Pare and slice the onions and put on top of the meat.
4. Sprinkle in some seasoning, and pour over about 1 gill of water, or stock.
5. Pare and slice the potatoes and pile on top of the onions.
6. Cover with a pie-dish the same size as the one containing the food.
7. Place in a hot oven. Cook gently for about 2½ hours. (Regulo 1.)
8. Serve very hot.

(Sufficient for 4 persons.)

IRISH STEW

Ingredients

1 *lb. neck of mutton.*   2 *Spanish onions.*   2 *lb. potatoes.*
Seasoning.   1 *oz. dripping.*

Method

1. Wipe the meat and trim it and cut it into pieces.
2. Melt the dripping and fry the meat lightly in it.
3. Slice the onions and fry these too.
4. Add ½ pint of water and cook slowly for 1 hour.   Add seasoning.
5. Pare and slice the potatoes, and put them in the pan with the meat and onions.
6. Cook for 1 hour longer.
7. Serve piled on a hot dish and garnish with parsley.

(Sufficient for 4 persons.)

LANCASHIRE HOT POT

Ingredients

¾ *lb. neck of mutton.*   ½ *lb. Flaky Pastry*   1½ *lb. potatoes.*
2 *Spanish onions.*   (see page 144).   *Seasoning.*

Method

1. Commence as for Hot Pot (see page 72).   When it has cooked for 1½ hours take it out and let it cool a little.
2. Cover with pastry as for Beef-Steak Pie (see page 62).
3. Serve hot.

(Sufficient for 4 persons.)

MEAT ROLL

Ingredients

1 *lb. round steak.*   2 *eggs.*   1 *oz. butter.*
1 *tablespoonful chopped onion.*   2 *oz. dripping.*
1 *breakfastcupful bread-crumbs.*   *Seasoning.*

Method

1. Mince the meat using the mincer.
2. Add seasoning and mix in the bread-crumbs.
3. Melt the butter and add.   Mix all ingredients.
4. Whisk the eggs and mix into the other ingredients.
5. Turn on to a floured board and shape into a roll.
6. Melt the dripping in a tin and place the roll in the tin.
7. Cook in the oven for about 1¼ hours.   (Regulo 5.)
8. Serve with Tomato Sauce (see page 126).
9. If to be served cold, place on a bed of lettuce.

(Sufficient for 4 persons.)

MIXED GRILL

Ingredients

4 *sausages.*	4 *sheep's kidneys.*	4 *tomatoes.*
4 *slices of undercut steak.*	4 *mushrooms.* *Seasoning.*	2 *oz. butter.*

Method

1. Trim the meat and prick the sausages.
2. Cut the kidneys in halves.
3. Place the meat, sausages, kidneys and other ingredients on a tin.   Put pats of butter on top of the meat.
4. Heat the grill, and when red hot put the tin under the heat.
5. Cook for about 6 minutes.
6. Turn and cook the second side.
7. Serve on a hot dish using the mushrooms and tomato as garnish.   (Sufficient for 4 persons.)

MUTTON AND KIDNEY HOT POT

Ingredients

¾ *lb. neck of mutton.*	2 *Spanish onions.*	2 *lb. potatoes.*
2 *sheep kidneys or* ½ *ox kidney.*	1 *oz. seasoned flour.* ½ *pint water or stock.*	1 *oz. dripping.*

Method

1. Cut the meat in pieces and halve the kidneys.
2. Dip each part in seasoned flour.
3. Melt the dripping and fry the parts lightly in the dripping.
4. Fry the onions till a golden brown.
5. Place the meat and onions in a casserole and add ½ pint of stock or water.
6. Cook for 1 hour with the lid on.
7. Pare and slice the potatoes and put on top of meat.
8. Cook for 1 hour longer.
9. Serve very hot.   (Sufficient for 4 persons.)

PICKLED MEAT

Ingredients

4 *or* 5 *lb. silverside, lightly pickled.*	1 *carrot.* 1 *onion.*	1 *turnip.*

Method

1. Wash the meat and put it on to boil in cold water.
2. Cook slowly for 1 hour.
3. Drain off the water and refill with boiling water and cook for 1 hour.

4. Prepare and cut up the vegetables and add.

5. Cook for 2 hours longer.

6. Lift out the meat, wrap in a clean towel, press between two plates with a weight on top.

7. Serve cold.

8. The meat may be glazed and decorated with savoury butter and aspic.

PORK PIE

Ingredients

1 *lb. pork.*   *Seasoning.*

Pastry

¾ *lb. flour.*	*A pinch salt.*	¼ *lb. lard.*
1 *gill milk.*	1 *egg white.*	

Method

1. Take all the bones from the meat and put the bones on to boil in a little water.

2. Cup up the meat finely, but do not mince.

3. Season well.

4. Boil the lard and milk together.

5. Mix the flour and salt and stir in the lard mixture.

6. Cool for a few minutes.

7. Turn on to a floured board.

8. Cut off ⅓ and lay aside.

9. Knead the other part till smooth and raise into a pie; you can either use a pie-shaper, a bowl or just the hands.

10. Fill up with the seasoned meat and add some of the stock from the bones.

11. Make the small piece of pastry into a lid and cover the pie. Make an opening in the centre.

12. Brush over with beaten egg-white.

13. Decorate as desired.

14. Cook in a hot oven for 1½–2 hours.

15. Fill up with the remainder of the stock.

16. Serve cold, garnished with parsley.

RAGOÛT OF OX KIDNEY

Ingredients

1 *ox. kidney.*	1 *carrot.*	1 *small turnip.*
1 *onion.*	1 *oz. dripping.*	1 *pint stock.*
1 *gill fresh peas.*	*Seasoning.*	

Method

1. Wipe the kidney and cut up in neat pieces.

2. Lightly fry in the dripping.

3. Place in a casserole.

4. Prepare and cut up the vegetables and fry lightly—do not fry the peas.

5. Season well and put the vegetables in the casserole with the meat.

6. Add the stock and a little more seasoning.

7. Add the green peas and put on the lid.

8. Cook for 45 minutes in a slow oven.   (Regulo 5.)

9. Serve hot.

(Sufficient for 4 persons.)

RAGOÛT OF VEAL

Ingredients

1 lb. veal cutlets.	1 carrot.	1 onion.
A small piece of turnip.	1 gill peas. Seasoning.	½ pint stock. 1 oz. butter.

Method

Cook as for Ragoût of Ox Kidney (see page 75), but fry in butter instead of dripping.   (Sufficient for 4 persons.)

ROAST IN A SAUCEPAN

Ingredients

1 small roast about 2½ lb.   1 oz. dripping.

Method

1. Trim the meat and cut off any excess fat.

2. Melt the dripping and fry the meat on both sides.

3. Put on the lid and cook for 1½ hours.

4. Lift out the meat and strain off the fat.

5. Pour in ½ pint of stock and mix in the brown sediment. Season and serve in a sauce-boat.

Note.—Only small joints are suitable for Pot Roasting.

ROLLED STUFFED STEAK

Ingredients

1 lb. round steak.	2 oz. bread-crumbs.	1 oz. suet.
1 oz. flour.	1 oz. dripping.	1 pint stock.
1 teaspoonful chopped parsley.	¼ teaspoonful mixed herbs.	Seasoning. 1 egg.

Method

1. Trim the steak and cut off any excess fat.

2. Mix the bread-crumbs, suet, parsley, herbs and seasoning. Bind with a beaten egg. Spread on the steak and roll up. Tie with string.

3. Melt the dripping and lightly fry the roll. Lift out.

4. Add the flour and stir till brown.

5. Add the stock and stir till boiling.
6. Put in the roll and stew gently for 1½–2 hours.
7. Lift out and remove the string.
8. Serve with the gravy poured over the steak.

(Sufficient for 4 persons.)

SAUSAGE ROLLS

Ingredients

½ *lb. Rough Puff or Flaky Pastry*
(see pages 147 or 144).

¾ *lb. sausages.*
1 *egg.*

Method

1. Pour boiling water over the sausages, leave for 1 minute and then skin them, and lay them aside till required.
2. Roll the pastry out into an oblong.
3. Place four sausages at regular intervals along the top edge.
4. Place four at the opposite edge.
5. Wet all round the edge of the pastry, across the centre and down between each row of sausages.
6. Fold over the top edge to the centre.
7. Fold up the bottom edge to the centre.
8. Press down the pastry between each sausage.
9. Cut into eight sausage rolls.
10. Make three cuts on the top and raise the edges with a knife.
11. Brush with beaten egg and bake in a hot oven for 20–25 minutes. Regulo 8 reduced to 7 after 10 minutes.
12. Serve hot or cold.

Note.—These rolls can be made with sausage meat if desired, or with a mixture of pork and beef, or one or the other.

SAVOURY ROLY-POLY

Ingredients

½ *lb. Suet Pastry* (see page 135).   ½ *lb. sausage meat.*

Method

1. Roll out the pastry into a long, thin strip.
2. Spread over the sausage meat.
3. Roll up tightly.
4. Put on a pan of water to boil.
5. Tie the roll in a floured cloth, fixing the ends very securely.
6. Plunge the roll into fast-boiling water. Boil steadily for 3 hours.
7. Serve with a good brown sauce.

(Sufficient for 4 persons.)

SEA PIE

Ingredients

¾ lb. skirt of beef.	1 carrot.	1 onion.
Seasoning.	1 oz. dripping.	½ oz. flour.
½ pint stock or water.	A piece of turnip.	

Pastry

6 oz. flour.	½ teaspoonful baking-powder.	A pinch of salt.
2½ oz. suet.		

Method

1. Trim the meat and cut up in pieces.
2. Melt the dripping and fry the meat till brown. Lift it on to a plate.
3. Pare and cut up the vegetables and fry them lightly. Lift these on to the plate with the meat.
4. Add the flour to the dripping and stir till brown.
5. Gradually add the stock and stir till boiling.
6. Add the meat and vegetables and simmer slowly for 1 hour.

To Prepare the Pastry

1. Measure out the flour and add salt.
2. Chop the suet and add.
3. Sprinkle in the baking-powder and mix well.
4. Mix to an elastic dough with cold water.
5. Turn on to a floured board and form into a round the size of the pan.
6. Season the stew and place the pastry on top.
7. Cook for 1 hour longer.
8. Divide the pastry into six or eight wedges and use it as a garnish for the meat.
9. Pile the vegetables in little heaps at the ends of the dish and serve very hot.　(Sufficient for 4 persons.)

SHEEP'S HEAD STEW

Ingredients

1 sheep's head.	Seasoning.	1 turnip.
1 pint water or stock.	1 oz. flour.	1 onion.
A little chopped parsley.	2 tablespoonfuls bread-crumbs.	1 egg.
1 oz. dripping.		1 carrot.

Method

1. Wash the head well and remove the brains and tongue.
2. Soak in salt water for 1 or 2 hours.
3. Split the head lengthwise.

4. Melt the dripping.
5. Add the flour and stir till brown.
6. Add the stock and stir till boiling.
7. Drain the water off the head and add head to the sauce. Prepare and add the vegetables.   Season.
8. Stew gently for about 2½ hours till tender.
9. The tongue may be cut in slices.

The Brains

1. Drain the water from the brains.
2. Boil in salted water for 20 minutes.
3. Chop well and add 2 tablespoonfuls of bread-crumbs, add a little parsley, seasoning, and brush with egg.
4. Fry in smoking hot fat till a golden brown.
5. Serve the stew on a dish using the brain cakes as a garnish.

SPICED BEEF

Ingredients

Piece of beef bought	*1 carrot.*	*½ turnip.*
spiced, about 4 lb.	*1 onion.*	

Method

1. Put the meat on to boil in boiling water.
2. Boil gently for 1 hour.
3. Prepare and cut up the vegetables and add to the meat.
4. Cook for 2½ hours.
5. Take out the meat and drain well on a clean towel.
6. Press between two plates with a weight on top.
7. Serve, using vegetables as a garnish.
8. The meat may be glazed and decorated with savoury butter and aspic.
9. Do not add this stock to the stock-pot, as it contains spice.

STEAMED CHOPS

Ingredients

4 chops, cut thin.   *1½ oz. butter.*

Method

1. Trim the fat and beat with a wooden spoon.
2. Place on a buttered plate and put a pat of butter on each. Cover with a second plate.
3. Steam over a pan of boiling water till tender.   This takes rather a long time, hence the need for the chops being cut thin.
4. Serve very hot.   (Sufficient for 4 persons.)

STEAMED STEAK

Ingredients

1 lb. shoulder or round steak.	1 onion.	1 small turnip.
1 oz. flour.	1 carrot.	½ pint stock.
	Seasoning.	

Method

1. Trim the meat and cut it up into neat pieces.
2. Measure the flour and add seasoning.
3. Dip each piece of meat in the seasoned flour.
4. Place a layer in a pudding-basin.
5. Cover with a layer of prepared vegetables.
6. Continue adding layers till all is used.
7. Pour the stock over all.
8. Cover with a buttered paper and place in a steamer.
9. Cook for 3 hours.
10. Serve very hot.

(Sufficient for 4 persons.)

STEWED BREAST OF VEAL

Ingredients

Piece of breast of veal (about 1 lb.).	1 onion.	1 oz. flour.
1 oz. dripping.	½ pint stock.	Seasoning.

Method

1. Melt the dripping.
2. Slice the onion and fry lightly and lift out.
3. Add the flour and blend it with the dripping.
4. Add ½ pint of stock and stir till boiling.
5. Add the meat and onion and simmer gently for 2½ hours. Season.
6. Serve very hot.
7. Garnish the dish with water-cress.

(Sufficient for 4 persons.)

STEWED HEART

Ingredients

1 heart.	1 carrot.	½ turnip.	1 onion.
1 oz. dripping.	1 oz. flour.	½ pint stock.	

Method

1. Cut the heart through the divisions.
2. Wash well in cold water and squeeze.
3. Leave to soak in water for 1 hour.
4. Prepare the sauce as for Stewed Breast of Veal (see above).

5. Place in the heart and cook for 1½ hours.
6. Serve using the vegetables as a garnish.

Note.—Hearts may be stewed, baked, stuffed and roasted, or boiled.

STEWED SWEETBREADS

Ingredients

4 *sweetbreads.*	4 *oz. butter.*	2 *oz. flour.*
2 *gills milk.*	*Seasoning.*	

Method

1. Wash the sweetbreads well in water with a little salt added.
2. Soak in cold water for 1½ hours.
3. Boil for 10 minutes.
4. Cut into slices.
5. Melt the butter and add the flour.
6. Pour in the milk and stir till boiling.
7. Add the slices of sweetbreads and simmer gently for 1½ hours.
8. Serve hot.   (Sufficient for 4 persons.)

STUFFED AND BAKED PORK

Ingredients

     1 *leg of pork.*   1 *oz. dripping.*

Stuffing

1 *oz. chopped suet.*	2 *oz. bread-crumbs.*	1 *egg.*
A pinch of thyme.	1 *teaspoonful chop-*	½ *apple, chopped.*
Rind of ½ a lemon.	*ped parlsey.*	*Seasoning.*

Method

1. Bone the leg.
2. Prepare the stuffing by mixing all the ingredients together and bind with the beaten egg.
3. Stuff the leg and tie with string.
4. Melt the dripping.
5. Place in the meat and baste well.
6. Cook in a hot oven till tender, allowing 25 minutes and 25 minutes over.   (Regulo 7.)
7. Remove the string and serve with Apple Sauce (see page 118) and brown gravy, if liked.

TRIPE AND ONIONS

Ingredients

1 *lb. dressed tripe.*	2 *Spanish onions.*	1 *pint milk.*
1 *oz. flour.*	*Seasoning.*	

Method

1. Cut up the tripe in neat pieces.
2. Pare and slice the onions.
3. Put the onions on to boil in the milk and cook for ¾ hour.
4. Add the tripe and cook for ¾ hour longer.
5. Add seasoning.
6. Blend the flour with a little cold milk and stir into the milk.
7. Stir till boiling.
8. Serve very hot.   (Sufficient for 4 persons.)

TOAD-IN-THE-HOLE

Ingredients

1 *lb. sausages.*   ¼ *lb. Batter* (see page 129).   *Seasoning.*

Method

1. Prepare the batter and lay it aside for 2 hours.
2. Dip the sausages in boiling water and remove the skins.
3. Butter a pie-dish and place the sausages in it.
4. Pour over the prepared butter.
5. Bake in a hot oven for ¾–1 hour.   (Regulo 6.)
6. Serve very hot.

7. If pork sausages are used, apple sauce may be served with them.   (Sufficient for 4 persons.)

VEAL AND HAM PIE

Ingredients

¾ *lb. veal.*   ¼ *lb. ham.*   1 *gill stock.*
½ *lb. Flaky Pastry*   2 *hard-boiled eggs.*   *Seasoning.*
(see page 201).

Method

1. Cut the veal into neat pieces and put a layer at the bottom of the pie-dish.
2. Cover the veal with a layer of ham.
3. Cover that with a layer of sliced eggs.
4. Continue until all the veal, ham and egg is used up.
5. Season the stock and pour it over the meat mixture.
6. Cover with the pastry as for Beef-Steak Pie (see page 62).
7. Brush with beaten egg and cook for 10 minutes. (Regulo 7.)
8. Reduce to Regulo No. 4 and cook for 1½ hours.
9. Serve cold.   (Sufficient for 4 persons.)

VEAL MOULD

Ingredients

¾ *lb. fillet of veal.*   1 *teaspoonful chop-*   ½ *lemon.*
½ *oz. gelatine.*   *ped parsley.*   *Stock.*
2 *hard-boiled eggs.*   ¼ *lb. bacon, cut in slices.*   *Seasoning.*

Method

1. Butter a mould and decorate with slices of hard-boiled eggs.
2. Cut up the veal into very small pieces.
3. Put the cut-up veal and sliced bacon alternately into the mould.
4. Add seasoning, chopped parsley, lemon juice and stock.
5. Cover with a buttered paper and steam for 2 hours.
6. Dissolve the gelatine and pour it in.
7. Lay aside to set.
8. Turn out and serve with salad.

(Sufficient for 4 persons.)

VEAL OLIVES

See recipe for Beef Olives (page 61).

MEAT LEFT-OVERS

BAKED MEAT MOULDS

Ingredients

1 *lb. cold meat.*	6 *oz. cooked potatoes.*	1 *egg.*
½ *teaspoonful chopped parsley.*	1 *small parboiled onion.*	*Seasoning.*
		1 *gill stock.*

Method

1. Mince the meat, using the mincer.
2. Sieve the potatoes.
3. Chop the onion.
4. Mix all three together.
5. Add seasoning and chopped parsley.
6. Add the stock and beaten egg.
7. Butter six individual moulds and sprinkle with bread raspings.
8. Fill up with the mixture and cover with buttered paper.
9. Bake for a few minutes in a hot oven.
10. Serve either hot or cold.
11. The mixture can be made in one large mould and sliced.

(Sufficient for 4 persons.)

COLD MEAT MOULD

Ingredients

½ *lb. cooked meat.*	1 *pint good stock.*	2 *hard-boiled eggs.*
3 *tablespoonfuls finely chopped celery.*	2 *tablespoonfuls pickles.*	½ *oz. gelatine.*
		Seasoning.

Method

1. Chop up the meat very finely, leaving out fat or gristle.
2. Chop up one egg and cut the other in slices and lay aside for decoration.
3. Chop the celery and pickles.
4. Mix all together and add seasoning.
5. Wet a mould and decorate with egg-slices.
6. Dissolve the gelatine in the seasoned stock and pour over the mixture.
7. Pour all carefully into the wet and prepared mould and lay aside to set.
8. Turn out when set and serve with salad and cream.

Note.—Cold beef, pork, or mutton may be used in this way. In the case of pork, add 1 apple finely chopped.

(Sufficient for 4 persons.)

CURRY OF COLD MEAT

Ingredients

¾ lb. cold meat.	1 onion.	1 gill milk or cream.
3 oz. butter.	1 apple.	A little apple chutney.
2 teaspoonfuls curry powder.	¾ pint stock.	Seasoning.
	1 oz. flour.	

Method

1. Trim the meat and remove bones, fat or gristle.
2. Melt the butter.
3. Pare and slice the onion and fry in the fat.
4. Add the curry powder, and flour and stir.
5. Pare and chop the apple, and add.
6. Pour in the stock and a little seasoning.
7. Simmer very slowly for ½ hour.
8. Add the chutney, chopped meat and milk or cream and stir well till boiling.
9. Serve with boiled rice as a border.

(Sufficient for 4 persons.)

DURHAM CUTLETS

Ingredients

¼ lb. cold beef or mutton.	1 teaspoonful chopped parsley.	Bath of fat to fry.
1 oz. flour.	1 small boiled onion.	1 oz. butter.
Seasoning.	Egg and bread-crumbs for coating.	1 gill stock.
½ oz. macaroni.		

Method

1. Chop the meat very finely.
2. Melt the butter and stir in the flour. Cook for a few minutes.

3. Add the stock and stir till boiling. Draw from the heat and form into a lump.

4. Chop the onion and add it and the meat, seasoning and parsley.

5. Spread on a plate to cool.

6. Form into cutlets and put a piece of macaroni on the end of each for a cutlet bone.

7. Dip in beaten egg and toss in bread-crumbs.

8. Fry in deep fat till a golden brown.

9. Serve immediately with fried parsley and tomato sauce.

(Sufficient for 4 persons.)

HASH

Ingredients

1 lb. cold meat cut in thin slices.   1 tablespoonful Worcester sauce.
Seasoning.   1 pint gravy.   1 boiled onion.

Method

1. Trim the meat and place in a casserole.

2. Sprinkle with seasoning.

3. Cut the onion in slices and place on the meat.

4. Add Worcester sauce to the gravy and pour over the meat.

5. Put on the lid and heat in a very moderate oven for ½ hour.   (Regulo 3.)

6. Do not allow the hash to boil.

(Sufficient for 4 persons.)

KROMESKIES

Ingredients

½ lb. streaky bacon.   1 mushroom.   Seasoning.
1 egg.   Bread-crumbs.   Bath of fat.
2 or 3 sheep's kidneys.   1 teaspoonful flour.   ½ gill stock.
1 teaspoonful butter and 1 oz. butter.   1 small onion (parboiled).

Method

1. Wash the kidneys.   Skin them and cut up very finely.

2. Chop the onion and mushroom.

3. Melt 1 oz. of butter and in it fry the kidney, mushroom and onion.

4. Make a panada (as for Durham Cutlets, see page 84), with ¼ oz. flour, butter and ½ gill of stock.

5. Add the fried kidney, mushroom and onion and season well.

6. Spread out the bacon slices and put a teaspoonful of the kidney mixture on each slice.

7. Roll up tightly.

8. Dip in beaten egg and bread-crumbs.

9. Fry in fat till a golden brown.
10. Serve at once.

(Sufficient for 4 persons.)

Note.—Remains of turkey, duck, chicken or pork may be used up in this way.

MEAT CROQUETTES

Ingredients

½ *lb. cold meat.*	1 *oz. flour.*	1 *oz. butter.*
1 *gill milk.*	*Seasoning.*	*Fat to fry.*
Worcester sauce or mushroom ketchup.		*Egg and bread-crumbs.*

Method

1. Make the panada as before (see page 84, Durham Cutlets), using flour, butter and stock (milk).
2. Chop up the meat and add to the panada.
3. Season well and add sauce if desired.
4. Turn on to a lightly floured board and form into croquettes, ovals, rounds, balls or sausage-shaped cakes.
5. Egg and crumb each and fry in hot fat till brown.
6. Serve at once.

Note.—Beef, mutton, pork or fowl may be used for croquettes.

(Sufficient for 4 persons.)

MEAT IN BATTER

Ingredients

¾ *lb. sliced cold meat.*   *Fat to fry.*   ¼ *lb. Batter* (see page 130).

Method

1. Prepare the batter and lay aside for 2 hours.
2. Put on the fat to heat.
3. Trim the meat and remove any excess fat.
4. A few minutes before it is required, dip each slice in the prepared batter.
5. Fry till nicely browned and puffy.
6. Serve at once.

(Sufficient for 4 persons.)

MEAT PATTIES

Ingredients

½ *lb. cold meat.*	*Seasoning.*	½ *oz. butter.*
½ *oz. flour.*	½ *gill milk or sauce.*	1 *egg.*
6 *oz. Flaky Pastry* (see page 144).		

Method

1. Prepare the pastry and lay it aside for 1 hour.
2. Chop the meat up finely.

3. Make a panada with butter, flour and sauce (see page 84, Durham Cutlets).

4. Add seasoning and chopped meat, and lay aside till cool.

5. Roll out the pastry till it is about ¼ inch thick.   Cut into rounds with a straight-edged cutter.

6. Place a spoonful of the mixture on half the number of rounds and wet the edges.   Cover with the other rounds.

7. Press the edges together well and then raise with a knife— that is, separate the flakes using the knife to the cut edge.

8. Make a few cuts on the top of each and brush with beaten egg.

9. Cook in a good oven till nicely browned.   (Regulo 8.)

10. Serve hot or cold.   (Sufficient for 4 persons.)

MEAT RISSOLES

Make as for meat croquettes, only form into balls (see page 86).

MINCED MEAT

Ingredients

½ pint good stock.   ¾ to 1 lb. cold meat   1 oz. dripping.
1 oz. flour.   (minced).   Seasoning.

Method

1. Melt the dripping and stir in the flour.

2. Cook till brown, stirring all the time.

3. Add stock and stir till boiling.

4. Add the minced meat and cook very slowly for 20 minutes. Season.

5. Worcester sauce or mushroom ketchup may be added, if liked.

6. Serve at once.   (Sufficient for 4 persons.)

RICE CUTLETS

Ingredients

½ lb. cold chopped meat.   1 gill tomato sauce.   Fat to fry.
½ teacupful rice.   2 oz. butter.   Seasoning.
1 onion boiled and chopped.   Egg and bread-crumbs.

Method

1. Boil the rice till tender and drain well.

2. Melt the butter and add the rice, and cook very slowly till the butter is absorbed.

3. Add seasoning and tomato sauce.

4. Stir in the chopped meat and onion and spread on a plate to cool.

5. Form into cutlets, and egg and crumb and fry as for Durham Cutlets (see page 84).

6. Serve at once.

(Sufficient for 4 persons.)

ROLLED MEAT

Ingredients

¾ *lb. cold meat cut in very thin slices.*   *Seasoning.*
½ *pint tomato sauce.*

Method

1. Spread out each thin slice and season well.
2. Roll up and secure with a tiny skewer.
3. Heat the sauce and place the rolls in it.
4. Heat very slowly for about 20 minutes.
5. Lift out the rolls and remove the skewers.
6. Pour the sauce over and serve at once.

(Sufficient for 4 persons.)

ROMAN PIE

Ingredients

½ *lb. Short Pastry (see page 139).*   1 *cooked rabbit (small).*
Seasoning.   1 *oz. grated cheese.*   3 *oz. macaroni.*
1 *onion.*   1 *gill cream.*   *Vermicelli.*

Method

1. Carefully remove the rabbit flesh from the bones.
2. Boil the macaroni in boiling salted water.
3. When tender cut it into short lengths. Mix these with the rabbit.
4. Add chopped onion, grated cheese, seasoning and cream.
5. Prepare the pastry.
6. Butter a cake tin, about 6 inches across and 4 or 5 inches high. Sprinkle with crushed vermicelli.
7. Line the tin with two-thirds of the pastry.
8. Fill up with the mixture.
9. Form the small part of the pastry into a lid and put on the pie.
10. Bake in a hot oven, Regulo 7, reduced to 6 after ½ hour, and cook for 1 hour.
11. Turn out and serve with cheese or tomato sauce.

(Sufficient for 4 persons.)

SHEPHERD'S PIE

Ingredients

1 *lb. cold meat.*   1 *oz. butter.*
1½ *lb. mashed potatoes.*   1 *parboiled onion.*
3 *or* 4 *tablespoonfuls good gravy.*   *Seasoning.*

Method

1. Mince the meat and season well.
2. Cut up the onion and add to the meat.
3. Add the gravy and mix well.
4. Pile the potatoes on top and put some pats of butter on the potatoes.
5. Reheat in a slow oven for about 20 minutes. (Regulo 7.)

(Sufficient for 4 persons.)

17. POULTRY AND GAME

A. ROAST FOWL

Ingredients

    1 *fowl.*   *¼ lb. bacon.*   *Sausage meat stuffing.*

Method

To Clean

1. Pluck out the feathers and singe the bird without discolouring the flesh.
2. Break off the feet.
3. Lay the fowl with the head towards you.
4. Cut off the head and slit the skin down about 3 inches.
5. Cut off the neck, but leave the skin fastened to the bird.
6. Loosen the internal organs at the neck end.
7. Now turn the bird round and make an opening at the tail end.
8. Insert the fingers and draw out the organs.
9. Wipe out with a clean towel wrung out of hot water.

To Truss for Roasting

10. Fold back the skin and turn the wings to lie across the back.
11. Skewer through from one wing to the other.
12. Tie the legs in position and fasten to the tip of the tail.

To Cook

Method

1. Stuff the fowl before trussing.
2. Place the slices of bacon over the breast and cover with a buttered paper.
3. Cook in a quick oven for ½ hour and reduce the heat. (Regulo 7.) Cook for ½–1 hour according to size.
4. Serve with brown sauce and bread sauce.

The Trimmings of a Fowl

Giblets

1. Remove the gall-bladder from the liver.
2. Use the neck, liver and gizzard.
3. Split the gizzard open and clean it out.
4. Wash and scrape the feet and remove the nails.
5. Use the giblets for soup, gravy or add to the stock-pot.

B. ROAST GAME

1. Game is hung before using, and for this a cool, airy place should be chosen. The time for hanging depends on individual taste, as some like game mild and others very high.
2. Pluck out the feathers and singe as for a fowl.
3. Leave on the feet, and wash and scrape the feet and legs.
4. Truss as for Roast Fowl (see page 89).

C. BOILED FOWL

1. Pluck and singe as for Roast Fowl (see page 89).
2. Draw in the same manner.
3. Cut off the feet and loosen the skin and pocket the legs.
4. Truss the wings as for Roast Fowl (see page 89).
5. After stuffing, tie the tips of the legs to the tail.
6. Use oatmeal or other stuffing. Giblets may be used as for Roast Fowl. Vegetables may be added to flavour the fowl.
7. A piece of ham boiled in the same water as the chicken helps the flavour, but sometimes slightly discolours the white flesh.

Note.—To serve, remove the strings and skewers and serve with white sauce, egg or parsley sauce.

BLANQUETTE OF RABBIT

Ingredients

1 *rabbit.*	1 *oz. flour.*	1 *oz. butter.*
1 *pint milk.*	1 *egg.*	*Seasoning.*

Method

1. Cut the rabbit into joints and remove the kidneys, liver and heart. Take out the gall-bladder.
2. Soak the rabbit in water for 1 hour.
3. Melt the butter and add the flour. Stir for a few minutes.
4. Add the milk and stir till boiling.
5. Add the pieces of rabbit and stew gently for 1½ hours.
6. Remove the pieces of rabbit and keep hot.
7. Season the sauce and add a well-beaten egg carefully.
8. Pour this sauce over the rabbit and serve at once.

(Sufficient for 4 persons.)

BOILED RABBIT

Ingredients

1 *rabbit.*   2 *onions.*   1 *carrot.*   ½ *turnip.*

Method

1. Prepare as for Blanquette of Rabbit (see page 90).
2. Prepare and cut up the vegetables.
3. Put the rabbit on to boil in sufficient water to cover.
4. Add the vegetables and seasoning.
5. Cook slowly till tender.
6. Lift out the rabbit and use the vegetables as a garnish.
7. Serve with white or parsley sauce.

(Sufficient for 4 persons.)

CHICKEN EN CASSEROLE

Ingredients

1 *chicken.*   1 *oz. butter.*   ½ *oz. flour.*   1 *onion.*
1 *bunch herbs.*   1 *gill stock.*   *Seasoning.*

Method

1. Draw the fowl, wipe it out and joint.
2. Melt the butter and lightly fry the fowl.
3. Pare and slice the onion and fry.
4. Put chicken and onion in the casserole and pour over the stock.
5. Add seasoning and herbs.
6. Cook in a moderate oven for 1 hour.   (Regulo 5.)
7. Thicken the gravy with a little blended flour and add to the chicken.
8. The chicken may be served in the casserole.

(Sufficient for 4 persons.)

CHICKEN PIE

Ingredients

1 *chicken.*   2 *oz. ham.*   1 *hard-boiled egg.*
1 *slice of round steak.*   1 *egg-yolk.*   ½ *pt. stock.*
½ *lb. Rough Puff Pastry (see page 147).*   *Seasoning.*

Method

1. Joint the chicken after cleaning.
2. Pile the pieces in a pie-dish.
3. Cut up the steak and put in a layer of meat.
4. Now put in a layer of ham.   The chicken, meat and ham may be mixed instead of in layers if preferred.
5. Season the stock.
6. Cut up the hard-boiled egg and place in the slices among the meats.

7. Pour over the stock.
8. Cover with pastry as for Beef-Steak Pie (see page 62).
9. Brush over with beaten egg-yolk.
10. Cook in a hot oven (Regulo No. 8) for 20 minutes, then reduce to No. 4.
11. Cook for 1¼ hours longer.
12. If the pie gets too brown cover it with a buttered paper.
13. Serve hot or cold.
14. Place some freshly-washed parsley in the centre.

(Sufficient for 4 persons.)

CHICKEN SAUTE

Ingredients

1 *small chicken.*	2 *oz. butter.*	1 *teacupful stock.*
A bunch of herbs.	1 *onion.*	½ *pint tomato sauce.*
A few cooked mushrooms.		*Seasoning.*

Method

1. Melt the butter.
2. Pare and slice the onion and fry in the butter.
3. Joint the chicken and lightly fry in the butter.
4. Pour over the stock and add seasoning and herbs.
5. Cook gently for about 1 hour.
6. Prepare the tomato sauce and mix with it the liquid in which the chicken was cooked.
7. Carefully add the joints of chicken.
8. Serve very hot, using the mushrooms to garnish.

(Sufficient for 4 persons.)

COMPÔTE OF PIGEONS

Ingredients

2 *pigeons.*	¼ *lb. ham.*	1 *cooked mushroom.*	¾ *pint stock.*
1 *teacupful bread-crumbs.*	1 *onion.*	1 *oz. butter.*	*Seasoning.*

Method

1. Bone the pigeons and remove the liver.
2. Chop the ham and liver together and fry lightly in 1 oz. of butter.
3. Add the bread-crumbs and seasonings.
4. Stuff the pigeons.
5. Put the stock on to heat and when boiling place in the pigeons.
6. Cook for 1 hour.
7. Serve on slices of fried bread.
8. Use the chopped mushroom as a garnish.

(Sufficient for 4 persons.)

CURRIED PIGEONS

Ingredients

2 *pigeons.*	1 *oz. butter.*	1 *pint stock.*
½ *teaspoonful curry*	¼ *lb. almonds.*	3 *onions.*
powder.	2 *oz. flour.*	*Seasoning.*

Method

1. Chop one onion and fry it in butter.
2. Mix the flour and seasoning.
3. Joint the pigeons and dip each part in the seasoned flour.
4. Fry lightly and stir in the curry.
5. Add the stock and cook for 1 hour.
6. Slice the two remaining onions.
7. Blanch and shred the almonds.
8. Fry in butter.
9. Dish the curry and garnish with fried onions and almonds.

(Sufficient for 4 persons.)

FRICASSÉE OF CHICKEN

Ingredients

1 *cold chicken.*	2 *oz. flour.*	2 *oz. butter.*
1½ *pints stock.*	1 *gill cream.*	*Seasoning.*

Method

1. Melt the butter and add the flour and cook lightly.
2. Add the stock and stir till boiling.
3. Season well.
4. Cut up the chicken, removing the skin.
5. Place the parts in the sauce and reheat.
6. Add the cream before serving.
7. Serve with chopped ham and tongue.

(Sufficient for 4 persons.)

JUGGED RABBIT OR HARE

Ingredients

1 *rabbit.*	¼ *lb. bacon.*	2 *onions.*	1 *oz. flour.*
2 *hard-boiled eggs.*	1 *clove.*	*Stock.*	*Seasoning.*

Method

1. Joint and soak the rabbit.
2. Place the jointed rabbit in a stew jar.
3. Pare and slice the onions and add.
4. Trim and cut up the bacon and lay over the onion.
5. Shell and slice the hard-boiled eggs and keep for a garnish.
6. Pour the stock and seasonings over the rabbit and cook for 2½ hours.

7. Remove the rabbit and thicken the gravy with 1 oz. of flour.

8. Use the egg as a garnish for the dish.

9. Forcemeat balls may be prepared and cooked with it.

(Sufficient for 4 persons.)

PIGEON PIE

Ingredients

5 or 6 pigeons.	2 slices round of beef.	6 oz. bread-
½ pint stock.	3 hard-boiled eggs.	crumbs.
½ lb. Flaky Pastry	1 teaspoonful chopped	1 oz. butter.
(see page 144).	parsley.	Seasoning.

Method

1. Clean the birds and wipe out well.

2. Reserve four of the feet and scrub and scrape well and soak in cold water.

3. Make a forcemeat with the bread-crumbs, parsley, butter and seasoning.

4. Fill the pigeons with the forcemeat.

5. Lay a slice of beef at the bottom of the pie-dish.

6. Lay the pigeons on top, breast downwards.

7. Slice the eggs and lay over the birds.

8. Place the other slice of meat over the eggs.

9. Pour in ½ pint of good stock.

10. Cover with flaky pastry as for Beef-Steak Pie (see page 62).

11. Dry the feet and place in the centre of the pie before serving.

RABBIT HOT POT

Ingredients

1 rabbit.	1 onion.	1 oz. flour.	Seasoning.
1½–2 lb. potatoes.	1 oz. dripping.	¼ lb. ham.	½ pint stock.

Method

1. Joint the rabbit and soak in cold water, and salt. Use the heart, kidneys and liver.

2. Melt the dripping.

3. Mix the seasoning into the flour and dip each part of rabbit in it.

4. Fry in the melted dripping.

5. Pare and slice the onion and fry till a nice brown.

6. Place in a stew-jar or casserole.

7. Lightly fry the ham and lay on top of the rabbit and onion.

8. Pour over the stock and put on the lid.

9. Cook for ½ hour in a good oven.

10. Pare and slice the potatoes and pile on top of the rabbit.

11. Cover again and cook for 1 hour, or until the potatoes are soft and the rabbit is tender.   (Regulo 5.)

12. Serve very hot.

13. Rabbit Hot Pot may be served in the casserole in which it is cooked.

(Sufficient for 4 persons.)

RABBIT PIE

Ingredients

1 *rabbit.*	½ *lb. breast of mutton.*	1 *onion.*
1 *oz. dripping.*	*Seasoning.*	1 *oz. flour.*
½ *lb. Rough Puff Pastry (see page* 147).		½ *pint stock.*

Method

1. Joint the rabbit as for Hot Pot and put to soak.

2. Cut up the mutton.

3. Mix the flour and seasoning.

4. Melt the dripping.

5. Dip each part of meat in the seasoned flour.

6. Fry lightly in the melted dripping.

7. Pare and slice the onion and fry.

8. Place all in a pie-dish and pour over the stock.

9. Cover the pie with the pastry as for Beef-Steak Pie (see page 62).

10. Cook until nicely browned and then put a buttered paper over the top.

11. Time required is usually about 1–1¼ hours.

12. It is often best to cook the rabbit separately for ½ hour and allow it to cool before covering.   If the rabbit is large or an old one, this is advisable.

13. Place some freshly-washed parsley in the opening before serving.

(Sufficient for 4 persons.)

ROAST DUCK

Ingredients

1 *Duck*

Stuffing

4 *oz. bread-crumbs.*	*A little sage.*	2 *boiled onions.*
Seasoning.	1 *egg.*	

Method

1. Pluck the duck; draw and singe it, and wipe it out well with a clean towel.

2. Cut off the first bone of the wing and scald and peel the feet and twist round the feet to lie along the back.

3. Prepare the stuffing and put it in the body of the bird.
4. Butter a paper and wrap the bird in it.
5. Bake in a good oven for 1½ hours. (Regulo 7.)
6. Serve with brown sauce and orange salad.

ROAST GROUSE

Ingredients

Brace of grouse.   1 oz. flour.   Seasoning.
2 slices toasted or fried bread.   2 slices ham.

Method

1. Pluck the grouse and truss as for Roast Fowl (see page 89).
2. Place a slice of ham—rather fat—on the breast of each bird.
3. Roast in a moderate oven for ½ hour. (Regulo 6.)
4. Remove the ham. Dredge the birds with flour. Baste till nicely browned.
5. Toast the bread and place the slices under the birds to catch the gravy.
6. Dish the birds on the slices of bread.
7. Serve with Brown Sauce (see page 119) and Bread Sauce (see page 119) and a few fried bread-crumbs.

ROAST RABBIT OR HARE

Ingredients

1 rabbit.   ½ lb. sausage-meat.   ¼ lb. streaky bacon.
Seasoning.   1 oz. dripping.

Method

1. Wash the rabbit and soak for ½ hour. Dry.
2. Skewer the legs and skewer through the neck, mouth and neck at the other side.
3. Season the sausage-meat, place it inside and sew up.
4. Melt the dripping in a tin and lay in the rabbit.
5. Place the slices of bacon on the top.
6. Bake in a good oven for 1¼ hours. (Regulo 6.)
7. Undo the sewing and place on a hot dish.
8. Garnish with parsley and baked tomatoes, and serve with Brown Sauce (see page 119).

ROAST PARTRIDGE OR PHEASANT

Ingredients

1 pheasant.   4 mushrooms.   1 oz. butter.   Seasoning.
1 slice bread fried in dripping.   4 oz. streaky bacon.

Method

1. Pluck the pheasant and truss as for Roast Fowl (see page 89).

2. Melt the butter and chop the mushrooms, mix together and season well and place inside the pheasant.

3. Place the slices of bacon on the breast.

4. Roast in a good oven for ½ hour. (Regulo 6.)

5. Serve on a slice of fried bread.

6. Serve with Brown Sauce (see page 119) and Bread Sauce (see page 119). (Sufficient for 4 persons.)

ROAST PIGEON

Ingredients

2 *pigeons.*   4 *slices of bacon.*   2 *slices of fried bread.*

Method

1. Pluck the pigeon and truss as for Roast Fowl (see page 89).

2. Wrap it in bacon.

3. Roast in a good oven for 20 to 30 minutes. (Regulo 6.)

4. Serve on a slice of fried bread.

5. Serve with Brown Sauce and Bread Sauce (see page 119). (Sufficient for 4 persons.)

ROAST TURKEY

Ingredients

1 *turkey.*   4 *oz. bacon.*   *Piece of leaf suet.*

Stuffing

½ *lb. chestnuts.*   4 *oz. bread-crumbs.*   4 *oz. sausage-meat.*
Seasoning.   *Rind of ½ lemon.*   2 *eggs.*
A small grating of nutmeg.   ½ *teaspoonful dried*
½ *teaspoonful chopped parsley.*   *herbs.*

Method

1. Make the stuffing. Bake the chestnuts for 10 minutes.

2. Take off the two skins and rub through a sieve.

3. Mix all the ingredients together.

4. Pluck and draw the bird and truss as for Roast Fowl (see page 89). Wipe out.

5. Place the stuffing in the breast.

6. Cover the breast with the slices of bacon.

7. Lay the leaf suet over the top of the bird.

8. Roast in a quick oven for 1½ hours. If it is a large bird it will take longer. (Regulo 6.)

9. Serve with gravy and Bread Sauce (see page 119).

D

STEAMED FOWL

Ingredients

1 *fowl.*   1 *lemon.*   1 *oz. dripping.*

Method

1. Pluck and truss the fowl as for Boiled Fowl (see page 90).
2. Cut the lemon in slices and place on the breast.
3. Wrap in a buttered paper.
4. Place in a steamer and steam for 2 hours.
5. Melt an ounce of dripping in a roasting-tin.
6. Remove the paper from the fowl and lay in the dripping. Baste over.
7. Bake till a golden-brown colour.
8. Serve using parsley and fried or baked sausages as a garnish.

Note.—This is a good method of using up old fowl, as it makes it very tender.

STEWED RABBIT

Ingredients

1 *rabbit.*   1 *onion.*   1 *carrot.*   ½ *turnip.*
1 *oz. flour.* 1 *oz. dripping.*   1 *pint stock.*

Method

1. Joint the rabbit and soak it in cold water.
2. Melt the dripping.
3. Lightly fry the pieces of rabbit.
4. Pare and slice the onion.
5. Lift out the pieces of rabbit, and add the flour to the dripping.
6. Stir till brown.
7. Add the stock and stir till boiling.
8. Place in the pieces of rabbit and fried onion.
9. Cook for ½ hour.
10. Pare the carrot and turnip and cut them up in dice, and add them to the stew.
11. Cook for 1 hour.
12. Season and serve.

(Sufficient for 4 persons.)

POULTRY LEFT-OVERS

CROQUETTES

Ingredients

1 *oz. flour.*   1 *oz. butter.* 1 *gill milk.*
Egg and bread-crumbs.   *Seasoning.*   *Fat to fry.*
½ *lb. cold chicken or other fowl.*

Method

1. Chop the chicken and remove all bones.
2. Melt the butter and add the flour.   Cook for 1 minute.
3. Add the milk and stir till thick.
4. Add the chicken and seasoning.
5. Spread on a plate to cool.
6. Form into croquettes.
7. Egg and crumb each and fry in smoking hot fat till a golden brown.
8. Serve garnished with parsley.

(Sufficient for 4 persons.)

RISSOLES

Ingredients

8 oz. cold fowl. *Egg and bread-crumbs.*
6 oz. sieved potatoes. *Fat to fry.*   *Seasoning.*

Method

1. Chop the meat and remove all bones.
2. Mix with the potatoes.
3. Season well.
4. Form into oval rissoles.
5. Egg and crumb each and fry in smoking hot fat till a golden brown.
6. Serve very hot.
7. Garnish with parsley.   (Sufficient for 4 persons.)

FILLING FOR OMELETS

Chopped fowl or rabbit may be used as a filling for omelets.

18. VEGETABLES

BAKED POTATOES IN JACKETS

Ingredients

6 or 8 *large potatoes.*

Method

1. Choose potatoes of the same size and free from blemishes.
2. Scrub them well in cold water until the skins are white.
3. Place in a hot oven and cook for 1 hour.   (Regulo 7.)
4. Reduce the heat and cook for about 1 hour longer, according to the size of the potatoes.
5. The potatoes when done should feel perfectly soft when pressed.
6. Before serving, make a cut all round the centre of the potatoes, so that they may be easily peeled.

(Sufficient for 4 persons.)

BOILED ARTICHOKES

Ingredients

1 *lb. artichokes.*   *Salt.*   *Water to boil.*

Method

1. Pare the artichokes carefully under water to preserve the colour, and leave in cold water till required.
2. Boil the water and add the salt.
3. Put in the artichokes and cook for 30 minutes.
4. Drain and serve with white sauce.

(Sufficient for 4 persons.)

BOILED ASPARAGUS

Ingredients

1 *bunch asparagus.*   *Water to boil.*
½ *teaspoonful sugar.*   *Salt.*

Method

1. Trim the asparagus and scrape very lightly.
2. Wash under cold running water.   Soak till required.
3. Butter a paper and place it round the tips.
4. Boil in salted water with sugar added.
5. Drain well on a sieve and serve with melted butter.

Note.—Asparagus may also be steamed.

(Sufficient for 4 persons.)

BOILED BEETROOT

Ingredients

1 *lb. beetroot.*   *Water to boil.*   *Vinegar.*

Method

1. Wash the beetroot very carefully, but do not pare or scrape, and do not break off any of the fibres.
2. Boil in fast-boiling water till soft; usually from 1½ to 2 hours.
3. Allow to cool, and then remove the skin.
4. Cut in slices and serve hot, or cold in a glass dish with vinegar poured over it.

(Sufficient for 4 persons.)

BOILED BRUSSELS SPROUTS

Ingredients

1 *lb. sprouts.*   *Salt.*

Method

1. Trim the sprouts, removing all soiled outer leaves.
2. Score the stalk end across.

3. Soak in cold water and salt for 1 to 2 hours.
4. Put on to boil in fast-boiling salted water and boil with the lid off.
5. Drain when soft.
6. Serve with melted butter.

Note.—A pinch of soda is often added to preserve the colour. This is not a good plan, as it destroys the mineral salts for which the vegetable is valuable. It is much better to sacrifice the colour a little than to do this. (Sufficient for 4 persons.)

BOILED CABBAGE

Ingredients

1 *cabbage (medium size).*   *Salt.*   *Water to boil.*

Method

1. Trim the outer leaves and trim the stalk.
2. Score across, and if large cut in halves.
3. Soak in cold water and salt.
4. Boil in fast-boiling water with salt till tender.
5. Drain well.
6. Chop up and add pepper and melted butter.
7. Serve hot.   (Sufficient for 4 persons.)

BOILED CARROTS

Ingredients

1 *lb. young carrots.*   *Salt.*   *A pinch of sugar.*

Method

1. Wash the carrots well in cold water.
2. Scrape off the outer skin.
3. Boil in water and salt with a little sugar added, until the carrots are tender; about 30 to 40 minutes usually.
4. Drain and serve with White Sauce (see page 127).
       (Sufficient for 4 persons.)

BOILED CAULIFLOWER

Ingredients

1 *cauliflower (medium size).*   *Salt.*   *Water to boil.*

Method

1. Trim the outer leaves and score across the stalk end.
2. Soak in cold salt water.
3. Put on to boil in fast-boiling salted water.
4. Boil till tender. Test the flower gently.
5. Drain and serve with White Sauce (see page 127).
       (Sufficient for 4 persons.)

BOILED LEEKS

Ingredients

1 *bunch of leeks.*   *Salt.*   *Water to boil.*

Method

1. Trim the leeks and cut off the feathery roots at the white end. Cut off the ragged tails.
2. Soak in salt and water.
3. Boil in fast-boiling water till tender.
4. Drain well and serve with White Sauce (see page 127).

Note.—Leeks may also be steamed or stewed.

(Sufficient for 4 persons.)

BOILED ONIONS

Ingredients

1 *lb. Spanish onions.*   *Salt.*   *Water to boil.*

Method

1. Peel the onions and put on to boil in boiling salted water.
2. Boil till tender.
3. Drain well and serve with White Sauce (see page 127).

(Sufficient for 4 persons.)

BOILED PARSNIPS

Ingredients

1 *lb. parsnips.*   *Salt.*   *Water to boil.*

Method

1. Pare or scrape the parsnips and soak in cold water.
2. Put on to boil in fast-boiling salted water.
3. Boil till tender.
4. Drain and serve with White Sauce or Parsley Sauce (see pages 127 or 125).   (Sufficient for 4 persons.)

BOILED TURNIP

Ingredients

1 *swede turnip (medium size).*   1 *oz. butter.*   *Seasoning.*

Method

1. Peel the turnip and cut it up in thin slices.
2. Boil in fast-boiling salted water till tender.
3. Drain well.
4. Mash and add pepper and butter. Reheat and serve at once.

(Sufficient for 4 persons.)

BOILED VEGETABLE MARROW

Ingredients

1 *marrow.*   *Salt.*

Method

1. Pare the marrow rather thickly and cut in four.
2. Remove the seeds and soft part.
3. Cut in squares.
4. Boil till tender in salted water for about 30 minutes.
5. Drain well and serve with White Sauce (see page 127).

BRAISED CELERY

Ingredients

3 *small heads of celery.*	*Seasoning.*	1 *carrot.*
1 *oz. flour.*	1 *onion.*	½ *turnip.*
1 *pint stock.*	1 *oz. butter.*	

Method

1. Trim the celery and scrub it well in cold water.
2. Separate the stalks, and if these are very long, half each piece.
3. Pare and cut up the carrot, turnip and onion.
4. Place the prepared vegetables in a casserole and add some seasoning.
5. Lay the celery on top and pour on the stock.   Put the lid of the casserole on.
6. Cook for 1½ hours in a moderate oven.   (Regulo 5.)
7. Blend 1 oz. of flour and stir into the sauce.
8. Lastly add 1 oz. butter.
9. Reheat and serve at once.

(Sufficient for 4 persons.)

BRAISED STUFFED ONIONS

Ingredients

4 *Spanish onions.*	¼ *lb. sausage-meat.*	1 *oz. bread-crumbs.*
½ *pint stock.*	1 *oz. flour.*	½ *oz. butter.*
1 *carrot.*	1 *onion.*	¼ *turnip.*	*Seasoning.*

Method

1. Mix the sausage-meat and bread-crumbs.
2. Peel the onions and parboil them.   Scoop out the centres.
3. Mix the onion which is taken out with the sausage-meat and bread-crumbs.
4. Stuff the onions with the mixture.
5. Pare and chop the carrot, turnip and onion and lay in a casserole and sprinkle in the seasoning.

6. Lay the stuffed onions on top and add the stock.

7. Put on the lid and bake till tender.   (Regulo 6.)   About 1 hr.

8. Thicken the sauce and add the butter, and serve.

(Sufficient for 4 persons.)

BROAD BEANS

Ingredients

1 *lb. broad beans.*   *Seasoning.*   ½ *oz. butter.*

Method

1. Shell the beans and peel off the outer skin.

2. Boil in fast-boiling salted water for about 40 minutes or till tender.

3. Drain and add some seasoning and butter, and serve.

(Sufficient for 4 persons.)

CAULIFLOWER AU GRATIN

Ingredients

1 *cauliflower.*   *Water.*   *Salt.*
A pinch of sugar.   ½ *pint Cheese Sauce.*   2 *oz. grated cheese.*

Method

1. Prepare and cook the cauliflower as for Boiled Cauliflower (see page 101).

2. Pour over the Cheese Sauce (see page 120).

3. Sprinkle with grated cheese.

4. Serve at once.   (Sufficient for 4 persons.)

CHIPPED POTATOES

Ingredients

1 *lb. small potatoes.*   *A bath of fat.*

Method

1. Peel the potatoes and cut into little wedges.

2. Rinse in cold water and then dry on a clean towel.

3. Fry in the boiling fat till a golden brown.

4. Drain and season well.

5. Serve very crisp.   (Sufficient for 4 persons.)

CREAMED POTATOES

Ingredients

1 *lb. mashed potatoes.*   2 *oz. butter.*   2 *egg-yolks.*
Seasoning.   1 *egg.*

Method

1. Mix the mashed potatoes, seasoning, butter and egg-yolks together.
2. Put into a bag with a large-rose pipe.
3. Pipe on to an oven shelf.
4. Brush over with beaten egg.
5. Bake till lightly browned.   (Regulo 7.)
6. Serve at once.

(Sufficient for 4 persons.)

DRIED BEANS OR PEAS

Ingredients

1 *lb. beans or peas.*   *Salt.*
1 *pint White Sauce* (see page 127).

Method

1. Soak the beans or peas over-night.
2. Boil in boiling salted water till tender.
3. Drain and serve with White Sauce.

(Sufficient for 4 persons.)

FRENCH BEANS

Ingredients

1 *lb. French beans.*   *Salt.*   1 *oz. butter.*

Method

1. String the beans and cut in thin shreds.
2. Put on to steam and cook till tender—about 20 minutes.
3. Add seasoning and butter and shake well to mix.
4. Serve hot.   (Sufficient for 4 persons.)

GREEN PEAS

Ingredients

1 *lb. peas.*   *Salt.*   1 *teaspoonful sugar.*
Small piece of mint.   1 *oz. butter.*   *Seasoning.*

Method

1. Shell and wash the peas.
2. Put water to boil and put in the sugar and salt.
3. When boiling, add the peas and cook for a few minutes, and then put in the mint.
4. Cook till tender.
5. Drain and add seasoning and melted butter.
6. Serve at once.

(Sufficient for 4 persons.)

GRILLED MUSHROOMS

Ingredients

1 lb. mushrooms.	Seasoning.	1 lemon.
2 oz. butter.	Toast.	

Method

1. Cut off the stalk and peel the mushrooms.
2. Wash well and dry carefully.
3. Lay on a grilling tin and sprinkle on the seasoning and lemon juice.
4. Add some little pats of butter.
5. Grill for 5 minutes on the first side.
6. Turn and grill the second side.
7. Serve on hot toast.   (Sufficient for 4 persons.)

MASHED POTATOES

Ingredients

1 lb. cooked potatoes.	2 oz. butter.	Seasoning.
2 tablespoonfuls hot milk.		

Method

1. Rub the potatoes through a sieve or use a potato presser.
2. Add seasoning and 1 oz. butter.
3. Stir in the hot milk and beat well.
4. Place in a buttered pie-dish and mark the top with a fork.
5. Place the other ounce of butter on top in little pats.
6. Brown under a grill.
7. Serve at once.   (Sufficient for 4 persons.)

NEW POTATOES

Ingredients

1 lb. new potatoes.	Salt and pepper.	Water to boil.
½ teaspoonful chopped parsley.		1 oz. butter.

Method

1. Scrub the potatoes till quite clean.
2. Put on to boil in boiling water till tender.
3. Add the salt when almost ready.
4. Drain off the water.
5. Add the butter, chopped parsley and pepper.
6. Re-heat and serve at once.   (Sufficient for 4 persons.)

POTATO CROQUETTES

Ingredients

¾ lb. mashed potatoes.	1 oz. butter.	Seasoning.
Egg and bread-crumbs.	1 egg.	Fat to fry.
½ teaspoonful chopped parsley.		

Method

1. Mix the potatoes, butter, seasoning, parsley and egg-yolk together.
2. Whisk the egg-white and fold in carefully.
3. Form into balls, and egg and bread-crumb each.
4. Fry in deep fat till brown and puffy.
5. Drain and serve very hot and crisp.

(Sufficient for 4 persons.)

POTATO RIBBONS

Ingredients

4 *large potatoes.*   *Fat to fry.*

Method

1. Pare the potatoes and cut in thick slices.
2. Pare round the outside of the slices to form ribbons. Wash well and dry in a clean towel.
3. Fry in hot fat till nicely browned.
4. Serve at once.

(Sufficient for 4 persons.)

POTATO STRAWS

Ingredients

4 *large potatoes.*   *Fat to fry.*

Method

1. Pare the potatoes and cut in half lengthwise.
2. Cut in very thin strips about $1\frac{1}{2}$ in. long.
3. Soak for 1 hour in cold water.
4. Drain and dry well.
5. Fry in hot fat.
6. Drain and serve at once.

(Sufficient for 4 persons.)

SALSIFY

Ingredients

1 *lb. salsify.*   1 *lemon.*   *Salt.*

Method

1. Scrape the vegetable till nice and white, and soak in cold water and lemon juice.
2. Boil in boiling salted water with lemon added for about an hour.
3. Drain and serve with White Sauce (see page 127).

(Sufficient for 4 persons.)

SEA-KALE

Ingredients

1 *bundle of kale.*	*Salt.*
Lemon.	2 *oz. butter.*

Method

1. Cut off the roots and wash the kale, and tie it in bundles.
2. Boil in fast-boiling salted water with the lemon juice added.
3. Drain well.
4. Serve on toast with melted butter poured over.

(Sufficient for 4 persons.)

SPINACH

Ingredients

1 *lb. spinach.*	1 *oz. flour.*	½ *pint milk.*	⅛ *gill of cream.*
1 *oz. butter.*	*A pinch of sugar.*	*Seasoning.*	

Method

1. Cut off the stalk and wash the leaves in several cold waters.
2. Boil in salted water till tender, generally about 15 minutes.
3. Drain well and chop.
4. Add the butter, flour, seasoning, cream, milk and sugar.
5. Re-heat and serve at once. (Sufficient for 4 persons.)

STUFFED POTATOES

Ingredients

4 *large potatoes.*	1 *oz. dripping.*	*Seasoning.*
½ *lb. sausage-meat.*	2 *tomatoes.*	1 *oz. bread-crumbs.*

Method

1. Peel the potatoes and cut a piece off the end to make a base on which each can stand.
2. Cut a piece off the other end and scrape out the centre. (These bits can be put in the stock pot.)
3. Mix the sausage-meat, bread-crumbs and seasoning together.
4. Fill up the potatoes.
5. Melt the dripping and put it in the potatoes.
6. Put on the lids and roast until the potatoes are soft. (Regulo 7.)
7. Slice the tomatoes.
8. Remove the lids of the potatoes and lay on a slice of tomato. Replace the lids.
9. Decorate with parsley. (Sufficient for 4 persons.)

STUFFED TOMATOES

Ingredients

4 *tomatoes*.	*Seasoning*.	2 *oz. chopped ham*.
½ *boiled onion*.	1 *oz. butter*.	1 *oz. grated cheese*.
2 *tablespoonfuls bread-crumbs*.		

Method

1. Scoop out the centres of the tomatoes.
2. Melt the butter and fry the onion and chopped ham.   Stir in the bread-crumbs and seasoning.
3. Fill up the tomatoes.
4. Lay on a buttered tin and cover with a buttered paper.
5. Cook for 10 to 15 minutes in a moderate oven. (Regulo 4.)
6. Sprinkle a little grated cheese on each and serve on toast.

(Sufficient for 4 persons.)

STUFFED VEGETABLE MARROW

Ingredients

1 *small marrow*.	*Fat to fry*.
Egg and bread-crumbs.	*Stuffing*.

Method

1. Peel the marrow, take out the seeds and soft parts, and boil for about 10 minutes.
2. Drain and stuff with any desired stuffing.
3. Rub over with flour.
4. Egg and bread-crumb, and fry in hot fat till a golden brown.
5. Drain and serve. (Sufficient for 4 persons.)

VEGETABLE LEFT-OVERS

BAKED CABBAGE OR SPROUTS

Ingredients

½ *lb. cabbage or sprouts (cooked)*.	½ *pint stock*.
1 *tablespoonful chopped onion*.	½ *lb. mashed potatoes*.
1 *teaspoonful mixed herbs*.	¼ *lb. bread-crumbs*.
1 *tablespoonful chopped parsley*.	

Method

1. Chop the green vegetables finely.
2. Add the potatoes, bread-crumbs, onion, parsley and herbs, and mix well.
3. Add the stock and mix again.
4. Put into a greased pie-dish and bake in a moderate oven (Regulo 4) for 20 minutes. (Sufficient for 4 persons.)

COLCANNON

Ingredients

1 *breakfastcupful cold potatoes.*   1 *breakfastcupful cold cabbage.*
Seasoning.   *Bread raspings.*   1 *oz. dripping.*

Method

  1. Grease a basin and sprinkle with bread raspings.
  2. Mash the potatoes and chop the cabbage.   Mix.
  3. Add seasoning and dripping.
  4. Turn into a greased basin and heat in the oven.
  5. Turn out and serve.

(Sufficient for 4 persons.)

DICED VEGETABLES

Ingredients

1 *lb. cooked carrots, turnips, and parsnips.*   *A few capers.*
2 *tablespoonfuls chopped parsley.*   1 *oz. butter.*
2 *tablespoonfuls mushroom or tomato sauce.*

Method

  1. Dice the vegetables.
  2. Heat them in the butter to which the chopped parsley, capers, and sauce are added.   Stir constantly until the butter is absorbed.
  3. Put the mixture in a pie-dish and keep hot till served.

(Sufficient for 4 persons.)

FRIED MASHED POTATOES

Ingredients

1 *lb. cold potatoes.*   *Fat.*   *Seasoning.*

Method

  1. Melt some dripping in a pan and when hot add the potatoes.
  2. Stir about well and see that they brown evenly all over.
  3. Sprinkle in some seasoning and serve very hot.

(Sufficient for 4 persons.)

19. SALADS

BEETROOT AND POTATO SALAD

Ingredients

4 *small beetroots.*   2 *hard-boiled eggs.*   1 *bunch spring onions.*
French Dressing (see page 228).   4 *whole boiled potatoes.*

Method

1. Boil the beetroots and when cool peel them.
2. Slice very thinly.
3. Trim the onions and chop roughly.
4. Slice the potatoes.
5. Shell the eggs and slice.
6. Put a layer of beetroot in a glass dish, then layers of potato, onion and egg.
7. Continue till all is used.
8. Arrange the egg on the top as neatly as possible.
9. The dressing may be poured over or handed separately.

(Sufficient for 4 persons.)

CAULIFLOWER SALAD

Ingredients

1 *cauliflower* (*boiled*).   1 *tablespoonful chopped parsley.*
Salad Dressing (see page 229).   1 *tablespoonful vinegar.*

Method

1. Divide the cauliflower into sprigs and dip each in the chopped parsley.
2. Arrange in a dish.
3. Pour a little vinegar over and lay on ice.
4. Before serving pour over the Salad Dressing.

(Sufficient for 4 persons.)

CELERY AND CREAM-CHEESE SALAD

Ingredients

1 *head of celery.*   1 *cream cheese.*
French Dressing (see page 228).

Method

1. Wash the celery and cut the very white parts into lengths and then into little straws.
2. Chop the rougher parts.
3. Cut the cheese in small cubes and mix with the chopped celery.
4. Pile in a dish.
5. Place the straws on the top and put a generous grating of hard cheese over all.
6. Lay on ice and just before serving pour over the French Dressing.

(Sufficient for 4 persons.)

CELERY AND TOMATO SALAD

Ingredients

I *head of celery.*   3 *or* 4 *tomatoes.*
French Dressing (see page 228).

Method

1. Pour boiling water over the tomatoes and peel them.
2. Cut in slices.
3. Scrub the celery and cut in straws.
4. Arrange in alternate layers in a glass dish.
5. Pour the dressing over before serving.

(Sufficient for 4 persons.)

CRAB SALAD

Ingredients

I *crab.*   I *lettuce.*   *A few capers.*
Salad Dressing or Mayonnaise (see pages 229 or 228).

Method

1. Cook the crab in fast-boiling water for about ½ hour.
2. Lay aside till cold.
3. Take out the flesh and divide finely.
4. Add Salad Dressing and chopped capers.
5. Wash the lettuce and drain well.
6. Arrange in a dish and place the crab mixture on top.
7. Put aside on ice till required.

(Sufficient for 4 persons.)

CUCUMBER SALAD

Ingredients

½ *cucumber.*   4 *or* 5 *cubes of pineapple.*
½ *teaspoonful chopped parsley.*   *Salad Dressing* (see page 229).

Method

1. Wipe the cucumber, but do not peel.
2. Trim the ends and score lengthwise with a vegetable cutter so that there are alternate white and green stripes running lengthwise.
3. Cut in very thin slices.
4. Chop the pineapple and sprinkle with parsley.
5. Put alternate layers of cucumber and pineapple in the dish.
6. Pour over the dressing.

(Sufficient for 4 persons.)

DRESSED GREEN SALAD

Ingredients

1 *lettuce.*	*Watercress.*	*Mustard and cress.*
Pepper.	1 *head of endive.*	1 *cucumber.*
1 *tablespoonful white wine vinegar.*		3 *tablespoonful salad oil.*

Method

1. Discard any coarse or discoloured leaves from the lettuce, endive or watercress.

2. Wash the lettuce leaves, the endive, watercress and mustard and cress quickly in well-salted water and dry by shaking in a vegetable strainer.

3. Break the lettuce leaves with the fingers.

4. Rub the inside of a salad bowl with a piece of onion and put in the prepared green stuffs.

5. Slice the cucumber thinly, and add.

6. Pour a tablespoonful of white wine vinegar over the salad, turning the leaves so that all are covered.

7. Next add 3 tablespoonfuls salad oil and again turn the leaves.

8. Add pepper, turning the leaves again.

(Sufficient for 4 persons.)

EGG SALAD

Ingredients

4 *hard-boiled eggs.*	4 *or* 5 *capers.*	*Chopped parsley.*
Mayonnaise (see page 228).		1 *lettuce.*

Method

1. Shell the eggs and cut the whites in rings.

2. Sieve the yolks and mix with parsley, chop the capers and add to the yolk mixture.

3. Wash and drain the lettuce.

4. Arrange in a dish and lay the egg rings round the outside.

5. Pile the yolk mixture in the centre.

6. Pour over the Mayonnaise.

7. Lay aside on ice till required.

(Sufficient for 4 persons.)

FISH SALAD

Ingredients

1 *lb. cooked fish.*	1 *lettuce.*	*Seasoning.*	2 *eggs.*
Mayonnaise (see page 228).		*A few gherkins and capers.*	

Method

1. Flake the fish.

2. Chop the gherkins and capers and add to the flaked fish.

3. Wash and drain the lettuce and arrange it in a dish.
4. Cut up the egg-whites and sieve the yolks.
5. Add the yolks to the fish mixture and season well.
6. Pile on top of the lettuce. Lay the egg-white rings round the edge as a garnish.
7. Serve the Mayonnaise separately.

(Sufficient for 4 persons.)

FRENCH SALAD

Ingredients

4 or 5 tomatoes.   Seasoning.   Salad oil.
Vinegar.   Chopped parsley.

Method

1. Dip the tomatoes in boiling water, skin them and cut in slices.
2. Mix the salad oil and vinegar together, using 1 part of vinegar to 2 parts of oil. Add seasoning.
3. Arrange the tomatoes in a dish and sprinkle in a little parsley.
4. Pour the dressing over.

(Sufficient for 4 persons.)

LETTUCE AND TOMATO SALAD

Ingredients

1 lettuce.   4 tomatoes.   Watercress.
Salad Dressing (see page 229).

Method

1. Wash the lettuce and watercress and drain them well.
2. Peel and slice the tomatoes.
3. Arrange in alternate layers in a salad bowl.
4. Pour over the dressing or, if liked, hand it separately.

(Sufficient for 4 persons.)

LETTUCE AND PINEAPPLE SALAD

Ingredients

1 lettuce.   1 apple.   Watercress.
1 small tin of pineapple.   Grated Parmesan cheese.
Salad Dressing (see page 229).   Chopped parsley.

Method

1. Cut each pineapple cube in four pieces and dip in chopped parsley.
2. Wash and drain the watercress.
3. Wash and drain the lettuce.

4. Peel and chop the apple.
5. Chop the coarser leaves of lettuce.
6. Mix the chopped lettuce, apple and pineapple.
7. Put a layer of lettuce in a glass dish.
8. Put a layer of the mixture on top.
9. Put a layer of watercress on top of that.
10. Continue till all is used up.
11. Sprinkle a little Parmesan cheese over the top.
12. Hand the dressing separately.

(Sufficient for 4 persons.)

LOBSTER SALAD

Ingredients

1 *lobster or* 1 *tin of lobster.*   *A few gherkins and capers.*
Salad Dressing (see page 229).   *Truffles and chilli pods.*
Watercress.   1 *lettuce.*   1 *beetroot.*   *Seasoning.*

Method

1. Cut up the lobster.
2. Wash and drain the lettuce and cress.
3. Chop the gherkins and capers and the outer leaves of the lettuce and add seasoning.
4. Peel and slice the beetroot and mix it in.
5. Add the lobster and mix with the Salad Dressing.
6. Make a bed of lettuce in a dish and pile in the mixture.
7. Decorate with truffles and chilli pods.
8. Lay on ice until required.

(Sufficient for 4 persons.)

MIXED VEGETABLE SALAD

Ingredients

4 *tomatoes.*   *Half a cucumber.*   1 *dozen radishes.*
1 *bunch of onions.*   2 *hard-boiled eggs.*   1 *apple.*
Salad Dressing (see page 229).   1 *lettuce.*

Method

1. Peel and slice the tomatoes.
2. Slice the cucumber.
3. Wash the lettuce and onions and drain well.
4. Chop the onions and roughly divide the lettuce.
5. Wash and slice the radishes.
6. Peel and chop the apple.
7. Shell and slice the eggs.
8. Arrange all as neatly as possible in a glass dish.
9. Pour over the Salad Dressing.

(Sufficient for 4 persons.)

ORANGE SALAD

Ingredients

4 or 5 oranges.   4 oz. sugar.   1 pint water.

Method

1. Peel the oranges and cut them in thin slices.
2. Grate the rind of one and put it on to boil with the water and sugar.
3. Boil for 1 hour and lay aside to cool, then pour it over the orange slices.
4. Lay on ice till required.

(Sufficient for 4 persons.)

POTATO SALAD

Ingredients

1 beetroot.   6 potatoes (cooked).   Seasoning.
Salad Dressing (see page 229).   1 teaspoonful chopped parsley.

Method

1. Use beetroot that has been well soaked in vinegar.
2. Cut the potatoes in dice, season them, and mix in the parsley.
3. Pour over the Salad Dressing.
4. Pile in a dish, decorating the salad with the beetroot cut in shapes.

(Sufficient for 4 persons.)

RUSSIAN SALAD

Ingredients

1 teacupful chopped meat.   1 or 2 cold boiled potatoes.
1 teacupful green peas.   1 tablespoonful chutney.
Salad Dressing (see page 229).   2 pickled onions.
3 oz. cheese.   1 lettuce.   Watercress.

Method

1. Chop the onions and mix with the green peas.
2. Mix the chutney and the meat together.
3. Add the potatoes cut in dice.
4. Wash and drain the lettuce and arrange it in a dish.
5. Mix all the other ingredients, cutting up the cheese very finely before adding.
6. Pile all on top of the lettuce.
7. Put a few sprigs of watercress on top as a garnish, and serve very cold with Salad Dressing.

(Sufficient for 4 persons.)

SPRING SALAD

Ingredients

1 *lettuce.*	1 *bunch radishes.*	4 *tomatoes.*
Watercress.	1 *bunch onions.*	2 *hard-boiled eggs.*

Salad Dressing (see page 229).

Method

1. Peel and slice the tomatoes.
2. Wash and drain the lettuce and watercress.
3. Chop the coarser leaves and shred the fine ones.
4. Trim the onions and cut up.
5. Wash and slice the radishes.
6. Shell and slice the eggs.
7. Arrange all in a glass dish, and serve with Salad Dressing.

(Sufficient for 4 persons.)

TOMATO SALAD

Ingredients

4 *tomatoes.*	*Seasoning.*	*Salad Dressing* (see page 229).
1 *onion.*	*Mustard.*	1 *teaspoonful chopped parsley.*

Method

1. Peel and slice the tomatoes.
2. Slice the onion.
3. Put a layer of tomatoes in a dish and sprinkle with a little parsley, seasoning and mustard.
4. Cover with a layer of thinly-sliced onion and season.
5. Continue till full.
6. Pour over the dressing. (Sufficient for 4 persons.)

WALDORF SALAD

Ingredients

4 *oz. cold ham or chicken.*	*Mayonnaise.*	1 *cucumber.*
A few gherkins. *Seasoning.*	1 *lettuce.*	4 *oz. tongue.*

Method

1. Chop the ham and tongue. Chop the gherkins and add.
2. Season well and mix in some Mayonnaise.
3. Cut the cucumber lengthwise and remove the seedy part.
4. Fill up the hollow with the mixture.
5. Cut in strips and serve on a bed of lettuce.

(Sufficient for 4 persons.)

WINTER SALAD

Ingredients

1 *head of celery.*	1 *beetroot.*	½ *lb. cold sprouts.*
½ *cold cauliflower.*	2 *or* 3 *cold potatoes.*	2 *hard-boiled eggs.*
1 *teaspoonful finely chopped parsley.*		*Salad Dressing.*

Method

1. Cut up all the ingredients small and arrange in as pleasing a manner as possible in a glass dish.
2. Serve with Salad Dressing.

(Sufficient for 4 persons.)

20. SAUCES

ANCHOVY SAUCE

Ingredients

1 oz. flour.	1 oz. butter.	½ pint milk.
2 teaspoonfuls anchovy essence.		Seasoning.

Method

1. Melt the butter and add the flour.
2. Cook for a few minutes, but do not discolour.
3. Gradually add the milk and stir till boiling.
4. Add seasoning and essence and cook for 5 minutes.
5. Serve in a sauce-boat.

(Sufficient for 4 persons.)

APPLE SAUCE

Ingredients

¾ lb. apples.	1 oz. butter.	1 clove.
¼ gill water.	2 oz. sugar.	

Method

1. Pare and core the apples.
2. Cut in slices.
3. Cook in a little water with the sugar added.
4. When soft, beat with a fork and add the other ingredients.
5. Serve either hot or cold.

(Sufficient for 4 persons.)

BÉCHAMEL SAUCE

Ingredients

2 oz. butter.	2 oz. flour.	1 gill cream.
½ pint white stock.	Seasoning.	½ pint milk.

Method

1. Melt the butter, add the flour and cook for 2 minutes.
2. Add the stock and milk gradually and stir till boiling.
3. Add seasoning and cream.
4. Serve hot.

(Sufficient for 4 persons.)

BREAD SAUCE

Ingredients

4 oz. bread-crumbs.   1 small onion.   3 peppercorns.
Seasoning.   1 oz. butter.   ½ pint milk.
1 tablespoonful cream.   1 clove.

Method

1. Warm the milk and add the onion cut in slices, clove and peppercorns.
2. Cook slowly for ½ hour.
3. Strain over the bread-crumbs.
4. Bring slowly to the boil and add seasoning, cream and butter.
5. Serve hot.   (Sufficient for 4 persons.)

BROWN SAUCE

Ingredients

1 oz. butter.   1 oz. flour.   1 pint stock.
1 onion.   2 tomatoes.   Seasoning.
Small pieces of carrot and turnip.   1 oz. chopped ham.

Method

1. Melt the butter and add the flour.
2. Stir till well browned.
3. Gradually add the stock.
4. Stir till boiling.
5. Prepare and cut up the vegetables and add to the stock.
6. Chop the ham and add.
7. Cook with the lid on for 1 hour.
8. Season and strain into a sauce-boat.
                                       (Sufficient for 4 persons.)

CAPER SAUCE

Ingredients

1 oz. butter.   1 oz. flour.   Seasoning.
2 teaspoonfuls capers.   1 gill milk.
1 tablespoonful vinegar.   1 gill stock.

Method

1. Melt the butter and add the flour.
2. Cook for 1 minute.
3. Gradually add the milk and stock.
4. Stir till boiling.
5. Cook for 5 to 7 minutes.
6. Season and add vinegar and chopped capers.
7. Serve hot.
                                       (Sufficient for 4 persons.)

CARAMEL SAUCE

Ingredients

½ *pint milk.*   1 *oz. sugar.*   1 *teaspoonful castor sugar.*

Method

1. Put 1 oz. of sugar in a pan with a little water.
2. Cook slowly till it becomes nicely browned.
3. Add the milk and heat slowly until the caramel dissolves.
4. Add castor sugar and serve.
5. If desired the sauce may be thickened with 1 teaspoonful of blended cornflour.

(Sufficient for 4 persons.)

CHEESE SAUCE

Ingredients

½ *pint milk.*   1 *oz. flour.*   1 *oz. butter.*
1½ *oz. grated cheese.*   Seasoning.

Method

1. Melt the butter in a saucepan and remove from the heat.
2. Add seasoning and flour and stir into the butter.
3. Add the milk, a little at a time, stirring all the time.
4. Heat the milk mixture to boiling point still stirring constantly.
5. Cook for 3 minutes.
6. Add the grated cheese and reheat but do not allow the sauce to boil.

(Sufficient for 4 persons.)

CHOCOLATE SAUCE

Ingredients

½ *pint water.*   1½ *oz. Supex chocolate.*   1 *oz. rice-flour.*
½ *teaspoonful vanilla essence.*   2 *teaspoonfuls castor sugar.*

Method

1. Dissolve the chocolate powder in ½ pint of water. Stir till boiling.
2. Blend the rice-flour in a little milk or water and stir in.
3. Stir till boiling.
4. Add the sugar and vanilla essence.
5. Serve hot or cold.   (Sufficient for 4 persons.)

CORNFLOUR SAUCE

Ingredients

½ *pint milk.*   1 *oz. cornflour.*   1 *egg-yolk.*   1 *oz. butter.*
A few drops of flavouring essence.   1 *teaspoonful castor sugar.*

Method

1. Melt the butter and add the cornflour. Cook for 2 minutes.
2. Add the milk gradually and stir till boiling.
3. Add the sugar, egg-yolk, and essence.
4. Beat well.
5. Serve hot. (Sufficient for 4 persons.)

CUSTARD SAUCE

Ingredients

½ *pint milk.* *A few drops of vanilla essence.*
1 *teaspoonful castor sugar.* 1 *egg-yolk.*

Method

1. Beat the egg-yolk and sugar together.
2. Warm the milk and pour it over the egg.
3. Return to the pan and cook very slowly until it thickens.
4. Add the vanilla essence and serve.
   (Sufficient for 4 persons.)

EGG SAUCE

Ingredients

1 *oz. butter.* 1 *oz. flour.* ½ *pint milk.*
Seasoning. 1 *hard-boiled egg.*

Method

1. Melt the butter and add the flour. Cook for 2 minutes.
2. Add the milk gradually and stir till boiling.
3. Cook for 5 minutes.
4. Chop the egg and add.
5. Season and serve. (Sufficient for 4 persons.)

GRAVY SAUCE (unthickened)

Ingredients

Seasoning. *Sediment after lifting out the roast.*
½ *pint water, stock, or potato water.*

Method

1. Remove the roast from the tin and strain off the fat.
2. Pour in the liquid and gather all the brown sediment into it.
3. Stir till boiling.
4. Season.
5. Serve with roast beef.

Note.—The water from boiled potatoes makes the best gravy. Remember when using it that very little if any extra salt is needed. (Sufficient for 4 persons.)

GRAVY SAUCE (thickened)

Ingredients

Sediment from roast.   Seasoning.
1 oz. flour.   ½ pint potato water or stock.

Method

1. Lift out the roast mutton or pork from the tin.
2. Strain off the fat.
3. Mix 1 oz. of flour into the sediment.
4. Stir till well mixed.
5. Add the liquid and stir till boiling.
6. Season.
7. Serve with mutton or pork.

(Sufficient for 4 persons.)

HARD SAUCE

Ingredients

¼ lb. fresh butter.   2 or 3 bitter almonds.   3 sweet almonds.
2 oz. castor sugar.   1 tablespoonful sherry.

Method

1. Blanch the almonds by putting them in water and bringing it to the boil.
2. Cool and peel off the brown skin.
3. Cut up the almonds and pound in a mortar.
4. Cream together the butter and sugar.
5. Add the almonds and sherry.
6. Serve very cold.

(Sufficient for 4 persons.)

HOLLANDAISE SAUCE

Ingredients

2 egg-yolks.   ½ lemon.   Water.
1 tablespoonful cream.   Seasoning.

Method

1. Whisk the eggs and add about one tablespoonful water.
2. Add the lemon juice, seasoning and cream.
3. Stir very slowly till boiling.

Note.—This sauce is best cooked in a double saucepan.

(Sufficient for 4 persons.)

HORSE-RADISH SAUCE

Ingredients

4 tablespoonfuls cream.   3 teaspoonfuls vinegar.
1 saltspoonful mixed mustard.   4 tablespoonfuls horse-radish.
¼ teaspoonful sugar.   1 tablespoonful milk.   Seasoning.

Method

1. Add the milk to the cream and beat together.
2. Add the seasonings, grated horse-radish, sugar and vinegar.
3. Whisk all together.
4. Serve very cold.   (Sufficient for 4 persons.)

JAM SAUCE

Ingredients

½ pint water.	Juice of ½ lemon.
1 oz. sugar.	2 tablespoonfuls jam.

Method

1. Put all the ingredients into a small saucepan.
2. Cook for 15 minutes rather slowly.
3. Strain and serve.
4. If the colour is not good, add a few drops of colouring: the colour added, of course, is the same as the colour of the jam—yellow, green or red.   (Sufficient for 4 persons.)

MAÎTRE D'HÔTEL BUTTER

Ingredients

1 teaspoonful chopped parsley.	Juice of ½ lemon.
2 oz. fresh butter.	Seasoning.

Method

1. Beat the butter to a cream.
2. Add lemon juice, parsley and seasoning.
3. Lay on ice to get very hard.
4. Cut up in tiny squares and serve.

(Sufficient for 4 persons.)

MARMALADE SAUCE

Ingredients

2 oz. marmalade.	½ pint water.	1 oz. sugar.

Method

1. Make as for Jam Sauce (see above).
2. It is not necessary to strain this sauce.

(Sufficient for 4 persons.)

MELTED BUTTER SAUCE

Ingredients

1 small onion.	1 tablespoonful vinegar.	3 oz. butter.

Method

1. Peel and chop the onion and mix with the vinegar.
2. Cook very slowly for 5 or 6 minutes. By that time the vinegar will have evaporated.

3. Add the butter slowly, little bits at a time.
4. Stir constantly until it thickens.
5. Serve at once.

(Sufficient for 4 persons.)

MINT SAUCE

Ingredients

2 *tablespoonfuls mint.*   1 *gill vinegar.*
½ *gill hot water.*   1 *oz. sugar.*

Method

1. Pick, wash and dry the mint and chop it finely.
2. Put the sugar into the sauce-boat.
3. Pour the hot water over the sugar.
4. Add the vinegar and stir in the mint.

(Sufficient for 4 persons.)

MORNAY SAUCE

Ingredients

1 *pint Béchamel Sauce* (see page 118).   *Cayenne pepper.*
Grated cheese (*to taste*).

Method

1. Prepare the Béchamel Sauce.
2. Add the grated cheese and beat up again but do not allow the sauce to boil.
3. Add cayenne pepper to taste before serving.

(Sufficient for 4 persons.)

MUSTARD SAUCE

Ingredients

1 *gill White Sauce* (see page 127).   1 *teaspoonful vinegar.*
1 *tablespoonful made mustard.*   *Juice of* ½ *lemon.*

Method

1. Make the White Sauce and add the other ingredients.
2. Serve hot.

(Sufficient for 4 persons.)

ONION SAUCE

Ingredients

½ *pint White Sauce* (see page 127).   *Seasoning.*
2 *boiled onions.*

Method

1. Make as for White Sauce.
2. Chop the onions and add to the sauce.
3. Season well and serve very hot.

(Sufficient for 4 persons.)

OYSTER SAUCE

Ingredients

4 or 5 oysters.	1 gill milk.	1 gill oyster liquor.
1 tablespoonful cream.	1 oz. butter.	Juice of ½ lemon.
	1 oz. flour.	Seasoning.

Method

1. Cook the oysters till tender.
2. Melt the butter and add the flour. Cook for 2 minutes.
3. Add the liquor from the oysters and 1 gill of milk.
4. Stir till boiling.
5. Add cream, lemon juice, and seasoning.
6. Cut up the oysters and add.

(Sufficient for 4 persons.)

PARSLEY SAUCE

Ingredients

1 oz. flour.	1 oz. butter.	½ pint milk.
2 teaspoonfuls chopped parsley.		Seasoning.

Method

1. Melt the butter and add the flour.
2. Cook for 2 minutes.
3. Add the milk and stir till boiling.
4. Add chopped parsley and seasoning. Cook for 5 minutes.
5. Serve.

(Sufficient for 4 persons.)

PIQUANTE SAUCE

Ingredients

½ pint White Sauce (see page 127).	Juice of ½ lemon.
4 (cooked) small mushrooms.	Cayenne pepper.
1 tablespoonful cream.	Seasoning.

Method

1. Make the White Sauce.
2. Add the lemon juice, seasoning and cayenne.
3. Chop the mushrooms and add.
4. Just before serving add the cream.

(Sufficient for 4 persons.)

SHRIMP SAUCE

Ingredients

½ pint White Sauce (see page 127).	2 egg-yolks.
A little red colouring.	Shrimps.
2 teaspoonfuls cream.	Seasoning.

Method

1. Prepare the White Sauce.
2. Add seasoning and colouring.
3. Add egg-yolks and beat well.
4. Add cream and a few prepared shrimps.
5. Serve hot.

(Sufficient for 4 persons.)

SYRUP SAUCE

Ingredients

6 *tablespoonfuls syrup.*   *Juice of ½ lemon.*

Method

Melt the syrup very slowly and add the lemon juice.

(Sufficient for 4 persons.)

SOUBISE SAUCE

Ingredients

½ *pint White Sauce (see page 127).*   1 *boiled onion.*
1 *tablespoonful cream.*   *Seasoning.*

Method

1. Sieve the onion and add to the White Sauce.
2. Add seasoning and cream.
3. Re-heat and serve.

(Sufficient for 4 persons.)

TARTARE SAUCE

Ingredients

1 *tablespoonful lemon juice.*   1 *tablespoonful vinegar.*
1 *teaspoonful chopped capers.*   ¼ *teaspoonful pepper.*
1 *teaspoonful chopped parsley.*   ¼ *teaspoonful mustard.*
1 *gill salad oil.*   1 *egg-yolk.*   *Sugar.*
¼ *teaspoonful salt.*   1 *cooked egg-yolk.*

Method

1. Mix the raw yolk of egg with the cooked yolk.
2. Add the salad oil very gradually.
3. Add vinegar and all other ingredients.
4. Keep stirring evenly and in the one direction.

(Sufficient for 4 persons.)

TOMATO SAUCE

Ingredients

4 *or* 5 *tomatoes.*   1 *small onion.*   2 *oz. butter.*
2 *teaspoonfuls sugar.*   1 *oz. flour.*   *Seasoning.*
½ *pint stock.*

Method

1. Cook the tomatoes and onion slowly for ½ hour.
2. Rub through a hair sieve.
3. Return all to the pan and add the stock.
4. Blend the flour and add it.
5. Add other ingredients and stir till boiling.
6. Serve hot.

(Sufficient for 4 persons.)

WHITE COATING SAUCE

Ingredients

1 oz. butter.   1 oz. flour.   Seasoning.   ½ pint milk.

Method

1. Melt the butter slowly in a pan.
2. Add the flour and cook for 1 minute.
3. Gradually add the milk and stir till boiling.
4. Cook for 5 minutes.
5. Season and use as required.
6. The sauce should coat the back of a wooden spoon quite thickly.

(Sufficient for 4 persons.)

WHITE (FLOWING) SAUCE

Ingredients

½ oz. butter.   ½ oz. flour.   Seasoning.   ½ pint milk.

Method

Make as for Coating Sauce (see above).

(Sufficient for 4 persons.)

21. SWEETS

BATTERS

Note.—Batters of all kinds should be mixed some time before they are used. This makes them lighter.

PANCAKES

Ingredients

¼ lb. flour.   A pinch of salt.   Castor sugar.
1 lemon.   2 eggs.   1 oz. butter.
1 breakfastcupful milk.

Method

1. Measure the flour and add the salt.
2. Whisk the egg-yolks and whites separately.

3. Add a little of the yolks and milk alternately to the flour.
4. Beat briskly till smooth.
5. Fold in the whites.
6. Lay aside for as long as possible.
7. Melt the butter in a small pan.
8. Pour it off when very hot.
9. Add a little more, and when melted pour in sufficient batter to cover the bottom of the pan.
10. When brown toss and fry the second side.
11. Turn on to a grease-proof paper dredged with sugar.
12. Sprinkle with lemon juice and sugar and roll up.
13. Continue till all are fried.
14. Serve hot on a paper doyley.

(Sufficient for 4 persons.)

BELGIAN PANCAKES

Ingredients

½ *pint milk.*	1 *dessertspoonful custard powder.*
½ *oz. butter.*	1 *oz. chopped walnuts.*
1 *oz. sugar.*	¼ *lb. Pancake Batter* (see page 127).

Method

1. Make batter as before and lay aside.
2. Blend the custard powder with a little milk, and boil the remainder.
3. Pour over the custard.   Stir till thick.
4. Add the sugar, butter and chopped nuts.
5. Keep hot.
6. Cook the pancakes, spread a little of the mixture on each.
7. Dust with sugar, roll up and keep hot.
8. Serve at once.

(Sufficient for 4 persons.)

BAKED APPLES IN BATTER

Ingredients

4 *apples.*   2–3 *oz. sugar.*   *A piece of butter.*
¼ *lb. Batter* (see page 129, Yorkshire Pudding).

Method

1. Pare and cut up the apples.
2. Lay in a buttered pie-dish.
3. Add the sugar and some small pats of butter.
4. Pour over a little water.
5. Prepare the batter and pour over.
6. Cook till brown and well risen.   (Regulo 7.)
7. Dust with sugar.
8. Serve at once.

(Sufficient for 4 persons.)

FRENCH PANCAKES

Ingredients

1 *small tin peaches.*	*Castor sugar.*	*A pinch of salt.*
2 *eggs.*	½ *pint milk.*	3 *oz. flour.*

Method

1. Measure the flour and add the salt.
2. Beat the yolks and add to the milk.
3. Gradually add to the flour and beat well.
4. Whisk the whites and fold in.
5. Lay aside for 1½ hours.
6. Cook as for ordinary Pancakes (see page 127).
7. Turn on to a sugared paper and place a slice of peach in each. Dust with sugar and roll up.
8. Serve at once.

(Sufficient for 4 persons.)

FRUIT IN BATTER

Ingredients

2 *lb. rhubarb.*	*Sugar.*
¼ *lb. Batter* (see below).	

Method

1. Trim and cut up the rhubarb into short lengths.
2. Place in a buttered pie-dish.
3. Sprinkle in the sugar, quantity according to taste, about 3 to 4 oz.
4. Prepare the batter and pour over the fruit.
5. Bake in a good oven till nicely browned and well risen. (Regulo 7.) Dust with castor sugar.
6. Serve at once.

(Sufficient for 4 persons.)

YORKSHIRE PUDDING

Ingredients

¼ *lb. flour.*	1 *egg.*	*A pinch of salt.*	½ *pint milk.*

Method

1. Measure out the flour and add the salt.
2. Whisk the egg and add the milk to it. Mix.
3. Add most of the milk mixture to the flour and beat till quite smooth.
4. Add the remainder and lay aside for 1 to 2 hours.
5. Put some dripping into a tin and melt it. Have sufficient when melted to cover the bottom of the tin.

E

6. Pour in the batter and bake for 30 minutes. (Regulo 7.)

7. Cut the batter in squares and serve with the meat.

8. If Yorkshire Pudding is to be used as a sweet dish, serve with sugar and with jam or stewed fruit.

(Sufficient for 4 persons.)

FRITTER BATTER

Ingredients

1 *egg.*	1 *tablespoonful salad oil.*	*A pinch of salt.*
3 *oz. flour.*	1 *small teacupful warm water.*	

Method

1. Measure out the flour and add the salt.

2. Separate the egg and mix the yolk with the salad oil and water.

3. Mix into the flour and beat till smooth.

4. Lay aside for 1½ hours.

5. Whisk the egg-white and fold it into the batter.

6. Use as required.

BANANA FRITTERS

Ingredients

4 *bananas.*   ¼ *lb. Batter.*   *Fat to fry.*   *Castor sugar.*

Method

1. Peel the bananas and cut them in two lengthwise.

2. Prepare the batter (see above), using 1 oz. bread-crumbs instead of 1 oz. flour.

3. Dip each piece of banana in the batter.

4. Fry in hot fat till brown.

5. Dust with sugar and serve at once.

(Sufficient for 4 persons.)

FRUIT FRITTERS

Ingredients

3 *apples.*	*Fat to fry.*
¼ *lb. Batter* (see above).	2 *oz. castor sugar.*

Method

1. Put on the fat to heat.

2. Pare and core the apples and cut them in rings.

3. Lift each with a skewer and dip in batter.

4. Fry till puffy and a golden brown.

5. Drain and dip in sugar.

6. Serve hot.

(Sufficient for 4 persons.)

MILK PUDDINGS

LARGE-GRAIN PUDDINGS

Allow 2 oz. grain to 1 pint of milk.

RICE PUDDING

Ingredients

2 oz. rice.	1 pint milk.	A small piece of
Sugar to taste.	½ oz. butter.	lemon rind.

Method

1. Wash the rice and place in a pudding-dish.
2. Add sugar and milk and leave for ½ hour.
3. Add a small piece of lemon rind and the butter and stir up.
4. Bake in a slow oven for 3 hours.   (Regulo 1.)
5. Remove the lemon rind before serving.

(Sufficient for 4 persons.)

CHOCOLATE TAPIOCA

Ingredients

2 oz. tapioca.	1 pint milk.	1 egg.
1 oz. sugar.	1 oz. grated chocolate.	1 oz. butter.

Method

1. Heat the milk and stir in the tapioca (if the very large grain is used, it is best to soak it for 1½ hours before using).
2. Stir till boiling.
3. Add the sugar, chocolate and butter.
4. Whisk the egg-yolk and white separately.
5. Stir in the yolk, and lastly fold in the white.
6. Pour into a buttered pie-dish and bake for 30 minutes. (Regulo 1.)
7. Serve hot.

(Sufficient for 4 persons.)

RICE AND SULTANA PUDDING

Ingredients

2 oz. rice.	1 oz. sultanas.	1 pint milk.
1 teaspoonful chopped suet.	1 oz. sugar.	A pinch of salt.

Method

1. Wash the rice and put it in a buttered pie-dish.
2. Clean the sultanas and add.
3. Add the sugar and pour over the milk.
4. Add salt and chopped suet.
5. Bake very slowly for 2 to 3 hours.   (Regulo 1.)

(Sufficient for 4 persons.)

TAPIOCA PUDDING

Ingredients

1 *pint milk.*   1 oz. sugar.   ½ oz. butter.
A few drops vanilla essence.   1 egg.   2 oz. tapioca.

Method

1. Soak the tapioca for 1½ hours.
2. Put it in a pie-dish.
3. Add the milk, sugar and vanilla.
4. Whisk the egg and add it and the butter.
5. Bake in a slow oven for 1½ hours. (Regulo 1.)
6. Serve hot.

(Sufficient for 4 persons.)

SAGO CREAM

Ingredients

2 oz. seed pearl sago.   1 *pint milk.*   1 oz. sugar.
A pinch of salt.   1 egg.   1 oz. butter.

Method

1. Wash the sago.
2. Warm the milk and stir in the sago. Stir till boiling.
3. Add the sugar, salt and butter.
4. Whisk the egg-yolk and stir in.
5. Beat well.
6. Whisk the egg-white and fold in.
7. Pour into a buttered pie-dish and cook slowly till nicely browned for about ¾ hour. (Regulo 1.)

(Sufficient for 4 persons.)

RICE CREAM

Make as for Sago Cream (see above), using rice instead of sago.

SMALL-GRAIN PUDDINGS

SEMOLINA PUDDING

Ingredients

1 *pint milk.*   *A pinch of salt.*   1 egg.
1 oz. sugar.   1 oz. butter.   2 oz. semolina.

Method

1. Heat the milk and stir in the semolina.
2. Stir till boiling.
3. Add sugar, salt and butter.
4. Beat the egg-yolk and stir it in.

5. Whisk the white and fold it in.
6. Pour all into a buttered pie-dish and cook for ½ hour. (Regulo 1.)
7. Serve hot.

(Sufficient for 4 persons.)

CORNFLOUR PUDDING

Ingredients

1 *pint milk.*	*A pinch of salt.*	2 *oz. cornflour.*
Raspberry or strawberry essence.		1½ *oz. sugar.*

Method

1. Blend the cornflour with a little of the milk.
2. Boil the remainder of the milk and pour over the blended cornflour. Stir well.
3. Return to the pan and cook for 2 minutes.
4. Add salt, sugar and flavouring.
5. Wet a mould and pour in the mixture.
6. Leave till set.
7. Turn out and serve cold with fruit.

(Sufficient for 4 persons.)

CUSTARDS

Custard puddings should be cooked slowly, otherwise the eggs may curdle. (Regulo 1.)

BAKED CUSTARD

Ingredients

1 *pint milk.*	2 *eggs.*	*A pinch of salt.*
1 *oz. sugar.*	*Grated nutmeg.*	

Method

1. Beat the eggs and sugar together.
2. Warm the milk and pour over. Mix well.
3. Add salt and strain into a buttered pie-dish.
4. Grate over with nutmeg.
5. Place the pie-dish in a tin of cold water and place in the oven.
6. Cook slowly for ½ to ¾ hour or till set. (Regulo 1.)

(Sufficient for 4 persons.)

COFFEE CUSTARD

Ingredients

1 *pint milk.*	1 *oz. sugar.*
1 *tablespoonful strained coffee.*	2 *eggs.*

Method

1. Mix the coffee and milk together and warm the mixture in a saucepan.

2. Beat the eggs and pour over the milk.   Add the sugar.

3. Strain into a buttered pie-dish.

4. Place in a tin of water and cook in a slow oven for ½ hour, or longer if not set.   (Regulo 1.)

(Sufficient for 4 persons.)

CUP CUSTARD

Ingredients

1 *pint milk.*   4 *eggs.*   1 *oz. sugar.*
A pinch of salt.   *Vanilla essence.*

Method

1. Warm the milk.

2. Beat the eggs and sugar together and pour it over the warmed milk.

3. Strain into buttered cups and cover with buttered paper.

4. Place in boiling water so that the water comes half-way up the cup, and let it stand at the side of the fire without boiling for 20 minutes.

5. Turn out and serve.

(Sufficient for 4 persons.)

STEAMED CUSTARD

Ingredients

4 *eggs.*   1 *pint milk.*   4 *teaspoonfuls sugar.*

Method

Make as for Cup Custard (see above), and steam in a basin

(Sufficient for 4 persons.)

CARAMEL CUSTARD

Ingredients

For Caramel

3 *oz. sugar.*   *Juice of* 1 *lemon.*

For Custard

1 *pint milk.*   4 *eggs*
A few drops of vanilla essence.   1 *oz. sugar.*

Method

1. Put the sugar and lemon juice into a small saucepan and cook till a golden-brown colour.

2. Draw from the heat and leave till brown.

3. Butter some small moulds and run in a little caramel in each.   Leave to set.

4. Prepare custard as before, and strain into the moulds.
5. Cover with buttered paper and steam till set—20 minutes.
6. Turn out and serve.

(Sufficient for 4 persons.)

CAMBRIDGE PUDDING

Ingredients

    1 *pint custard.*   6 *sponge cakes.*   *Raisins.*

Method

1. Butter a basin and paper for covering.
2. Cut up the sponges and lay in the basin.
3. Add the cleaned raisins.
4. Pour over the custard. Cover with greased paper and steam for 40 minutes. Turn out and serve.

(Sufficient for 4 persons.)

PASTRY-MAKING

General Hints

1. Everything should be kept as cool as possible.
2. Only the tips of the fingers should be used to rub in the fat.
3. Rolling should be light and even.
4. Only enough flour should be used on the baking-board to prevent the pastry from sticking.
5. Rich pastry requires greater heat for cooking than does plain pastry.
6. Pastry containing baking-powder should be baked immediately it is made.
7. For puffy and flaky pastries the pastry should be mixed to the consistency of the fat used in it.

SUET PASTRY

Ingredients

½ *lb. flour or 6 oz. flour and 2 oz. bread-crumbs.*   *Water to mix.*
½ *teaspoonful baking-powder.*   *A pinch of salt.*   ¼ *lb. suet.*

Method

1. Chop the suet very finely. Remove all skin and shreds.
2. Add the salt to the flour.
3. Mix in the suet and baking-powder.
4. Mix to an elastic dough with cold water.
5. Suet pastry is best boiled, steamed or stewed, and may be used for dumplings or savoury balls, etc.
6. The puddings are much lighter with the addition of bread-crumbs in place of some of the flour.

(Sufficient for 4 persons.)

APPLE DUMPLING

Ingredients

½ lb. Suet Pastry (see page 135).   1 lb. apples.
¼ lb. sugar.   Water.   4 cloves.

Method

1. Prepare the pastry and turn on to a floured board. Cut off about ¼.
2. Line a pudding-basin with the larger portion.
3. Pare and core and slice the apples.
4. Put half into the basin and then add sugar and cloves.
5. Put in the remainder of apples and a little water.
6. Roll out the small piece of pastry and form into a round to fit the top of the basin.
7. Place on and press down the edges.
8. Cover with a greased paper and steam for 2 hours.
9. Any fruit in season can be used in place of apples.

(Sufficient for 4 persons.)

BACHELOR'S PUDDING

Ingredients

4 oz. flour.   ½ teaspoonful baking-powder.   A pinch of salt.
4 oz. currants.   ¼ lb. bread-crumbs.   ¼ lb. sugar.
4 oz. suet.   1 apple.   2 eggs.

Method

1. Pare and chop the apple, clean the currants.
2. Chop the suet.
3. Mix all the dry ingredients together.
4. Whisk the eggs and add to the mixture.
5. If necessary, add a little milk.
6. Cover with a greased paper and steam for 2 to 2½ hours.
7. Turn out and serve with a custard sauce.

(Sufficient for 4 persons.)

FIG PUDDING

Ingredients

½ lb. figs, finely chopped.   Milk to mix.   4 oz. flour.
½ teaspoonful baking soda.   A pinch of salt.   1 egg.
1 teaspoonful cream of tartar.   4 oz. suet.
4 oz. bread-crumbs.   4 oz. sugar.

Method

1. Put on a pan of water to boil.
2. Prepare basin, and butter a paper to cover.
3. Chop the figs finely.

4. Shred the suet, removing all stringy parts.
5. Mix all the dry ingredients together.
6. Mix to an elastic dough with the egg and milk.
7. Turn into a greased basin, cover with greased paper and steam for 2–2½ hours.
8. Turn out and serve with Custard Sauce (see page 121).
(Sufficient for 4 persons.)

FRUIT PUDDING

Ingredients

½ lb. Suet Pastry (see page 135).   Water.   ¼ lb. sugar.
A piece of lemon rind, finely grated.   1 lb. plums.

Method

1. Prepare the suet pastry.
2. Line the basin as for apple dumpling.
3. Stone the plums and put in half of them.
4. Add sugar, and lemon rind grated.
5. Add remainder of plums and a little water.
6. Cover with the remainder of the pastry.
7. Cover with buttered paper and steam for 2–2½ hours.
8. Serve with Custard Sauce (see page 121).
(Sufficient for 4 persons.)

GOLDEN PUDDING

Ingredients

½ lb. bread-crumbs.   6 oz. suet.   3 oz. flour.
2 oz. demerara sugar.   ½ pint milk.   2 eggs.
¼ lb. apricot or other jam.

Method

1. Chop the suet finely.
2. Add all dry ingredients and mix well.
3. Mix the jam in the milk, whisk eggs and add to the milk and pour over the other ingredients and allow to stand for 1 hour.
4. Pour into a greased basin and cover with a greased paper.
5. Steam for 2½–3 hours.
6. Turn out and serve with Jam Sauce (see page 123).
(Sufficient for 4 persons.)

LEMON PUDDING

Ingredients

4 oz. bread-crumbs.   2 eggs.
Grated rind and juice of 2 lemons.   4 oz. sugar.
1 teaspoonful baking-powder.   4 oz. flour.
1 tablespoonful syrup.   4 oz. suet.

Method

1. Grease a basin and paper.
2. Mix all the dry ingredients together.
3. Whisk eggs and beat in. Add lemon juice and syrup. Add a little milk if necessary.
4. Turn into a greased basin and cover with greased paper.
5. Steam for 2–2½ hours.
6. Turn out and serve with a suitable sauce.

(Sufficient for 4 persons.)

MARMALADE PUDDING

Ingredients

½ *lb. bread-crumbs.*   *Almost* 1 *pint of milk.*   4 *oz. marmalade*
3 *oz. sugar.*   2 *oz. butter.*   *A pinch of salt.*   2 *eggs.*

Method

1. Heat the milk and pour over the bread-crumbs.
2. Add the butter, sugar, marmalade and salt.
3. Whisk the eggs and beat in.
4. Turn into a greased basin and cover with a buttered paper.
5. Steam gently for 1 hour.
6. Allow to shrink and then turn out.
7. Serve with Marmalade Sauce (see page 123).

Note.—The pudding can be varied by using orange marmalade, lemon marmalade, grapefruit or ginger marmalade.

(Sufficient for 4 persons.)

ROLY POLY

Ingredients

6 *oz. Suet Pastry* (see page 135).   *Jam.*

Method

1. Prepare the pastry and turn out on to a floured board.
2. Roll out into a square.
3. Spread with jam and roll up tightly.
4. Tie in a cloth which has been scalded and dusted with flour.
5. Plunge into fast-boiling water and boil for 3 hours.
6. Turn out and serve very hot with Jam Sauce (see page 123).

Note.—Mincemeat may be used instead of jam.

(Sufficient for 4 persons.)

STEAMED JAM PUDDING

Ingredients

> 6 oz. Suet Pastry made with half bread-crumbs,
> half flour (see page 135).   Jam.

Method

1. Prepare the pastry.
2. Butter a basin and spread the bottom with jam.
3. Divide the pastry into four or five pieces.
4. Form one into a round and lay on top of the jam.
5. Spread with jam and continue till all is used up, finishing with pastry.
6. Cover with greased paper.
7. Steam for 2–2½ hours.
8. Turn out and serve hot.   (Sufficient for 4 persons.)

SYRUP SPONGE PUDDING

Ingredients

¼ lb. flour.   3 oz. suet.   ¼ lb. bread-crumbs.
½ teaspoonful baking-powder.   A pinch of salt.
Water or milk to mix.   2–3 oz. syrup.

Method

1. Grease a basin and put the syrup at the bottom.
2. Chop the suet and mix with the flour and bread-crumbs.
3. Add salt and baking-powder.
4. Mix to a rather soft dough with milk or water.
5. Turn into the basin, cover with greased paper and steam for 2½ hours.
6. Turn out and serve.
7. No sauce is necessary as the syrup runs all over the pudding.   (Sufficient for 4 persons.)

SHORT PASTRY

Ingredients

4 oz. butter ⎫ mixed.   1 lb. flour.   A pinch of salt.
4 oz. lard   ⎭
1 teaspoonful baking-powder.   Water.

Note.—To make the pastry rich for special dishes allow 12 oz. shortening to 1 lb. flour and mix with egg-yolks.

Method

1. Measure the flour and add salt.
2. Cut and then rub in the shortening till the whole is like fine bread-crumbs. Add the baking-powder.

3. Mix as stiffly as possible, using very cold water.
4. Turn on to a floured board and use as required.

APPLE AMBER

Ingredients

¼ lb. Short Pastry (see page 139).	2 oz. butter.	1 lb. stewed apples.
1½ ozs. castor sugar.	4 oz. sugar.	1 lemon.
	2 eggs.	

Method

1. Butter a pie-dish and line it with pastry.
2. Stew the apples and rub through a sieve.
3. Add the butter melted and lemon juice and rind.
4. Beat in the egg-yolks and pour over the pastry.
5. Brush the edges with egg and bake for ½ hour. (Regulo 6.)
6. Whisk the egg-whites and add 1½ oz. castor sugar.
7. Pile on top and return to the oven till pale brown. (Regulo ¼.)

(Sufficient for 4 persons.)

APPLE TART

Ingredients

½ lb. Short Pastry (see page 139).		2 oz. sultanas.
Water.	1 lb. apples.	3 oz. sugar.

Method

1. Prepare the pastry and leave in a cool place till required.
2. Pare and core the apples. Cut in slices.
3. Place half in a pie-dish and add the sugar, cleaned sultanas and a little water.
4. Cover with the remainder of the apples.
5. Turn the pastry on to a floured board and roll out to one size larger than the pie-dish.
6. Cut a strip all round.
7. Wet the edge of the pie-dish and lay on the strip. Wet the top of the strip.
8. See if the pastry fits the pie-dish by lifting it on the rolling pin.
9. If too small roll out a little.
10. Cover the pie and press down the edges.
11. Trim sharply with a knife.
12. Score up the edge.
13. Bake in a good oven for about 1 hour. (Regulo 6.)
14. Sprinkle with castor sugar and serve either hot or cold with custard.

(Sufficient for 4 persons.)

APPLE AND CRANBERRY PIE

Ingredients

1 *lb. cooking apples.*   ¼ *lb. sugar.*   ¼ *lb. cranberries.*
½ *lb. Short Pastry (see page 139).*   *Water.*

Method

1. Prepare the pastry and lay aside.
2. Peel and core the apples and slice.
3. Pick over the cranberries.
4. Place the apples, cranberries, sugar and a little water in a pie-dish and cover with the pastry as for Apple Tart (see page 140).
5. Serve either hot or cold.

(Sufficient for 4 persons.)

BAKEWELL TART

Ingredients

½ *lb. Short Pastry*   2 *oz. butter.*   2 *oz. bread-crumbs.*
   (see page 139).   2 *oz. castor sugar.*   *Any flavouring.*
2 *tablespoonfuls jam.* 1 *egg.*

Method

1. Line a tin with the pastry and spread over with jam.
2. Cream the butter and sugar.
3. Add the egg-yolk and beat well.
4. Add bread-crumbs and flavouring.
5. Whisk the white and fold into the mixture.
6. Pour over the jam and bake in a hot oven for 5–10 minutes.   (Regulo 6.)
7. Reduce the heat and bake for ½ hour.   (Regulo 5.)
8. Serve either hot or cold.

(Sufficient for 4 persons.)

CUSTARD TART

Ingredients

½ *lb. Short Pastry (see page 139).*   ½ *pint milk.*
1 *tablespoonful cornflour.*   3 *egg-yolks.*
1 *teaspoonful sugar.*   *Nutmeg.*

Method

1. Mix the sugar and cornflour.
2. Boil the milk and pour over the cornflour.
3. Add the egg-yolks and beat well.
4. Line a tin and bake the pastry before filling with custard.
5. Pour in the custard.   Grate the nutmeg over it.
6. Bake for 10 minutes (Regulo 6) and serve either hot or cold.

(Sufficient for 4 persons.)

CHOCOLATE CUSTARD TART

Ingredients

½ *lb. Short Pastry* (see page 139).   1 *oz. cornflour.*
2 *oz. chocolate.*   ½ *pint milk.*   3 *egg-yolks.*

Method

1. Make as for Custard Tart (see page 141), only dissolve the chocolate in a little of the milk and pour over the remainder.
(Sufficient for 4 persons.)

FRUIT FLAN

Ingredients

½ *lb. rich Short Pastry* (see page 139).   1 *gill cream.*
Any fruit desired.

Method

1. Line a flan ring with pastry.
2. Put some rice in a greased paper in the tin and bake till nicely browned.   (Regulo 5.)
3. Remove the rice and dry the part underneath.
4. Place on a pastry tray.
5. Slice the peaches or other fruit and lay in.
6. Decorate with whipped cream.
7. The syrup may be boiled till thick and served as a sauce.
(Sufficient for 4 persons.)

LEMON PIE

Ingredients

1 *lemon.*   1 *oz. butter.*   1 *egg.*
1 *gill water.*   4 *oz. sugar.*   1 *oz. cornflour.*
¼ *lb. Short Pastry* (see page 139).

Method

1. Line a tin with the pastry.
2. Mix the sugar and cornflour.
3. Boil the water and pour over, stirring all the time.
4. Add butter, lemon juice and grated rind.
5. Whisk the egg and beat in.
6. Cook for a few minutes till thick.
7. Pour into the tin and bake in a moderate oven for 20 minutes.   (Regulo 6.)
8. Serve either hot or cold.
(Sufficient for 4 persons.)

MINCE TARTLETS

Ingredients

½ lb. *Short Pastry* (see page 139).   1 oz. *castor sugar*.
8 oz. *mincemeat*.   1 *egg*.

Method

1. Prepare the pastry and turn on to a floured board. Divide in two.
2. Roll one part into a square and place on a baking-sheet.
3. Spread with mincemeat.
4. Roll out the other part to the same size.
5. Cover the mincemeat with it. Press the edges.
6. Divide into small squares by marking with a knife, but do not separate.
7. Brush with egg.
8. Cook in a hot oven for 15–20 minutes. (Regulo 6.)
9. Dust with sugar and divide down the knife marks.
10. Cool on a tray.

Note.—This is a good way of using mincemeat for people who do not like a lot of pastry, but are fond of mincemeat.

(Sufficient for 16 tartlets.)

NORFOLK APPLE TART

Ingredients

¼ lb. *Short Pastry* (see page 139).   ½ lb. *stewed apples*.
4 *tablespoonfuls marmalade*.   1 oz. *castor sugar*.

Method

1. Prepare the pastry and line a plate with half of it.
2. Spread with marmalade.
3. Spread a layer of apples on top.
4. Cover with the remainder of the pastry.
5. Cook for 20 minutes. (Regulo 6.)
6. Dust with castor sugar and serve either hot or cold.

(Sufficient for 4 persons.)

PINEAPPLE PUDDING

Ingredients

¼ lb. *Short Pastry* (see page 139).   1 *tin pineapple*.
2 oz. *castor sugar*.   2 *eggs*.

Method

1. Line a tin with the pastry.
2. Cook the pastry, using a filling of rice to keep it from rising. (Regulo 6.)
3. Remove the rice and paper and dry the bottom.
4. Drain the pineapple and arrange in the case.

5. Whisk the egg-whites and add the sugar.
6. Pile on top of the pineapple.
7. Place in a slow oven till pale brown.   (Regulo ¼.)
8. The egg-yolks can be made into a custard sauce to serve with the pudding.

(Sufficient for 4 persons.)

TREACLE TART

Ingredients

6 oz. *Short Pastry* (see page 139).   2 *tablespoonfuls syrup.*
½ *teaspoonful ground ginger.*   2 *oz. bread-crumbs.*

Method

1. Line a plate with the pastry.   Trim the edge.
2. Mix the bread-crumbs, ginger and syrup together.
3. Spread on the pastry.
4. Roll out the trimmings and cut in strips and place on in lattice work over the syrup mixture.
5. Bake in a hot oven for ½ hour.   (Regulo 6.)
6. Serve either hot or cold.

(Sufficient for 4 persons.)

WELSH CHEESE CAKE

Ingredients

1 *pint milk.*   3 *oz. currants.*   2 *oz. castor sugar.*   1 *egg.*
½ *lb. Short Pastry* (see page 139).   1 *dessertspoonful rennet.*

Method

1. Heat the milk and add the rennet.
2. Drain through a fine muslin bag.
3. Whisk the egg and beat it into the curd.
4. Add sugar and cleaned currants.
5. Line a tin with pastry and spread on the mixture.
6. Bake in a moderate oven.   (Regulo 6.)

(Sufficient for 4 persons.)

FLAKY PASTRY

Ingredients

1 *lb. flour.*   *A pinch of salt.*   8 *oz. shortening.*
1 *teaspoonful baking-powder.*   *Water to mix.*

If a richer pastry is required, use 12 oz. shortening and leave out the baking powder.

Method

1. Measure the flour, and add the salt.
2. Divide the shortening (which can be butter, margarine, lard, trex or a mixture of butter and lard) into 4.

3. Rub one portion into the flour.   Add baking-powder.

4. Mix with cold water to a stiff paste.

5. Turn on to a floured board and roll out into a long strip.

6. Take a portion of the shortening left and place it all over the strip in little pats.   Dust with flour and fold in three.

7. Press down the edges and half turn so that the cut edges are to and from you.

8. Roll out again and put on another quarter of the shortening.   Fold and turn.

9. Continue until all is used up.

10. Fold once more and lay aside in a cool place until required.

Note.—Flaky pastry is used for meat pies, patties, turn-overs, etc.

APPLE AND CURRANT CAKE

Ingredients

6 oz. *Flaky Pastry* (see page 144).   6 oz. *stewed apples.*
3 oz. *currants.*   ¾ oz. *castor sugar.*   ¾ oz. *butter.*

Method

1. Mix the butter into the apples.

2. Clean the currants and add.

3. Line a plate with pastry and spread on the mixture.

4. Cover with pastry.

5. Bake for 25 minutes.   (Regulo 7.)

6. Dust with sugar and serve either hot or cold.

(Sufficient for 4 persons.)

CANADIAN CURD PIE

Ingredients

6 oz. *Flaky Pastry* (see page 144).   ¼ *teaspoonful ground ginger.*
¼ *lb. curds.*   2 *eggs.*   2 oz. *currants.*
Rind of ½ *lemon.*   2 oz. *sugar.*   2 oz. *butter.*

Method

1. Squeeze the curds through muslin until quite dry.   Rub through a sieve.

2. Mix in the butter, ginger, lemon rind and sugar.

3. Separate the eggs, and beat the yolks into the mixture.

4. Whisk the whites and fold in.

5. Line a plate with pastry and sprinkle it with cleaned currants.

6. Pour on the mixture and bake for 30 minutes.   (Regulo 5.)

7. Serve with cream.

(Sufficient for 4 persons.)

KENILWORTH TARTS

Ingredients

6 oz. *Flaky Pastry* (see page 144).
2 oz. *butter*.
1 *orange*.
2 oz. *castor sugar*.
1 *egg*.
A pinch of salt.
3 oz. *flour*.
Apricot jam.

Method

1. Roll out the pastry and line some tins with it.
2. Put a teaspoonful of jam in each.
3. Cream the butter and sugar and add salt.
4. Add the egg and sifted flour alternately.
5. Add grated rind of half an orange and all the juice.
6. Slightly more than half fill the tins.
7. Bake for 20 minutes in a good oven.   (Regulo 7.)
8. Serve either hot or cold.

(Sufficient for about 18 tarts.)

MINCE PIES

Ingredients

½ lb. *Flaky Pastry*
(see page 144).
½ lb. *mincemeat*.
1 oz. *sugar*.

Method

1. Roll out the pastry and cut into rounds.
2. Line some tins with the rounds and half fill with mincemeat.
3. Cut some small rounds and fix on as covers.
4. Cut with a knife to let out the steam.
5. Cook in a hot oven for 15–20 minutes.   (Regulo 8.)
6. Dust with sugar and serve either hot or cold.

(Sufficient for about 18 pies.)

ORANGE CHEESE CAKES

Ingredients

Juice of 1 *orange*.
1 *tablespoonful cornflour*.
¼ lb. *Flaky Pastry* (see page 144).
1 *egg*.
4 oz. *sugar*.
1 oz. *butter*.
1 *gill water*.

Method

1. Roll out the pastry and line the tins.
2. Measure sugar and mix with the cornflour.
3. Boil the water and pour over.
4. Add the egg well beaten.   Add the orange juice.
5. Cook for 1 minute.
6. Pour on to the pastry and cook in a moderate oven for 15 minutes.   (Regulo 6.)
7. Serve either hot or cold.

(Sufficient for about 18 cakes.)

SAXON PUDDING

Ingredients

6 oz. *Flaky Pastry* (see page 144).   3 oz. *cake-crumbs.*
½ *teaspoonful ratafia essence.*   2 oz. *chopped peel.*
3 *eggs.*   2 oz. *sugar.*   ½ *pint milk.*   2 oz. *butter.*

Method

1. Line a tin with the pastry.
2. Cream the butter and sugar together and add the egg-yolks.
3. Whisk the whites and fold in.
4. Add the cake-crumbs and ratafia essence.
5. Mix in the peel and mix to an elastic consistency with milk.
6. Do not use the whole ½ pint unless necessary.
7. Pour over the pastry and cook for ½ hour. (Regulo 7.)
8. Serve hot or cold.

(Sufficient for 4 persons.)

ROUGH PUFF PASTRY

Ingredients

1 *lb. flour.*   A *pinch of salt.*   ½ *lb. shortening.*   *Water.*
1 *teaspoonful baking-powder.*   *Juice of* ½ *lemon.*

Method

1. Measure the flour and add salt and baking-powder.
2. Add the shortening and cut with a knife into small pieces; do not rub.
3. Mix to a firm dough with water and lemon juice.
4. Turn on to a floured board and roll out into a strip.
5. Flour lightly and fold in three. Half turn and seal the edges with the rolling-pin.
6. Repeat rolling and folding the pastry three times.
7. Lay aside in a cool place till required.

Note.—Use for meat pies, sausage rolls, etc., more so than for sweet dishes.

APPLE PUFFS

Ingredients

½ *lb. Rough Puff Pastry* (see above).   *Rind of* 1 *lemon.*
1 *egg.*   2 *apples.*   1 *oz. sugar.*

Method

1. Peel the apples, core and chop up finely.
2. Add the sugar and grated lemon rind.
3. Roll out the pastry and cut in squares.

4. Spread some of the mixture on each and fold over corner-wise to form envelopes.   Press the edges together.

5. Brush with beaten egg-white and dust with sugar.

6. Cook quickly for 15–20 minutes.   (Regulo 8.)

7. Cool on a tray.   (Sufficient for about 8 puffs.)

EVESHAM TART

Ingredients

6 oz. Rough Puff Pastry (see page 147).   1½ oz. castor sugar.
¾ lb. apples.   3 oz. sugar.   2 eggs.   1 lemon.

Method

1. Line a tin with the pastry.

2. Stew the apples with 3 oz. of sugar, and grated lemon rind and juice.

3. Beat in the egg-yolks.

4. Pour over the pastry and cook for ½ hour in a moderate oven.   (Regulo 7.)

5. Whisk the whites till stiff and add the castor sugar.

6. Pile on the top and return to the oven till a golden brown. (Regulo ¼.)

7. Serve hot or cold.   (Sufficient for 4 persons.)

GENOESE PASTRY

Ingredients

3 oz. butter.   3 oz. flour.   3 oz. castor sugar.   4 eggs.

Method

1. Whisk the eggs and sugar together.

2. Melt the butter and take off the froth.

3. Add the butter to the egg mixture.

4. Sieve the flour and fold into the mixture.

5. Pour into a buttered tin and bake for ¾ hour.   (Regulo 3.)

6. Cool and use as required.

Note.—Genoese Pastry is used as the basis of most small iced cakes, French cakes, etc.

CHOUX PASTRY

Ingredients

4 oz. flour.   2 oz. butter.   ½ pint water.
1 tablespoonful sugar.   3 eggs.

Method

1. Place the water, sugar and butter in a pan and heat slowly.

2. Sieve the flour and beat it in quickly.   Beat till quite smooth.

3. Lay aside to cool.
4. Whisk the eggs in one by one.
5. Use as required.

Note.—This pastry is used for cream slices, cream cakes, éclairs, etc.

OTHER SWEETS

AMERICAN PUDDING

Ingredients

¾ lb. apples.	3 oz. sugar.	4 oz. flour.
3 oz. castor sugar.	A pinch of salt.	3 oz. butter.
¼ teaspoonful baking-powder.		2 eggs.

Method

1. Pare, core and slice the apples and put them on to stew with 3 oz. of sugar.
2. When soft pour them into a pie-dish.
3. Cream the butter and sugar and add the salt.
4. Beat in the eggs one at a time.
5. Gradually add the flour and baking-powder.
6. If too stiff, add a little milk.
7. Put the mixture on top of the apples.
8. Cook in a moderate oven till well risen and nicely browned. (Regulo 4.)
9. Sift with sugar.
10. Serve either hot or cold.

(Sufficient for 4 persons.)

APPLE CHARLOTTE

Ingredients

1 lb. apples.	3 oz. sugar.	Milk.
2 slices of bread and butter.		1 oz. demerara sugar.

Method

1. Soak the slices of bread and butter in milk.
2. Pare, core and chop the apples.
3. Butter a pie-dish and half fill it with the chopped apples.
4. Sprinkle in the sugar and very little water.
5. Cover with slices of soaked bread and butter.
6. Sprinkle over some demerara sugar and bake in a slow oven for 1½ hours.   (Regulo 4.)
7. The top should be nicely browned and crisp.

(Sufficient for 4 persons.)

APPLE SNOW

Ingredients

3 *egg-whites.*
3 *apples.*

1 *tablespoonful castor sugar.*
1 *oz. finely chopped nuts.*

Method

1. Core the apples and bake them. When quite soft remove all the pulp and beat till smooth.
2. Whisk the egg-whites till very stiff and then add a little apple pulp and castor sugar alternately.
3. Continue till all is used up.
4. Do not add all the pulp at once or else the eggs will go flat.
5. Beat till very stiff and smooth.
6. Pile in a glass dish and decorate with the chopped nuts.
7. Lay on ice and serve very cold.

(Sufficient for 4 persons.)

BAKED APPLES

Ingredients

4 *apples.*   2 *oz. sugar.*   *A little mincemeat or jam.*

Method

1. Wipe and core the apples.
2. Fill up the core with mincemeat or jam.
3. Place on a tin and mix a little sugar and water together and pour it round the apples.
4. Bake slowly till soft. (Regulo 5.)
5. Serve hot or cold.

Note.—If preferred the core may be filled up with sugar instead of jam or mincemeat. (Sufficient for 4 persons.)

BERESFORD PUDDING

Ingredients

1 *egg.*
Its weight in butter, sugar and flour.

1 *orange.*
1 *tablespoonful bread-crumbs.*
½ *teaspoonful baking-powder.*

Method

1. Cream the butter and sugar.
2. Add the egg and beat well.
3. Add the grated rind and strained juice of the orange.
4. Mix the flour, baking-powder, and bread-crumbs and add.
5. Pour into a buttered basin and cover with a buttered paper.
6. Steam gently for 1 hour.
7. Turn out and serve with a suitable sauce.

(Sufficient for 4 persons.)

BIRD'S-NEST PUDDING

Ingredients

2 oz. sago.	1 *pint milk*.	1 *oz. sugar*.
4 *apples*.	1 *oz. jam*.	

Method

1. Wash the sago and soak in a pint of milk.
2. Add the sugar.
3. Pare and core the apples and place in the sago.
4. Fill up the centres with jam.
5. Bake in a moderate oven for 1 hour.   (Regulo 4.)
6. If the apples are not quite soft, bake a little longer.

(Sufficient for 4 persons.)

BLACK-CAP PUDDING

Ingredients

2 oz. *currants*.	1 *tablespoonful castor sugar*.
Syrup.	½ *pint Pancake Batter* (see page **127**).

Method

1. Butter a pudding-dish and paper to cover.
2. Clean the currants and mix with the sugar.
3. Put these in the bottom of the basin.
4. Pour over the batter and cover over with greased **paper**.
5. Steam for 1 hour.
6. Turn on to a hot dish and pour some golden syrup over the pudding.
7. Serve hot.

(Sufficient for 4 persons.)

BORDER OF PEARS

Ingredients

1 *small tin pears*.	1½ *oz. castor sugar*.
1 *small tin raspberries*.	1 *gill cream*.
1 *dessertspoonful cornflour*.	*Juice of* ½ *lemon*.

Method

1. Strain the pears and arrange in a border on an oval glass dish.   Lay on ice.
2. Strain the raspberries and rub through a sieve.
3. Add sugar and lemon juice.
4. Blend the cornflour and add.
5. Stir till boiling.   Lay on ice or freeze.
6. Pile the mixture in the centre of the pears.
7. Whisk the cream and decorate.
8. Serve very cold.

(Sufficient for 4 persons.)

BREAD-AND-BUTTER PUDDING

Ingredients

1 *pint milk.*	*Slices of bread and butter without*
1 *egg.*	*crusts about* (6 oz.).
1 *oz. sugar.*	2 *oz. currants or sultanas.*

Method

1. This is a good way of using up left-over bread and butter.
2. Cut off crusts.
3. Butter a pie-dish and lay in some of the pieces of bread and butter.
4. Sprinkle with currants.
5. Continue to fill the dish with slices of bread and currants alternately until it is three-quarters full.
6. Warm the milk and add the sugar.
7. Beat the egg and add it to the milk.
8. Pour over the bread and soak for 1 hour.
9. Bake in a moderate oven for $\frac{3}{4}$ hour. (Regulo 5.)
10. Serve hot.

(Sufficient for 4 persons.)

CABINET PUDDING

Ingredients

2 *oz. valencia raisins.*	4 *oz. bread.*	1 *oz. sugar.*
$\frac{1}{2}$ *pint milk.*	1 *egg.*	

Method

1. Stone the raisins.
2. Butter a basin and decorate with the stoned raisins.
3. Warm the milk. Add sugar and beaten egg.
4. Cut the bread in squares.
5. Put the bread in the basin and strain over the custard.
6. Soak for 30 minutes or longer.
7. Steam slowly for 1 hour, but do not boil.
8. Allow to cool before turning out.
9. Serve with Custard Sauce (see page 121).

(Sufficient for 4 persons.)

CAMP PUDDING

Ingredients

3 *oz. suet.*	3 *oz. sugar.*	3 *oz. bread-crumbs.*
3 *oz. flour.*	$1\frac{1}{2}$ *oz. currants.*	$1\frac{1}{2}$ *oz. raisins.*
$1\frac{1}{2}$ *oz. peel.*	1 *orange.*	1 *lemon.*
2 *eggs.*	*Milk to mix.*	

Method

1. Grease a basin and paper.
2. Chop suet and clean currants and raisins.
3. Chop the peel.
4. Mix all the dry ingredients.
5. Add the rind of the lemon and all the juice.
6. Add the rind of half the orange and all the juice.
7. Beat the eggs and add.
8. If necessary use a little milk, but if the fruit has been juicy, this should not be required.
9. Turn into a greased basin and cover with a greased paper.
10. Steam for 2 to 2½ hours.
11. Turn out and serve with Custard Sauce (see page 121).

(Sufficient for 4 persons.)

CASTLE PUDDING

Ingredients

2 *eggs.*   4 *oz. sugar.*   3 *oz. butter.*
½ *teaspoonful baking-powder.*   4 *oz. flour.*   *A pinch of salt.*

Method

1. Grease some moulds.
2. Cream the butter and sugar.
3. Sift the flour and baking-powder and salt together.
4. Add with the eggs alternately to the butter.
5. Half fill the moulds and cover with buttered paper.
6. Steam for ½ hour.
7. The moulds can be baked if liked.
8. Turn out and serve with Jam Sauce (see page 123).

(Sufficient for 4 persons.)

CHOCOLATE PUDDING

Ingredients

8 *oz. flour.*   *A pinch of salt.*   2 *oz. butter.*
2 *oz. castor sugar.*   1 *egg.*   *A little milk.*
½ *teaspoonful baking-powder.*   1 *tablespoonful Supex chocolate.*

Method

1. Cream the butter and sugar.
2. Add salt and baking-powder to the flour.
3. Add the egg well beaten to the sugar and butter.
4. Add the flour.
5. Dissolve the chocolate in a little milk and add.
6. Turn into a buttered basin, cover with a buttered paper and steam for 1½ hours.
7. Turn out and serve with Chocolate Sauce (see page 120).

(Sufficient for 4 persons.)

CHRISTMAS PUDDING

Ingredients

4 oz. flour.	8 oz. stoned raisins.
6 oz. finely-shredded suet.	8 oz. sultanas.
½ teaspoonful powdered cinnamon.	1 tablespoonful jam.
1 tablespoonful brandy.	4 eggs.
½ teaspoonful ground ginger.	4 oz. bread-crumbs.
Juice and grated rind of 1 lemon.	8 oz. brown sugar.
1 teaspoonful baking-powder.	8 oz. currants.
½ teaspoonful mixed spice.	A little milk.
3 oz. mixed candied peel (chopped finely).	3 oz. minced apple.

Method

1. Wash and dry the dried fruits and prepare the others.
2. Stone (if necessary) and chop the raisins.
3. Mix all the dry ingredients together.
4. Add the eggs (well-beaten), lemon juice, brandy, jam, and a little milk if necessary, and mix all to a stiff consistency.
5. Put all into greased pudding basins and cover with greased paper and then with pudding cloths.
6. Steam for 8 hours at first, filling up the steamer from time to time with boiling water.
7. Remove the puddings from the steamer. Take off the pudding cloths and cover with clean dry cloths.
8. Store in a cool dry place until needed.
9. Steam for another 2 hours before serving.
10. Serve with Hard Sauce (see page 122) or with White Sauce (see page 127).

EGG JELLY

Ingredients

3 gills water.   6 oz. sugar.   2 lemons.   2 eggs.

Method

1. Wash the lemons, dry and grate the rind.
2. Add the grated rind and the strained juice to the water.
3. Add the sugar and stir till boiling.
4. Allow to cool.
5. Beat the eggs and stir into the mixture.
6. Stir over a gentle heat, but do not boil.
7. Pour into small moulds. Turn out when set.

(Sufficient for 4 persons.)

FRUIT IN JELLY

Ingredients

1 packet lemon jelly.	1 small tin sliced peaches.
1 tin mandarine oranges.	2 bananas.

Method

1. Drain the syrup from the tins and make up to slightly less than 1 pint with water.
2. Make the jelly with this.
3. Peel and slice the bananas.
4. Put the fruit in a glass dish and pour over the jelly.
5. Lay on ice to set.
6. Serve with whipped cream.

(Sufficient for 4 persons.)

FRUIT MOULD

Ingredients

½ *lb. prunes.*	1 *lemon.*	3 *oz. syrup.*
2 *tablespoonfuls sherry.*	½ *oz. gelatine.*	1 *gill cream.*

Method

1. Soak the prunes over-night in a little water.
2. Boil with the syrup and grated rind of a lemon till soft.
3. Rub through a sieve.
4. Dissolve the gelatine and add, also lemon juice.
5. Add the sherry.
6. Pour into a mould and lay on ice.
7. Turn out and serve with whipped cream.

(Sufficient for 4 persons.)

FRUIT SALAD

Ingredients

1 *orange.*	1 *apple.*	1 *small tin pears.*
2 *oz. black grapes.*	2 *oz. white grapes.*	1 *banana.*
1 *small tin sliced peaches.*		1 *tin stoned cherries.*

Method

1. Drain the liquid from the tins of fruit. Mix well.
2. Boil and reduce to about one half. Cool.
3. Skin the grapes and remove the seeds.
4. Peel and slice the apple.
5. Peel the orange and divide into sections. Skin each section.
6. Peel and slice the banana.
7. Mix all the fruit in a salad bowl.
8. Pour over the syrup.
9. Lay on ice.
10. Serve with cream.

(Sufficient for 4 persons.)

GOOSEBERRY FOOL

Ingredients

¾ lb. gooseberries. I gill cream. I teacupful water.
3 oz. sugar. I egg-white.

Method

1. Stew the gooseberries and rub through a hair sieve.
2. Whisk the egg-white.
3. Whisk the cream and mix with the white.
4. Fold in the sieved gooseberries.
5. Serve in individual glasses with sponge fingers.

(Sufficient for 4 persons.)

JUNKET

Ingredients

I pint new milk. I oz. sugar.
Rennet. ½ gill cream.

Method

1. Warm the milk to blood heat. Add the sugar.
2. Add the quantity of rennet stated on the bottle.
3. Stir in and lay in a warm place.
4. A little chocolate flavouring may be added if liked.
5. Serve with castor sugar and cream.

(Sufficient for 4 persons.)

LEMON SPONGE

Ingredients

I pint lemon jelly. 3 egg-whites.

Method

1. Make the jelly and set aside to cool.
2. Whisk the whites till stiff.
3. Gradually mix in the jelly and whisk until the mixture starts to set.
4. Pour into a wetted mould and set on ice.
5. Turn out and serve with cream.

(Sufficient for 4 persons.)

MILK JELLY

Ingredients

I pint milk. I oz. gelatine.
Rind of I lemon. 2 oz. loaf sugar.

Method

1. Dissolve the gelatine in a little water.
2. Add the milk and grated lemon rind.
3. Add sugar.

4. Strain and set on ice to set.
5. Turn out and serve with cream.

(Sufficient for 4 persons.)

OMELETS
Ingredients

3 *eggs.*	*Seasoning.*
3 *oz. butter.*	3 *tablespoonfuls milk.*

Method

1. Beat the egg-yolks and whites separately.
2. Mix and add half the butter cut into little pieces.
3. Add the milk and seasoning.
4. Put the remainder of butter into the omelet pan and melt.
5. Pour in the egg mixture.
6. Cook till almost set.
7. Loosen round the edges.
8. Fold over.
9. Serve at once.   (Sufficient for 4 persons.)

Various fillings which may be added.

1. Jam.
2. Chopped kidney.
3. Grated cheese.
4. Chopped parsley.
5. Flaked cooked haddock.
6. Chopped mushrooms.
7. Asparagus tips.
8. Finely chopped ham.
9. Finely chopped tongue.
10. Chopped chicken.
11. Tomatoes (sliced).
12. Shrimps.

The foundation recipe is the same and the various fillings added. The filling gives the omelet its name.

PRINCE ALBERT PUDDING
Ingredients

1 *sponge loaf.*	4 *oz. castor sugar.*	1 *pint milk.*
3 *oz. cherries.*	2 *eggs.*	*A pinch of salt.*
½ *teaspoonful vanilla essence.*		1 *cupful bread-crumbs.*

Method

1. Warm the milk and pour over the bread-crumbs. Crush up the sponge loaf and add.
2. Chop the cherries and add with the sugar, salt and vanilla essence.
3. Add the egg-yolks and fold in the stiffly-beaten whites.

4. Turn into a greased basin, cover with greased paper and steam for 1½–2 hours.

5. Turn out and serve with Custard Sauce (see page 121).

(Sufficient for 4 persons.)

PRUNES EN CASSEROLE

Ingredients

1 *lb. prunes.*   *Water.*
4 *oz. sugar.*   *Cinnamon stick.*

Method

1. Soak the prunes over-night.

2. Place in a casserole with the sugar and a piece of cinnamon stick and the water they were soaked in.

3. Put on the lid and cook in the oven till tender. (Regulo 4.) About 1 hour is required.

4. The prunes should be plump and soft.

5. Serve hot or cold.   (Sufficient for 4 persons.)

QUEEN OF PUDDINGS

Ingredients

1 *pint milk.*   1 *oz. butter.*   2 *oz. sugar.*   2 *eggs.*
1½ *oz. castor sugar.*   3 *oz. bread-crumbs.*   *Raspberry jam.*

Method

1. Butter a pie-dish.

2. Soak the bread-crumbs in the milk.

3. Add 2 oz. of sugar and 2 egg-yolks.   Mix well.

4. Pour into the pie-dish and bake till set.   (Regulo 5.)

5. Cool slightly and spread with jam.

6. Whisk the whites and castor sugar.

7. Pile on top of the pudding.

8. Cook in a slow oven till brown.   (Regulo ¼.)

9. Serve hot.   (Sufficient for 4 persons.)

STEWED DRY FRUIT

Ingredients

1 *pint water.*   1 *lb. dried apricots or*
4 *oz. sugar.*   *other dried fruit.*

Method

1. Soak the fruit over-night in the water.

2. Stew in the water it was soaked in, adding the sugar.

3. Cook till tender—about ½ hour.

4. Serve cold.   (Sufficient for 4 persons.)

STEWED FRESH FRUIT

Ingredients

1 *lb. fresh plums.*	¼ *lb. sugar.*	*Water.*

Method

1. Remove the stalks and wipe.
2. Put on to stew with the water and sugar.
3. Cook slowly till tender, but do not break.
4. Serve cold.

(Sufficient for 4 persons.)

SULTANA PUDDING

Ingredients

¼ *lb. sultanas.*	¼ *lb. butter.*	¼ *lb. sugar.*
6 *oz. flour.*	*A pinch of salt.*	2 *eggs.*
½ *teaspoonful baking-powder.*		

Method

1. Cream the butter and sugar, and add salt.
2. Add the eggs well beaten.
3. Add the sifted flour and baking-powder.
4. Clean the sultanas and add.
5. If too stiff, use a little milk.
6. Turn into a buttered basin and cover with a buttered paper.
7. Steam for 2–2½ hours.
8. Turn out and serve with sauce.

(Sufficient for 4 persons.)

SUMMER BREAD PUDDING

Ingredients

1 *lb. raspberries or strawberries.*	1 *gill cream.*
Slices of bread and butter.	3 *oz. sugar.*

Method

1. Pick over the fruit and sprinkle on the sugar. Lay aside for 1 hour.
2. Butter a pudding-basin and line it with slices of bread and butter.
3. Strain off the liquid and place the fruit in the bowl.
4. Cover with pieces of bread and butter.
5. Warm the syrup and cook till thick.
6. Pour over the pudding.

7. Place a plate and weight on top and put aside or leave over-night.

8. Turn out and serve with cream.

9. Serve very cold.

(Sufficient for 4 persons.)

TRIFLE

Ingredients

1 *sponge loaf or 4 small sponges.*	*Raspberry jam.*
Glacé cherries, ratafias and angelica.	½ *pint custard.*
1 *tablespoonful brandy.*	½ *pint cream.*
1 *tablespoonful sherry.*	

Method

1. Divide the sponges and spread with plenty of raspberry jam. Lay in a dish.

2. Crush the ratafias over the sponges.

3. Pour over the sherry and brandy and the custard, which should be cold.

4. Lay aside for 1 hour.

5. Whip the cream, and flavour if liked.

6. Either pour on top or pipe over the custard.

7. Decorate with cherries and angelica.

8. Serve very cold.

(Sufficient for 4 persons.)

WEST-RIDING PUDDING

Ingredients

4 *slices bread.*	1 *oz. butter.*
Juice of 1 *lemon.*	¼ *lb. stewed dried apricots.*

Method

1. Spread the bread with butter and cut off the crusts. Divide each slice into four long strips.

2. Butter a pie-dish and place a few pieces of bread in the bottom.

3. Cover with the apricots.

4. Continue in alternate layers till all is used up, finishing with a layer of bread.

5. Add the lemon juice to the apricot juice and pour over the bread.

6. Bake in a moderate oven till nicely browned.   (Regulo 5.)

7. Serve hot.

(Sufficient for 4 persons.)

22. SAVOURIES

ANCHOVY AND EGGS

Ingredients

4 *eggs.*   1 *oz. butter.*   *Seasoning.*
Anchovy essence.   *A little milk.*   *Parsley for garnish.*
4 *rounds of buttered toast.*

Method

1. Whisk the eggs till light and frothy.
2. Add a little milk, seasoning and anchovy essence.
3. Melt the butter in a small pan.
4. Pour in the egg mixture and stir over a gentle heat until it thickens.
5. Pour on to the hot buttered toast.
6. Garnish with parsley and serve at once.

(Sufficient for 4 persons.)

CHEESE AIGRETTES

Ingredients

1½ *oz. grated cheese.*   1 *oz. grated cheese (extra).*
2 *oz. flour.*   *Seasoning.*   1 *egg.*
1 *yolk.*   1 *oz. butter.*   1 *gill water.*

Method

1. Heat the water and butter together.
2. Sift the flour and add to the water.   Beat briskly until it gets very thick and can be gathered into a ball.
3. Add the grated cheese, egg and seasoning.
4. Heat a bath of fat, and, when hot, cook the cheese mixture in spoonfuls.
5. Drain well and roll in the grated cheese.
6. Serve immediately.   (Sufficient for 4 persons.)

CHEESE BISCUITS

Ingredients

3 *oz. grated cheese.*   4 *oz. flour.*   2 *oz. butter.*
1 *egg-yolk.*   *Seasoning.*   *A pinch of cayenne.*

Method

1. Measure the flour and add the salt.
2. Rub in the butter till fine.
3. Add the seasoning and grated cheese.
4. Mix with beaten egg-yolk to a stiff dough.
5. Roll out on a floured board, and cut in biscuit shapes.
6. Cook for about 15 minutes in a moderate oven. (Regulo 5.)
7. Cool on a tray.   (Sufficient for 4 persons.)

F

CHEESE PYRAMIDS

Ingredients

4 *water biscuits.*	½ *cupful cream.*	*Parsley.*
Some cheese cut in slices.	1 *oz. grated cheese.*	*Seasoning.*

Method

1. Whip the cream and to it add the grated cheese and seasoning.
2. Put a little on each biscuit.
3. Decorate with small pieces of cheese and a tiny piece of parsley.
4. Serve in a dish of watercress.

(Sufficient for 4 persons.)

CHEESE SANDWICHES

Ingredients

6 *oz. Short Pastry* (see page 139).		
A pinch of sugar.	1 *oz. butter.*	*Juice of* ½ *lemon.*
¼ *lb. grated cheese.*	*Seasoning.*	1 *hard-boiled egg.*

Method

1. Prepare the pastry and keep in a cool place until required.
2. Melt the butter.
3. Pound the egg in a basin and add the melted butter.
4. Add the sugar, cheese, seasoning and lemon juice.
5. Roll out the pastry and cut in two.
6. Spread the mixture on one half and cover with the other. Trim the edges.
7. Cook on a baking sheet for 20 minutes. (Regulo 6.)
8. Cut in squares, and serve hot or cold.

(Sufficient for 4 persons.)

CHEESE SOUFFLÉ

Ingredients

1 *gill milk.*	1 *oz. flour.*	1 *oz. butter.*
4 *eggs.*	*Seasoning.*	4 *oz. grated cheese.*

Method

1. Prepare a soufflé tin or four small ones.
2. Melt the butter and add the flour.
3. Cook for 1 minute.
4. Add milk and beat till quite smooth.
5. Remove from heat and add the egg-yolks, beating each one separately.
6. Add seasoning and cheese.
7. Whisk the egg-whites and fold into the mixture.

8. Pour into the prepared tin and bake for 20–30 minutes. (Regulo 8.)

9. If small tins are used, cook for about 10 minutes.

10. Serve at once.

(Sufficient for 4 persons.)

CHEESE STRAWS

Ingredients

3 oz. grated cheese. Seasoning. 3 oz. flour.
2 oz. butter. 1 egg-yolk.

Method

1. Measure the flour and add seasonings and cheese.
2. Rub in the butter till fine.
3. Mix with beaten egg-yolk till very stiff.
4. Roll out thinly and cut in narrow strips.
5. Cut a few rings to hold the straws when they are baked.
6. Cook till a golden brown. (Regulo 5.)
7. Serve the straws in little bundles held together by the rings.
8. The ends of the straws may be dipped in red pepper.

(Sufficient for 4 persons.)

CHEESE TARTLETS

Ingredients

4 oz. Rough Puff Pastry (see page 147).
1 dessertspoonful flour. Seasoning. 1 oz. cheese.
½ gill milk. ½ oz. butter. 1 egg.

Method

1. Melt the butter, add the flour and cook for 1 minute.
2. Add the seasoning, cheese and milk, and cook for 1 minute after boiling.
3. Add the egg-yolk and then fold in the beaten egg-white.
4. Line some small tins with pastry and half fill each with the mixture.
5. Bake for about 20–30 minutes. (Regulo 8.)
6. Serve very hot.

(Sufficient for 4 persons.)

HADDOCK CROÛTES

Ingredients

4 small rounds of toast. Seasoning.
Some cooked Finnan haddock. Cheese Sauce (see page 120).

Method

1. Prepare the toast and keep it hot.
2. Flake the haddock and place a little on each round of toast.

3. Pour over the Cheese Sauce.

4. Heat for a few minutes in the oven (Regulo 5) and serve at once. *(Sufficient for 4 persons.)*

HAM TOAST

Ingredients

4 *rounds of toast.*
Cheese Sauce (see page 120).

4 *oz. grated cheese.*
4 *oz. chopped ham.*

Method

1. Butter the toast, allow three small slices for each person, and spread one with chopped ham.

2. Place one on top and spread with grated cheese.

3. Place another round on top of the cheese, buttered side down.

4. Arrange in an entrée dish and pour over the Cheese Sauce.

5. Heat for a few minutes in the oven before serving. (Regulo 5.) *(Sufficient for 4 persons.)*

HERRING ROES

Ingredients

¼ *lb. Fritter Batter* (see page 130).
3 *tomatoes.*
¼ *lb. streaky bacon.*

4 *roes.*
Parsley.

Seasoning.
Fat to fry.

Method

1. Wash and dry the roes.

2. Peel the tomatoes and cut in slices.

3. Cut up the roes and season.

4. Place a piece of roe on a piece of tomato and roll up in a slice of bacon. Continue till all is used up.

5. Dip in fritter batter and fry in hot fat till a golden brown.

6. Serve hot and garnish with parsley.

(Sufficient for 4 persons.)

SARDINES ON TOAST

Ingredients

1 *tin sardines.*
4 *rounds of buttered toast.*

Seasoning.

Method I

1. Prepare the toast.

2. Drain the oil from the sardines and arrange a few on each piece of toast. Sprinkle on a little seasoning.

Method 2

1. Instead of buttering the toast, melt the butter. Then pound the sardines and mix in the melted butter and seasoning.

2. Spread the mixture on toast and garnish with parsley and corraline pepper.

(Sufficient for 4 persons.)

SARDINE PYRAMIDS

Ingredients

4 rounds of fried bread.	Red pepper.	1 oz. butter.
Chopped parsley (dried).	4 sardines.	Seasoning.

Method

1. Pound the fish after removing the skin and bones.
2. Melt the butter and add.
3. Season well and pile on the fried bread, into little pyramids.
4. Decorate with parsley and red pepper.
5. Serve with watercress.

(Sufficient for 4 persons.)

STUFFED EGGS

Ingredients

4 hard-boiled eggs.	Fat to fry.	Seasoning.
Egg and bread-crumbs.	1 oz. butter.	Flour.
½ teaspoonful chutney.	1 oz. chopped ham.	

Method

1. Shell the eggs and cut in halves lengthwise. Remove the yolk.
2. Pound the yolks and add the melted butter.
3. Add chopped ham, chutney and seasoning.
4. Fill up the centres of the egg-whites with the mixture and join the halves.
5. Roll in flour.
6. Dip in egg and then bread-crumb each.
7. Fry till a golden brown. Serve hot.

(Sufficient for 4 persons.)

STUFFED MUSHROOMS

Ingredients

1 oz. butter.	Seasoning.	4 rounds of toast.
2 oz. chopped ham.	Juice of 1 lemon.	¼ lb. mushrooms.
1 oz. bread-crumbs.		

Method

1. Prepare the mushrooms. Peel and lay them on a hot dish.

2. Sprinkle on the seasoning and lemon juice, and grill the mushrooms.

3. Mix the ham and bread-crumbs together and season well.

4. Spread some on each mushroom and grill for a few minutes.

5. Serve on rounds of toast.

(Sufficient for 4 persons.)

STUFFED OLIVES

Ingredients

1 *dozen olives.*	*A few anchovies.*	*Seasoning.*
1 *hard-boiled egg-yolk.*	*Cayenne pepper.*	1 *oz. butter.*

Method

1. Stone the olives.

2. Bone the anchovies and pound with the egg-yolk.

3. Add butter and seasoning.

4. Rub the mixture through a hair sieve and put in an icing paper or paper bag.

5. Pipe into the olives.

6. Serve very cold.

(Sufficient for 4 persons.)

23. CHEESE DISHES

BAKED CHEESE

Ingredients

6 *oz. grated cheese.*	*Seasoning.*	6 *oz. bread-crumbs.*
3 *eggs.*	¾ *pint milk.*	1½ *oz. butter.*

Method

1. Melt the butter and pour over the bread-crumbs.

2. Boil the milk and pour it over the crumbs.

3. Add seasoning, grated cheese and egg-yolks.

4. Whisk the whites and fold into the mixture.

5. Pour into a buttered pie-dish and bake till nicely browned. (Regulo 7.)

6. Serve very hot.

(Sufficient for 4 persons.)

CHEESE AND CELERY

Ingredients

Celery.	4 oz. grated cheese.	2 oz. butter.
2 oz. flour.	1 gill milk.	Seasoning.
4 buttered rounds of toast.		

Method

1. Cook the celery till tender, and drain.   Chop finely.
2. Mix with the grated cheese.
3. Melt the butter and add the flour and milk.   Stir till boiling.
4. Add the other ingredients and seasoning and cook for a few minutes.
5. Serve on rounds of buttered toast.
6. Garnish with parsley and celery straws.

(Sufficient for 4 persons.)

CHEESE AND TOMATOES

Ingredients

4 rounds of toasted bread.		
1 oz. butter.	A little milk.	Seasoning.
4 oz. grated cheese.	Cayenne.	4 tomatoes.

Method

1. Cut the bread into rounds about the size of a slice of tomato.
2. Toast and butter and keep hot.
3. Place sliced tomato on each round of toast.
4. Melt 1 oz. of butter and add the grated cheese, milk and seasoning.
5. Stir over a gentle heat till quite smooth.
6. Put some on top of each tomato slice.
7. Serve at once.

(Sufficient for 4 persons.)

CHEESE FRITTERS

Ingredients

4 oz. cheese (grated).	2 egg-whites.	Seasoning.
½ gill milk.	Fat to fry.	Watercress.
2 tablespoonfuls flour.		

Method

1. Mix the cheese, flour and seasoning together.
2. Heat the milk and pour over.
3. Whisk the egg-whites and fold into the mixture.

4. Drop in spoonfuls into the hot fat and fry till golden-brown and puffy.

5. Serve immediately on a bed of watercress.

(Sufficient for 4 persons.)

GOLDEN BUCK RAREBIT

Ingredients

4 *eggs.*	*Seasoning.*	*Mustard.*
4 *rounds buttered toast.*		4 *oz. cheese (grated).*
1 *tablespoonful flour.*		1 *tablespoonful butter.*

Method

1. Prepare and butter the toast, and keep it hot.

2. Poach the eggs and keep them hot.

3. Melt the butter.

4. Add the flour, cheese and seasonings.

5. Pour over the rounds of toast and place one poached egg on top of each.

6. Serve hot.

(Sufficient for 4 persons.)

MACARONI CHEESE

Ingredients

¾ *pint White Sauce* (see page 127).	2 *oz. macaroni.*
4 *oz. grated cheese.* *Seasoning.*	1 *egg.*

Method

1. Boil the macaroni in salted water for about 45 minutes.

2. Drain and cut it up into rings.

3. Prepare the sauce and beat in 1 egg.

4. Add the cheese and macaroni to the sauce and season well.

5. Pour into a buttered pie-dish and cook in a moderate oven till brown.   (Regulo 7.)

6. Serve at once.

(Sufficient for 4 persons.)

WELSH RAREBIT

Ingredients

4 *slices of hot buttered toast.*	2 *tablespoonfuls milk.*
Seasoning. 2 *oz. butter.*	6 *oz. cheese.*

Method

1. Melt the butter and add the milk, grated cheese and seasoning.

2. When melted pour it over the hot buttered toast.

3. Serve at once.

(Sufficient for 4 persons.)

24. EGG DISHES

ANCHOVY EGGS

Ingredients

4 *eggs.*	4 *rounds of toast.*	1 *oz. butter.*
Anchovy essence.	*Seasoning.*	*Parsley.*

Method

1. Toast the bread, butter it and keep it hot.
2. Poach the eggs in boiling salted water.
3. Place one on each round of buttered toast.
4. Put a teaspoonful of anchovy essence on each and reheat in a slow oven.
5. Garnish with parsley and serve hot.

(Sufficient for 4 persons.)

BOILED EGGS

Ingredients

Boiling salted water.   4 *eggs.*   *Seasoning.*

Method

1. Put on a small pan of water to boil.
2. Add a little salt.
3. When boiling, carefully put in the number of eggs to be boiled.
4. There must be sufficient water to cover them easily.
5. Boil rather quickly for 1 minute.
6. Draw the pan to the side of the fire and cook for 4 minutes longer.

Note.—If cooking for a child or invalid 3 minutes is sufficient.

Hard-boiled eggs: put in boiling water and boil for 10 minutes.

(Sufficient for 4 persons.)

CHEESE CUSTARD

Ingredients

4 *oz. grated cheese.*	*Seasoning.*	2 *oz. butter.*
2 *gills milk.*	2 *eggs.*	1 *oz. cornflour.*

Method

1. Melt the butter and add the cornflour. Cook for 1 minute.
2. Add milk and stir till boiling.
3. Add seasoning, well-beaten egg, and grated cheese.
4. Pour into a buttered pie-dish and bake for 20 minutes. (Regulo 6.)
5. Serve hot.   (Sufficient for 4 persons.)

CURRIED EGGS

Ingredients

4 *hard-boiled eggs.*   *Seasoning.*   *Tomato sauce.*
½ *teaspoonful curry powder*   *Cayenne.*
Parsley and watercress.   1 *oz. bread-crumbs.*

Method

1. Shell the eggs and cut a piece off the ends.
2. Take out the yolks.
3. Pound the yolks with the curry powder.
4. Add seasoning, cayenne, bread-crumbs and tomato sauce.
5. Fill up the eggs with the mixture.
6. Garnish with parsley and watercress.
7. Serve with Tomato Sauce (see page 126).

(Sufficient for 4 persons.)

EGG CROQUETTES

Ingredients

1¼ *oz. flour.*   1¼ *oz. butter.*   1¼ *gills milk.*
Seasoning.   *Fat to fry.*   3 *hard-boiled eggs.*
Egg and bread-crumbs.   *Watercress.*

Method

1. Melt the butter and add the flour.
2. Stir in the milk and cook till boiling.
3. Add seasoning.
4. Shell and chop the eggs and add to the mixture.
5. Turn on to a plate to cool.
6. Form into eight cakes, and egg and crumb each.
7. Fry in deep fat till a golden brown.
8. Serve with watercress as a garnish.

(Sufficient for 4 persons.)

FRIED EGGS

Ingredients

4 *eggs.*   *Bacon fat.*   *Seasoning.*

Method

1. Melt the fat and heat till quite hot.
2. Break each egg separately.
3. Baste the fat over the eggs, but do not turn.
4. Cook until the white is set and the yolk coated with white.
5. Serve at once. Garnish with parsley.

(Sufficient for 4 persons.)

OMELETS

Recipes for Omelets are given in the Sweets Section, page 157.

POACHED EGGS

Ingredients

4 *eggs.*   *Water.*   *Salt.*   4 *slices buttered toast.*

Method

1. Put on a pan of water to boil.
2. Add a good quantity of salt, varying the amount with the quantity of water.
3. Break an egg into a saucer.
4. When the water is boiling, stir it briskly with a spoon.
5. When it is going round fast, pour in the egg.   This gives the egg a good shape.
6. Cook until the egg sets.
7. Lift out and drain off the water.
8. Serve on hot buttered toast.

(Sufficient for 4 persons.)

SCOTCH EGGS

Ingredients

6 *oz. sausage-meat.*	*Seasoning.*	*Fat to fry.*
Watercress.	*Parsley.*	4 *hard-boiled eggs.*
Egg and bread-crumbs.	*Flour.*	

Method

1. Shell the eggs and roll them in the flour.
2. Coat with the sausage-meat.
3. Dip in egg and toss in bread-crumbs.
4. Fry in deep fat till a golden brown.
5. Lift out and drain.
6. Cut in halves and decorate each with a sprig of parsley.
7. Serve on a bed of watercress.

(Sufficient for 4 persons.)

SCRAMBLED EGGS

Ingredients

3 *eggs.*	3 *tablespoonfuls milk.*	1 *oz. butter.*
Parsley.	4 *rounds of buttered toast.*	*Seasoning.*

Method

1. Break the eggs and separate the yolks and whites.
2. Beat the yolks and add the seasoning and milk.
3. Whisk the whites and fold in.
4. Melt the butter and pour in the mixture.
5. Stir over a gentle heat until it thickens.

6. Serve on rounds of hot buttered toast.

7. Garnish with parsley.

Note.—As a variety, chopped kidney may be added. Two sheep's kidneys lightly fried are sufficient for the quantities given above.

(Sufficient for 4 persons.)

SCRAMBLED EGGS AND TOMATOES

Ingredients

3 *eggs.*	4 *tomatoes.*	3 *tablespoonfuls milk.*
1 *oz. butter.*	*Seasoning.*	4 *rounds of toast.*

Method

1. Cook the eggs as for Scrambled Eggs (see page 171).

2. Slice the tomatoes and lay them on the buttered toast.

3. Grill for a minute or two.

4. Pile the egg mixture on top and decorate with a tiny piece of tomato.

5. Serve hot.

(Sufficient for 4 persons.)

25. USE OF DRIED EGGS

The Dried Eggs which are prepared under the direction of the Ministry of Food form a very important item of the housewife's store cupboard. When eggs are scarce, or when the arrival of unexpected visitors demands the use of more eggs than are available in their fresh state, they are invaluable.

Full directions are given on the packets or tins of dried egg for the method of reconstitution into liquid egg form. It is, however, advisable to use them dry, *i.e.*, unreconstituted, in plain cakes, puddings, batter mixtures, and in the making of biscuits. In such cases, the dry egg is mixed with the other dry ingredients. It is necessary to add two tablespoonfuls of water for each dried egg used, and this should be added to any other liquid appearing in the recipe.

Dried eggs can be used for all recipes in this Book, which do not demand that whites and yolks are separated.

The following additional recipes are suggested:

GOLDEN SOUP

Ingredients

2 *pints stock.*	1 *small onion.*	*Fat for frying.*
4 *small slices of bread about ½ inch thick.*	2 *eggs (reconstituted).*	*Seasoning.*

Method

1. Have the stock ready.
2. Cut the bread.
3. Reconstitute the eggs.
4. Dip the bread into the reconstituted eggs.
5. Prepare the onion, chop it finely, and fry it in the fat.
6. Next fry the bread on both sides.
7. Drain the onions and bread and add to the stock.
8. Season and serve, allowing 1 slice of bread to each person.

(Sufficient for 4 persons.)

HAKE IN SORREL

Ingredients

1 *lb. of hake.*	*Salt.*	*Red Pepper*
French mustard.	*Sorrel.*	*Juice of* 1 *lemon.*
2 *eggs (reconstituted).*	*Nutmeg.*	

Method

1. Boil the hake (see page 48).
2. Prepare the sorrel leaves and cook them in water to which salt and a little nutmeg have been added.
3. Mash the sorrel finely.
4. Add the reconstituted eggs and season with a little French mustard.
5. Arrange the sorrel on a dish and on it place the fish.
6. Sprinkle lemon juice and red pepper over the whole.

(Sufficient for 4 persons.)

STUFFED LIVER

Ingredients

1 *lb. liver.*	*Seasoning.*	$\frac{1}{2}$ *pint of stock.*
2 *oz. chopped bacon fat.*		*Fat for cooking.*
2 *finely chopped onions.*		2 *oz. chopped ham.*
2 *oz. bread soaked in stock.*		$\frac{1}{4}$ *lb. bread-crumbs.*
2 *eggs (reconstituted).*		*Seasoned flour.*

Method

1. Wash and prepare the liver and cut into fairly thick slices.
2. Dip each slice in seasoned flour and brown in fat in a saucepan.
3. Mix the bacon fat, chopped ham, bread, and onions together; add seasoning and eggs and spread the mixture on the slices of liver.
4. Sprinkle each slice with bread-crumbs.
5. Arrange the slices of liver in a casserole, add the stock, and brown in the oven.

(Sufficient for 4 persons.)

POTATO BALLS

Ingredients

¾ lb. cold potatoes.	¼ lb. flour.	Salt.
¼ oz. butter.	Pepper.	A little milk.
2 eggs (reconstituted).		2 oz. grated cheese.

Method

1. Mash the potatoes finely.

2. Add the reconstituted eggs, grated cheese, flour (sieved), butter, seasoning and milk, and mix well together to a soft consistency. Leave to stand for an hour.

3. Have a pan of boiling salted water ready.

4. Mould the mixture into balls and drop them into the water.

5. Cook for a quarter of an hour.

6. Serve with a meat or fish dish or alone as a supper dish with Mornay Sauce (see page 124).

(Sufficient for 4 persons.)

PORTUGUESE MACARONI

Ingredients

½ lb. macaroni.	1 oz. butter.	¼ lb. grated cheese.
Pepper.	Salt.	½ pint milk.
2 eggs (reconstituted).		¼ lb. bread-crumbs.
1 tablespoonful chopped onion.		1 teaspoonful parsley.
½ pint Tomato Sauce (see page 126).		

Method

1. Boil the macaroni in salted water for about 45 minutes.

2. Drain it and, if necessary, cut it up into suitable lengths.

3. Stew the onion and parsley in the butter until tender.

4. Grease a fireproof dish and put in a layer of the macaroni.

5. Cover with a layer of the onion, seasoning and cheese.

6. Continue until the macaroni is used up.

7. Beat up the eggs with the milk and pour over all.

8. Cover the top with bread-crumbs and a few tiny pieces of butter, and bake for about an hour in a moderate oven. (Regulo 5.)

9. Serve with hot Tomato Sauce.

(Sufficient for 4 persons.)

POTATO AND CHEESE SOUFFLÉ

Ingredients

1 lb. potatoes.	3 oz. flour.	Salt.
Pepper.	4 oz. grated cheese.	1 gill milk.
3 dried eggs (reconstituted).		1 teaspoonful baking-powder.

Method

1. Prepare the potatoes, boil them, and mash them finely.
2. Add the reconstituted eggs, grated cheese, flour (sieved), baking-powder, seasoning, and milk. Mix well together so that the consistency is soft.
3. Bake in a greased pie dish in a hot oven (Regulo 8) for half-an-hour.
4. Serve very hot.

(Sufficient for 4 persons.)

SCRAMBLED EGGS AND VEGETABLES

Ingredients

4 *dried eggs (reconstituted)*.	4 *tablespoonfuls milk.*
1 *tin of macedoine of vegetables.*	1 *oz. chopped parsley.*
1 *oz. chopped onion.* *Seasoning.*	1 *oz. butter.*

Method

1. Drain the vegetables and season with pepper and salt.
2. Add chopped parsley and chopped onion.
3. Add the milk and a pinch of salt to the reconstituted **eggs** and beat well.
4. Add half the seasoned vegetables to the egg mixture.
5. Melt the butter in a saucepan, add the egg-vegetable mixture, and cook over a low heat, stirring gently until the mixture sets.
6. Pour this mixture on to the middle of a dish.
7. Heat the remainder of the seasoned vegetables in a little butter and arrange round the egg and vegetables.

(Sufficient for 4 persons.)

STUFFED SAVOURY PANCAKES

Ingredients

4 *oz. flour.*	1 *oz. butter.*	½ *pint milk.*
4 *tablespoonfuls water.*	*Pinch of salt.*	2 *dried eggs (dry).*

Stuffing : A thick stew of mushrooms with tiny pieces of kidney, ham, or left-over meat.

Method

1. Prepare the stew.
2. Make the pancakes according to the instructions on page 127.
3. Spread some of the savoury mixture on each pancake and roll up.
4. Serve very hot with or without a sauce.

(Sufficient for 4 persons.)

EGGS IN WATERCRESS

Ingredients

4 *dried eggs.*
1 *bunch of radishes.*

French Dressing (see page 228).
Watercress.

Method

1. Wash and prepare the watercress and chop it finely.
2. Cover it with French Dressing.
3. Make the dried eggs hard according to the Ministry of Food's recipe.
4. Slice the hard eggs, and place them on the dressed watercress.
5. Prepare the radishes and arrange them between the egg slices.

(Sufficient for 4 persons.)

GRAY'S CAKE

Ingredients

½ lb. flour.
¼ lb. butter.
½ teaspoonful baking-powder.
2 dried eggs (dry).

¼ lb. sultanas.
¼ lb. currants.

A little milk.
A pinch of salt.
¼ lb. granulated sugar.
4 tablespoonfuls water.

Method

1. Cream the butter and add the sugar.
2. Add the flour (sifted), the eggs, fruit, salt, and baking powder, and mix well.
3. Add the water and a little milk if necessary.
4. Beat all together for half-an-hour, then put in a greased cake tin, and bake in a moderate oven (Regulo 4) for about an hour.

ORANGE CAKE

Ingredients

¼ lb. butter.   ¼ lb. sugar.
Grated rind of 1 orange.
4 tablespoonfuls water.

3 oz. flour.   2 eggs (dry).
2 oz. ground almonds.
¼ teaspoonful baking-powder.

Filling:

Juice of 1 orange.   2 oz. ground almonds.   3 oz. sugar.

Method

1. Cream the butter and sugar until soft.
2. Add the flour, almonds, rind of orange, eggs and baking powder, and mix all together.
3. Add the water and beat well.
4. Put into a greased cake tin and bake in a moderate oven (Regulo 4) for about an hour.

5. Cool on a wire tray and when cold cut into three layers and spread with the orange filling.

Note.—To make the filling: Beat together the orange juice, almonds and sugar until smooth.

SIMNEL CAKE

Ingredients

¼ *lb. flour.*	¼ *lb. sultanas.*	¼ *lb. currants.*
A pinch of salt.	2 *oz. sugar.*	¼ *lb. butter.*
1 *tablespoonful milk, if necessary.*		
½ *teaspoonful ground ginger.*		Marzipan as filling:
½ *teaspoonful ground nutmeg.*		¼ *lb. ground almonds.*
2 *tablespoonfuls syrup.*		½ *lb. icing sugar.*
2 *dried eggs (dry).*		*Juice of* 1 *lemon.*
4 *tablespoonfuls water.*		*A little ratafia essence.*
½ *teaspoonful ground cinnamon.*		*Vanilla essence.*
1 *teaspoonful baking-powder.*		2 *eggs (reconstituted).*

Method

1. Cream the butter with sugar and syrup.
2. Mix the flour, dried egg, sultanas, currants, spices, baking-powder and salt.
3. Beat the mixture into the creamed butter and mix with the water to a stiff consistency, adding the milk if necessary.
4. Put half the mixture into a greased cake tin.
5. Over this put a layer of the marzipan.
6. Add the rest of the cake mixture.
7. Bake in a moderate oven (Regulo 4) for about 2 hours.
8. Decorate the top with a layer of the marzipan and brown in the oven.

To make the marzipan

1. Add the sugar, vanilla essence, ratafia essence, and lemon juice to the almonds, and mix.
2. Add enough of the reconstituted beaten egg to mix to a stiff consistency.

26. VEGETARIAN DISHES

GENERAL NOTE

Strict vegetarians exclude all forms of meat and poultry, butter and eggs from their dietary. Those who merely omit meat and bacon are not true vegetarians.

It is beyond the scope of this book to give many of the large number of vegetarian dishes. In the foregoing sections are many suitable recipes. The following are just a few to make the choice of vegetarian menus easier.

BRAISED CABBAGE WITH ONIONS AND CHESTNUTS

Ingredients

½ *lb. chestnuts.*   2 *Spanish onions.*   *Seasoning.*
1 *gill Household Stock* (see page 37).   1 *small cabbage.*

Method

1. Boil the chestnuts for 5 minutes.

2. Drain, shell and peel the nuts, and place them in a casserole.

3. Peel and slice the onions and mix them with the chestnuts.

4. Add seasoning and stock.

5. Wash and cut the cabbage in half.

6. Lay the cabbage on top of the chestnuts cut side down.

7. Put on the lid and cook in a moderate oven till tender. (Regulo 4.)

8. Serve hot.

(Sufficient for 4 persons.)

BRAISED LETTUCE

Ingredients

2 *lettuces.*   2 *carrots.*   2 *onions.*   *Seasoning.*
2 *gills Household Stock* (see page 37).   1 *turnip (small).*

Method

1. Prepare the carrots, turnip and onions and cut each into small cubes.

2. Place in a casserole.

3. Add the seasoning and pour over the stock.

4. Wash the lettuce and cut each in half.

5. Cook the vegetables in the oven for ½ hour.   (Regulo 4.)

6. Lay the lettuce on top and cook for half an hour longer.

7. Serve hot.

(Sufficient for 4 persons.)

BRUSSELS SPROUTS FRITTERS

Ingredients

1 *lb. young sprouts.*   ¼ *lb. Batter* (see page 130).   *Fat to fry.*

Method

1. Trim the sprouts and soak for 1 hour in salted water.

2. Drain well.

3. Dip in the batter and fry in smoking hot fat till golden brown.

4. Drain well and dust with seasoning.

5. Serve very hot.

Note.—If the sprouts are not quite fresh and young, it is necessary to parboil them before dipping them in the batter.

(Sufficient for 4 persons.)

BUTTER BEANS AND TOMATO SAUCE

Ingredients

1 *pint Tomato Sauce* (see page 126).　　1 *lb. beans.*
Seasoning.　　2 *onions.*

Method

1. Soak the beans over-night.
2. Boil with the sliced onions for about 1½ hours.
3. Strain the beans and onions.
4. Heat the Tomato Sauce and add the beans and onions.
5. Season well and cook slowly for 20 minutes.
6. Serve very hot.　　(Sufficient for 4 persons.)

CARROT SALAD

Ingredients

2 *bunches young carrots.*　　2 *lettuces.*　　*Watercress.*
Salad Dressing (see page 229).

Method

1. Wash the lettuce and watercress and soak in salted water.
2. Wash the carrots and grate them.
3. Chop a little of the cress and the coarser leaves of the lettuce.
4. Mix these with the carrot.
5. Make a bed of lettuce leaves and watercress. Put the sprigs of watercress round the sides.
6. Mix a little dressing with the chopped vegetables and pile all in the centre of the dish.
7. Decorate with small lettuce leaves and watercress.
8. Serve very cold.　　(Sufficient for 4 persons.)

CHESTNUT SOUP

Ingredients

1 *lb. chestnuts.*　　1 *oz. butter.*　　1 *oz. flour.*
1½ *pints Household Stock* (see page 37).　　1 *onion.*
A *small piece of celery.*　　*Seasoning.*

Method

1. Put the chestnuts on to boil in cold water. When boiling turn out and allow to cool. Shell and skin them.

2. Put the stock on to boil and add the chestnuts.
3. Prepare the vegetables and add to the soup.
4. Add the butter and bring to the boil.
5. Cook for 1 hour.
6. Mix the flour with a little cold milk and stir in.   Stir till boiling.   Season.
7. Reheat and serve.

(Sufficient for 4 persons.)

LENTIL CUTLETS

Ingredients

¼ *lb. lentils.*	¼ *lb. bread-crumbs.*	1 *oz. grated cheese.*
1 *oz. butter.*	*Seasoning.*	*Fat to fry.*
Tomato Sauce (see page 126).		*Egg and bread-crumbs.*

Method

1. Wash the lentils and tie in a small muslin bag.
2. Cook gently for about 1 hour.
3. Lift out and drain.
4. Mix with the bread-crumbs, grated cheese and seasoning.
5. Melt the butter and add.
6. Bind with a little Tomato Sauce.
7. Lay aside for 1 hour.
8. Form into cutlets.
9. Egg and crumb each and fry in smoking hot fat till brown.
10. Drain and serve on a bed of watercress.

(Sufficient for 4 persons.)

MOCK SWEETBREADS

Ingredients

1 *pint White Sauce* (see page 127).	*Seasoning.*
2 *gills peas.*	½ *lb. bread-crumbs.*	2 *egg-yolks.*

Method

1. Soak the peas over-night.
2. Cook until tender.
3. Mix with the bread-crumbs and seasoning.
4. Bind together with egg-yolk.
5. Form into a roll and slightly flatten out to resemble a sweetbread.
6. Prepare the white sauce.
7. Roll the mixture in flour and lay gently in the sauce.
8. Poach gently for about 15 minutes.
9. Serve at once, garnished with parsley and lemon.

(Sufficient for 4 persons.)

NUT SALAD

Ingredients

Walnuts.   Brazil nuts.   Almonds.   Watercress.
Salad Dressing (see page 229).   *Lettuce.*

Method

1. Shell and chop the nuts.
2. Wash the lettuce and cress and chop half of it.
3. Mix this with the nuts.
4. Bind with a little Salad Dressing.
5. Arrange some lettuce and cress on a dish and pile the nut mixture in the centre.
6. Decorate with lettuce and cress and a few whole nuts.

(Sufficient for 4 persons.)

PINEAPPLE AND CREAM-CHEESE SALAD

Ingredients

1 *small tin pineapple slices.*   *Chopped parsley.*
Salad Dressing (see page 229).   *Cream cheese.*
2 *lettuces.*   *Seasoning.*

Method

1. Wash and soak the lettuce.
2. Shred half of it.
3. Chop all the pineapple except one slice.
4. Cut the cream cheese in small cubes.
5. Mix together, add seasoning, and bind with a little dressing.
6. Make a bed of lettuce and pile the mixture in the centre.
7. Put a layer of small lettuce leaves on top.
8. Lay the pineapple slice in the centre and fill up the hole in the middle with tiny pieces of cheese rolled in chopped parsley.

(Sufficient for 4 persons.)

POTATOES AU GRATIN

Ingredients

1 *lb. small potatoes.*   *Seasoning.*
Cheese Sauce (see page 120).   *Chopped parsley.*
1 *oz. grated cheese.*   1 *oz. butter.*

Method

1. Peel the potatoes and steam them till tender.
2. Sprinkle with seasoning.
3. Place in a vegetable dish.

4. Mix some chopped parsley and grated cheese, and put on top of the potatoes. Add the melted butter.

5. Pour over the Cheese Sauce.

6. Serve immediately.

(Sufficient for 4 persons.)

POTATO PIE

Ingredients

1½ *lb. potatoes.*   1 *gill Household Stock* (see page 37).
Flaky Pastry (see page 144). 1 *Spanish onion.* *Seasoning.*

Method

1. Peel the potatoes and cut them in thin slices.

2. Lay them in a dish.

3. Peel the onion and slice thinly into rings and add to the potatoes.

4. Add seasoning and stock.

5. Cover with another dish and cook for 1 hour in a moderate oven. (Regulo 5.)

6. Allow to cool.

7. Prepare the pastry, and when the vegetables are cold, cover in the usual way.

8. When cooked, serve with a sprig of parsley in the centre.

(Sufficient for 4 persons.)

STUFFED ONIONS

Ingredients

4 *Spanish onions.*	1 *oz. bread-crumbs.*	2 *tomatoes.*
Seasoning.	1 *egg-yolk.*	*A little chutney.*
2 *oz. cooked peas.*		

Method

1. Peel the onions and boil for 35 minutes.

2. Lift out and drain and scoop out the centres.

3. Mix the parts of the onion removed with the crumbs.

4. Add the peas.

5. Skin the tomatoes, chop and add.

6. Add seasoning and a little chutney.

7. Bind with beaten egg-yolk.

8. Stuff the onions with the mixture and place on a buttered tin.

9. Bake in a moderate oven till tender. (Regulo 7.)

10. Serve with Tomato Sauce (see page 126).

(Sufficient for 4 persons.)

TOMATO TIMBALES

Ingredients

4 *tomatoes.*
A little cayenne.
2 *tablespoonfuls cream.*

1 *pint White Sauce* (see page 127).
1 *tablespoonful chopped parsley.*

Method

1. Pour boiling water over the tomatoes and peel them carefully.
2. Bake in a slow oven till tender but not broken. (Regulo 5.)
3. Prepare the sauce.
4. Add cayenne and cream.
5. Lay the tomatoes in a dish and pour over the sauce.
6. Sprinkle with chopped parsley.
7. Serve hot.   (Sufficient for 4 persons.)

TURNIPS AND MUSTARD SAUCE

Ingredients

½ *pint Mustard Sauce* (see page 124).
6 *small turnips.*   *Seasoning.*

Method

1. Pare the turnips and boil them in salted water till quite tender.
2. Drain them well.
3. Prepare the sauce.   Add the turnips and re-heat.
4. Serve at once.

(Sufficient for 4 persons.)

VEGETABLE CROQUETTES

Ingredients

1 *egg.*
1 *teacupful bread-crumbs.*
¼ *lb. shelled nuts finely chopped.*

¼ *of a cooked marrow.*
4 *oz. cold potatoes.*
Egg and crumbs.

Fat to fry.
2 *oz. butter.*
Seasoning.

Method

1. Mash the potatoes and marrow together.
2. Add the chopped nuts and bread-crumbs.
3. Melt the butter and add.
4. Season well.
5. Mix with beaten egg to bind together.
6. Form into oval cakes and egg and crumb each.
7. Fry in deep fat till a golden brown.   Drain well.
8. Serve garnished with parsley and watercress.

(Sufficient for 4 persons.)

VEGETABLE OMELET

Ingredients

4 *eggs.*	2 *tablespoonfuls cream.*	4 *tablespoonfuls water.*
2 *oz. butter.*	*Cooked vegetables.*	*Seasoning.*

Method

1. Choose whatever vegetables liked, or use a mixture of several.
2. Cut the vegetables into tiny cubes.
3. Tie in muslin and cook till tender.
4. Mix with cream and seasoning.
5. Separate the egg-whites and yolks.
6. Beat the whites till frothy.
7. Stir in the yolks and the water.
8. Melt the butter and pour in the omelet.
9. Cook till just set and lay the vegetables and cream in the centre.
10. Fold over and cook the edges.
11. Serve at once. (Sufficient for 4 persons.)

VEGETABLE PIE

Ingredients

1 *gill peas.*	1 *onion.*	1 *gill stock.*	*Seasoning.*
1 *bunch small carrots.*		1 *small cauliflower.*	
½ *lb. Flaky Pastry* (see page 144).		1 *bunch small turnips.*	

Method

1. Prepare all the vegetables according to kind.
2. Steam in a steamer till quite tender.
3. Drain thoroughly and place in a pie-dish.
4. Season the stock and pour over.
5. Cover the pie in the usual way.
6. Reserve a few peas, and pile them in the centre of the pie.
7. Serve hot. (Sufficient for 4 persons.)

VEGETABLE STEW

Ingredients

A mixture of new vegetables, peas, cauliflower, carrots, turnip and onion.	2 *egg-yolks.*	1 *oz. flour.*
	1 *oz. butter.*	*Seasoning.*
	½ *pint milk.*	

Method

1. Prepare the vegetables according to kind and steam in a steamer.
2. Drain and sprinkle on a little seasoning.

3. Melt the butter.
4. Add the flour and cook for 1 minute.
5. Stir in the milk and beaten egg-yolks, and stir till boiling.
6. Season.
7. Re-heat the vegetables in the sauce.
8. Cook slowly for 20 minutes.
9. Serve hot.

(Sufficient for 4 persons.)

27. CAKES AND BISCUITS

GENERAL HINTS ON CAKE-MAKING

1. For cake-making choose good-quality tins.
2. Buy them in several sizes and kinds.
3. For shortening the cake several fats may be used.

    (*a*) For very plain cakes, dripping.
    (*b*) Gingerbreads (plain), dripping or lard.
    (*c*) Margarine.
    (*d*) Trex—this gives very good results.
    (*e*) Spry.
    (*f*) Butter.
    (*g*) Mixture of butter and margarine.

4. Good fruit must be used, as the waste in cheaper qualities makes them the dearer in the long run. Choose good reliable brands.

5. Methods

    (*a*) For plain cakes the shortening is rubbed into the flour as for pastry.
    (*b*) For richer cakes and pound cakes the fat and sugar are beaten together with a wooden spoon until quite creamy.
    (*c*) For sponge cakes the eggs and sugar are beaten over hot water until creamy.
    (*d*) In a few cases the butter is melted and added.

6. To cream butter and sugar

Measure the butter into a basin. Add the castor sugar and beat with a wooden spoon until white and creamy. Do not allow to become oily, as it makes the cake heavy.

7. To sift flour and baking-powder

Measure out the flour and baking-powder, and rub through a sieve or use a flour-sifter. This aerates the flour and removes all lumps. The more air in the flour the lighter the cake.

8. To clean fruit

Currants: Place in the corner of a towel, add some flour, and rub thoroughly, then draw carefully from the flour. The stalks will be left behind.

Raisins: Pick off the stalks and remove any hard dry fruit.

Cherries: Roll in flour. If to be used for small cakes, chop.

9. To blanch almonds

Put on to boil in water to cover. When boiling, allow to boil for 2 minutes. Cool, and then remove the brown skin.

ALMOND CHEESE CAKES

Ingredients

2 oz. ground almonds.   ¼ lb. castor sugar.   Marmalade.
½ lb. Flaky or Short Pastry (see pages 144 or 139).   1 egg.

Method

1. Line some small cake tins with the pastry.

2. Put a small amount of marmalade in each case. Do not be tempted to put in a lot, as it only boils out and spoils the appearance of the cakes.

3. Mix the almonds and sugar together and add the egg-yolk.

4. Whisk the white and fold in.

5. Put a little of the mixture in each case and cook till a golden brown (Regulo 7)—about 15–20 minutes.

6. Cool on a tray.

BIDEFORD BUNS

Ingredients

¼ lb. ground rice.   3 oz. castor sugar.   ¼ lb. butter.
½ teaspoonful baking-powder. 2 oz. sultanas.   ¼ lb. flour.
½ teaspoonful ground ginger. Milk to mix.   2 eggs.

Method

1. Cream the butter and sugar.

2. Add the eggs, beating each in separately.

3. Add the rice to the flour and mix well.

4. Measure and add the baking-powder and ginger and mix into the egg mixture, using milk if necessary.

5. Clean the sultanas and add.

6. Grease some small tins and fill each three-quarters full with this mixture.

7. Bake in a sharp oven for about 20 minutes. (Regulo 5.)

8. Cool on a tray.

CHEESE CAKES

Ingredients

¼ *lb. Short Pastry* (see page 139).	*Apricot jam.*
1 *teaspoonful baking-powder.*	¼ *lb. castor sugar.*
6 *oz. flour.* ¼ *lb. butter.*	2 *eggs.*

Method

1. Line some tins with the pastry and put a little jam in each.
2. Cream together the butter and sugar.
3. Add the egg-yolks.
4. Mix the flour and baking-powder together.
5. Sift into the egg mixture.
6. Fold in the stiffly-beaten whites.
7. Half fill the tins with the mixture.
8. Roll out the trimmings of pastry and cut in very narrow strips.
9. Put a little cross of pastry on top of each cake.
10. Bake in a moderate oven for about 20 minutes. (Regulo 6.)
11. Cool on a tray.

CHERRY CAKE

Ingredients

½ *lb. butter.*	½ *lb. castor sugar.*	*A pinch of salt.*
4 *eggs.*	½ *lb. cherries.*	12 *oz. flour.*
½ *teaspoonful baking-powder.*		

Method

1. Line a cake tin with greased paper.
2. Cream the butter and sugar.
3. Add the eggs one at a time, and beat well.
4. Mix flour, salt and baking-powder.
5. Roll the cherries in flour.
6. Mix the flour into the egg mixture and lastly stir in the cherries.
7. Turn into the prepared tin.
8. Cook for ½ hour. (Regulo 4.)
9. Reduce to No. 3 and cook for 1½ hours longer.
10. Cool on a tray.

CHOCOLATE CAKE

Ingredients

½ *lb. flour.*	*A pinch of salt.*	6 *oz. butter.*
6 *oz. sugar.*	3 *eggs.*	*Milk.*
1 *teaspoonful baking-powder.*		¼ *lb. grated chocolate.*

Method

1. Cream the butter and sugar together.
2. Add the egg-yolks.
3. Mix the salt, baking-powder and flour together.
4. Dissolve the chocolate in a little milk and add to the egg mixture.
5. Stir in the flour.
6. Whisk the egg-whites and fold in.
7. Turn into a buttered tin and cook for $1\frac{1}{4}$ hours. (Regulo 4.)
8. Cool on a tray.
9. The cake may be coated with chocolate icing and decorated if desired.

CHOCOLATE SANDWICH

Ingredients

$\frac{1}{4}$ lb. butter.	A pinch of salt.	$\frac{1}{2}$ lb. flour.
4 oz. chocolate.	2 or 3 eggs.	Milk.
1 teaspoonful baking-powder.		$\frac{1}{4}$ lb. castor sugar.

Method

1. Butter two sandwich tins and dust with a mixture of 1 teaspoonful of castor sugar and 1 teaspoonful of flour. Shake out the loose flour.
2. Cream the butter and sugar.
3. Grate the chocolate and dissolve in the milk.
4. Add the eggs to the creamed butter and stir in the chocolate.
5. Mix the flour, salt and baking-powder together.
6. Sift into the mixture and mix well.
7. Turn into the two prepared sandwich tins and bake in a moderate oven for about 20 minutes. (Regulo 5.)
8. Cool and join with any filling desired.

COCONUT CAKE

Ingredients

$\frac{1}{2}$ lb. flour	$\frac{1}{4}$ lb. butter.	2 eggs.
$\frac{1}{2}$ teaspoonful baking-powder.		A pinch of salt.
2 oz. desiccated coconut.		$\frac{1}{4}$ lb. castor sugar.

Method

1. Cream the butter and sugar together.
2. Add the eggs one at a time and beat well.
3. Mix the flour, salt, coconut and baking-powder together, and stir into the mixture, using a little milk if necessary.
4. Turn into a well-greased tin and bake for $1\frac{1}{4}$ hours. (Regulo 4.)
5. Turn on to a tray to cool.

COFFEE CAKE

Ingredients

½ lb. flour.   ¼ lb. butter.   ¼ lb. sugar.
½ teaspoonful baking-powder.   A pinch of salt.
I teaspoonful coffee essence.   2 eggs.

Method

1. Grease a cake tin and dust with a mixture of 1 oz. flour and 1 oz. sugar. Shake out any loose flour.
2. Cream the butter and sugar.
3. Add the eggs, beating each separately.
4. Add the essence.
5. Mix the flour, salt and baking-powder and beat into the mixture.
6. Turn into the greased tin and cook for about 45 minutes. (Regulo 4.)
7. Cool on a tray.

CHRISTMAS CAKE

Ingredients

8 oz. butter or margarine.   8 oz. castor sugar.
8 oz. flour.   3 oz. raisins.   4 oz. currants.
4 oz. almonds.   3 oz. candied peel.   4 eggs.
I wineglass brandy.   ½ oz. mixed spice.   6 oz. cherries.
A little milk to mix, if necessary.   8 oz. sultanas.

Method

1. Prepare the fruit, blanch and slice the almonds finely, cut up the cherries, and chop the peel.
2. Cream the butter and sugar.
3. Add the eggs, well-beaten, alternately with the sifted flour.
4. Add the rest of the ingredients in small quantities, beating well.
5. Add the brandy and a little milk if necessary, so that the mixture is of a stiff consistency.
6. Turn into a tin lined with double kitchen paper and bake in a moderate oven (Regulo 2) for 3½ to 4 hours. Test and turn out.
7. When the cake is cold, ice it first with Almond Icing (page 199), and then with Royal Icing (page 201).

DUNDEE CAKE

Ingredients

½ lb. flour.   6 oz. butter.   4 oz. sugar.   4 eggs.
A pinch of salt.   ¼ lb. cherries.   ¼ lb. sultanas.
I tablespoonful ground almonds.   1 oz. chopped peel.
½ teaspoonful baking-powder.   1 oz. whole almonds.

Method

1. Line a cake tin with greased paper.
2. Clean the fruit. Chop the peel. Halve the cherries and roll in flour.
3. Cream the butter and sugar. Add the beaten eggs.
4. Mix the baking-powder and salt into the flour.
5. Sift into the mixture. Add the ground almonds.
6. Add all the prepared fruit and turn into the greased tin.
7. Blanch the almonds, halve and put on top.
8. Bake for about 2½ hours. (Regulo 2.)

GENOA CAKE

Ingredients

4 oz. butter.	4 oz. sugar.	6 oz. flour.
A pinch of salt.	2 oz. sultanas.	2 oz. currants.
2 oz. cherries.	2 oz. peel.	4 eggs.
1 small teaspoonful of baking-powder.		2 oz. chopped
Rind and juice of lemon.		almonds.

Method

1. Line a tin with buttered paper.
2. Prepare all the fruit and the almonds and peel.
3. Cream the butter and sugar and add the eggs. Mix flour, salt and baking-powder together.
4. Sift into the mixture.
5. Add the fruit and grated rind and juice.
6. Turn into prepared tin and bake for 2½ hours. (Regulo 2.)

GINGER BISCUITS

Ingredients

½ lb. flour.	¼ lb. Demerara sugar.
¼ lb. butter or margarine.	¼ oz. ground ginger.
½ oz. finely-chopped lemon rind.	¼ lb. treacle.

Method

1. Sieve the flour and rub the butter into it.
2. Add the sugar, ginger and lemon rind.
3. Melt the treacle and add it to the mixture. Mix well.
4. Roll out on a board until the paste is ¼ in. thick; cut into rounds, place on a greased tin, and bake in a moderate oven for about 15 minutes. (Regulo 2.)

GINGER BREAD

Ingredients

½ lb. flour.	¼ lb. sugar.	Milk. 2 eggs.
A pinch of salt.	3 oz. treacle.	¼ lb. sultanas.
¼ lb. currants.	2 oz. almonds.	¼ lb. butter.
1 teaspoonful each of ginger, cinnamon and bicarbonate of soda.		

Method

1. Cream the butter and sugar together.
2. Stir in the treacle and then beat in the eggs.
3. Mix the flour, salt, spices and soda together and beat into the mixture.
4. Add the prepared fruit and almonds, and beat well. Add milk if necessary.
5. Turn into a greased tin and bake for 2 hours. (Regulo 4.)
6. Cool on a tray.

LONDON BUNS

Ingredients

½ lb. flour.	2 oz. lard.	Milk. 2 eggs.
A pinch of salt.	2 oz. citron peel.	2 oz. sugar.
1 teaspoonful of baking-powder.		1 oz. sultanas.

Method

1. Measure the flour and add the salt and baking-powder.
2. Rub in the lard till fine.
3. Add the sugar.
4. Clean the fruit and chop the peel and add.
5. Whisk one egg and add some milk and stir into the mixture. Mix to a light dough.
6. Grease a baking-sheet and place on the mixture formed into little balls.
7. Brush with beaten egg and put the sugar from the peel on top.
8. Cook for 15 minutes. (Regulo 6.)
9. Cool on a tray.

LUNCHEON CAKE

Ingredients

¾ lb. flour.	A pinch of salt.	6 oz. sugar.
¼ lb. sultanas.	¼ lb. currants.	1½ oz. peel.
6 oz. lard and butter mixed.		2 eggs.
½ teaspoonful bicarbonate of soda.		Milk if necessary.
1 teaspoonful each spice, ginger, cinnamon and cream of tartar.		

Method

1. Measure the flour and add the salt. Rub in the fat till fine.
2. Add all the dry ingredients.
3. Add all the prepared fruits.
4. Whisk the eggs and add a little milk.
5. Mix to a rather moist consistency.
6. Turn into a greased tin and bake in a hot oven for 15 minutes. (Regulo 6.) Reduce the heat and bake for 2 hours.

MACAROONS

Ingredients

4 oz. ground almonds.   1 oz. almonds.
1½ tablespoonfuls ground rice.   Rice-paper
6 oz. castor sugar.   3 egg-whites.

Method

1. Lay the rice-paper on a baking-tray.
2. Whisk the egg-whites till very stiff.
3. Gradually add the sugar.
4. Mix in the ground almonds and ground rice.
5. Put the mixture on the rice-paper in spoonfuls.
6. Blanch the almonds and place a half on each cake.
7. Bake for 25 minutes.   (Regulo 3.)
8. Cool on a tray.

MADEIRA CAKE

Ingredients

6 oz. butter.   A pinch of salt.   ½ lb. flour.
Strips of citron peel.   5 oz. castor sugar.   4 eggs.
½ teaspoonful baking-powder.

Method

1. Line a tin with greased paper.
2. Cream the butter and sugar, and gradually add the beaten eggs.
3. Mix the flour, salt and baking-powder.
4. Sift into the mixture.
5. Turn into the prepared tin.
6. Place the strips of citron peel on top.
7. Cook for 1½–2 hours.   (Regulo 3.)
8. Cool on a tray.

MAIDS OF HONOUR

Ingredients

½ lb. Short Pastry (see page 139).   2 oz. desiccated coconut.
2 oz. butter.   2 oz. castor sugar.   1 lemon.   1 egg.

Method

1. Line some cake tins with the pastry.
2. Cream the butter and sugar.
3. Add the egg and beat well.
4. Add the coconut and grated lemon rind and strained juice.
5. Half fill the tins and cook for 15 minutes.   (Regulo 5.)
6. Cool on a tray.

MILK BISCUITS

Ingredients

¼ lb. flour.
¼ teaspoonful baking-powder.

½ gill milk.
A pinch of salt.

Method

1. Measure the flour and add the salt and baking-powder.
2. Add the milk and mix well.
3. Turn on to a floured board and roll out very thin.
4. Cut into biscuits and cook on an oven shelf.
5. Cook for about 8 minutes. (Regulo 6.)
6. Do not allow the biscuits to get too brown.
7. Store in a tin.

MIXED FRUIT CAKE

Ingredients

½ lb. butter.
½ lb. castor sugar.
3 tablespoonfuls sherry.
2 tablespoonfuls ground almonds.
1 teaspoonful baking-powder.

10 oz. flour.
A pinch of salt.
5–6 eggs.

¼ lb. cherries.
3 oz. rice-flour.
¼ lb. mixed peel.
¼ lb. currants.
¼ lb. sultanas.

Method

1. Line a tin with well-greased paper.
2. Make as for Genoa Cake (see page 190).
3. When the cake is cooked pour the sherry in the centre.
4. Keep for 1 week in an air-tight tin.
5. Ice and decorate as desired.

OATMEAL BISCUITS

Ingredients

¼ lb. flour.
4 oz. castor sugar.

2 egg-yolks.
A pinch of salt.

¼ lb. medium oatmeal.
4 oz. butter or margarine.

Method

1. Cream the butter and sugar together.
2. Mix the flour, oatmeal and salt together.
3. Add 2 egg-yolks to the butter and sugar.
4. Add the flour and other dry ingredients.
5. Mix to a stiff dough.
6. Turn on to a floured board and knead till smooth.
7. Roll out very thinly.
8. Cut into biscuits and lay on a greased baking-sheet.
9. Cook in a moderate oven till golden brown. (Regulo 5.)
10. Cool on a tray and store in an air-tight tin.

G

ORANGE CAKE

Ingredients

6 *oz. flour.*	4 *oz. sugar.*	1 *teaspoonful baking-powder.*
3 *oz. butter.*	3 *eggs.*	*Juice and rind of 2 oranges.*

Method

1. Cream the butter and sugar together.
2. Add the egg-yolks.
3. Mix the flour and baking-powder together.
4. Stir into the mixture.
5. Add orange rind and strained juice.
6. Whisk the egg-whites and fold into the mixture.
7. Turn into a greased tin and bake in a moderate oven till well risen and nicely browned—about ¾ hour. (Regulo 5.)
8. Cool on a tray.

PARKINS

Ingredients

¼ *lb. flour.*	*A pinch of salt.*
¼ *lb. medium oatmeal.*	1 *oz. lard or margarine.*
½ *teaspoonful spice.*	¼ *teaspoonful cinnamon.*
½ *teaspoonful ginger.*	2 *oz. blanched almonds.*
3 *tablespoonfuls syrup.*	1 *tablespoonful treacle.*
1 *teaspoonful of bicarbonate of soda.*	1 *egg.*

Method

1. Mix the treacle and syrup together and put to melt slowly.
2. When melted add the lard.
3. Mix all the dry ingredients together.
4. Cool the syrup mixture and beat in 1 egg.
5. Mix into the flour to form a stiff dough.
6. Form into little balls and place a good distance apart on a greased shelf.
7. Place a half of a blanched almond on each.
8. Cook in a moderate oven (Regulo 3) till ready.
9. Cool on a tray and store in tins.

POUND CAKE

Ingredients

½ *lb. butter.*	½ *lb. sugar.*	10 *oz. flour.*
2 *oz. chopped peel.*	¼ *lb. sultanas.*	¼ *lb. currants.*
1 *teaspoonful baking-powder.*	*A pinch of salt.*	*Rind of 1 lemon.*
	4 *eggs.*	

Method

1. Cream the butter and sugar.
2. Add the eggs one at a time. Beat well.
3. Prepare the fruit. Chop the peel finely.
4. Add the baking-powder and salt to the flour and sift into the butter mixture.
5. Lastly add the fruit and grated lemon rind.
6. Line a tin with greased paper and turn in the mixture.
7. Bake in a good oven for 2½ hours. (Regulo 2.)
8. Cool on a tray.

QUEEN CAKES

Ingredients

2 *eggs.* ¼ *lb. currants.* *Rind of ½ lemon.*
The weight of the eggs in castor sugar, butter and flour.
½ *teaspoonful baking-powder.*

Method

1. Cream the butter and sugar.
2. Add the egg-yolks and beat well.
3. Mix the flour and baking-powder together.
4. Fold into the mixture.
5. Add the currants and lemon rind.
6. Whisk the egg-whites and fold in.
7. Turn into small greased Queen Cake tins and bake for 20 minutes. (Regulo 5.)
8. Cool on a pastry tray.

RASPBERRY BUNS

Ingredients

3 *oz. butter.* 3 *oz. sugar.* 8 *oz. flour.*
1 *teaspoonful baking-* *Raspberry jam.* 1 *egg.*
  powder. *A pinch of salt.* *Rind of ½ lemon.*

Method

1. Cream the butter and sugar.
2. Add the egg well beaten.
3. Mix the flour, salt and baking-powder together.
4. Add to the mixture and add the grated lemon rind.
5. Turn on to a floured board and divide into about ten pieces. Form into balls.
6. Make a hole in the centre of each with the finger. Put in a little jam.
7. Close up the hole again and lay on a greased baking-sheet.
8. Bake in a good oven for about 20 minutes. (Regulo 6.)

RICE CAKE

Ingredients

4 oz. flour.	2 eggs.	½ teaspoonful baking-powder.
4 oz. butter.	2 oz. rice-flour.	
4 oz. sugar.	A pinch of salt.	Grated rind of ½ lemon.

Method

1. Cream the butter and sugar together.
2. Mix the flour, salt, baking-powder and rice-flour together.
3. Add the egg-yolks to the butter and beat well.
4. Add the flour and grated rind.
5. Whisk the egg-whites and fold in.
6. Turn into a greased tin and bake for 1¼ hours.   (Regulo 3.)
7. Cool on a tray.

ROCK CAKES

Ingredients

½ lb. flour. 2 oz. sugar.	A pinch of salt. 1 egg.	
2 oz. butter or margarine.	¼ teaspoonful cinnamon.	
3 oz. currants and raisins mixed.	1 teaspoonful baking-powder.	
	½ teaspoonful ground ginger.	

Method

1. Measure the flour and add the salt.
2. Rub in the fat till fine.
3. Add all dry ingredients.
4. Beat the egg and add a little milk.
5. Mix into the flour and make into a stiff dough.
6. Grease a baking-sheet and put on the mixture in little rough piles.
7. Bake in a hot oven for 20 minutes.   (Regulo 6.)
8. Cool on a tray.

SANDWICH CAKE

Ingredients

4 oz. butter.	4 oz. sugar.	6 oz. flour.
A pinch of salt.	2 eggs.	½ gill cream.
1 teaspoonful baking-powder.		Flavouring.

Method

1. Cream the butter and sugar.
2. Add the salt and baking-powder to the flour.
3. Beat the eggs and add to the butter mixture.
4. Fold in the flour lightly.
5. Grease two sandwich tins and dust with a mixture of 1 teaspoonful of castor sugar and 1 teaspoonful of flour.
6. Shake off any excess flour.
7. Divide the mixture into the tins.

8. Bake for about 15 minutes.   (Regulo 6.)

9. Cool.

10. Whisk the cream and add a little sugar and flavouring. Spread on one cake and place the other on top.

SEED CAKE

Ingredients

4 oz. butter.	4 oz. sugar.	8 oz. flour.
A pinch of salt.	2 eggs.	1 oz. carraway seeds.
1 teaspoonful baking-powder.		

Method

1. Cream the butter and sugar.

2. Add the eggs well beaten.

3. Mix the flour, salt and baking-powder together, and add to the mixture.

4. Stir in the seeds.

5. Turn into a greased tin and bake rather slowly for $1\frac{1}{2}$ hours.   (Regulo 3.)

6. Cool on a tray.

SHORTBREAD

Ingredients

1 lb. flour.	4 oz. castor sugar.	$\frac{1}{2}$ lb. fresh butter.

Method

1. Mix the flour and sugar together on a pastry board.

2. Put the butter on the board and start kneading the flour mixture into the butter.

3. Add the flour to the butter very slowly and knead occasionally.

4. Continue kneading until quite smooth and all the flour is worked in; no liquid must be added.

5. Form into a round cake or cut out in small cakes.

6. Place on an oven shelf and bake slowly for $\frac{3}{4}$ hour. (Regulo 3.)

7. Cool before trying to lift on to a tray.

SPONGE CAKE

Ingredients

4 oz. flour.	3 eggs.
1 teaspoonful baking-powder.	4 oz. sugar.

Method

1. Grease a beehive mould and dust with castor sugar and flour, using 1 teaspoonful of each.

2. Whisk the egg-yolks and sugar over boiling water till white and very stiff.

3. Remove from the heat and whisk till cold.
4. Mix the flour and baking-powder together.
5. Sieve and fold into the mixture.
6. Whisk the egg-whites till quite stiff and fold in.
7. Turn into the prepared tin and bake for about ¾ hour. (Regulo 3.)
8. Cool on a tray.

SULTANA CAKE

Ingredients

8 oz. butter.	8 oz. castor sugar.	12 oz. flour.
A pinch of salt.	4 eggs.	8 oz. sultanas.
½ teaspoonful baking-powder.		

Method

1. Cream the butter and sugar.
2. Add the eggs, beating each one in separately.
3. Mix the flour, baking-powder and salt and add to the mixture.
4. Clean the fruit and add.
5. Line a cake tin with greased paper and pour in the mixture.
6. Cook in a hot oven for ¾ hour.   (Regulo 4.)
7. Reduce the heat to Regulo 3 and cook for 1 hour.
8. Cool on a tray.

SWISS ROLL

Ingredients

4 oz. flour.	4 oz. sugar.	Jam.
A pinch of salt.	Castor sugar.	3 eggs.
1 teaspoonful baking-powder.		

Method

1. Whisk the egg-whites till white and stiff.
2. Add the yolks one at a time.
3. Add the sugar and beat until the mixture is quite thick and almost white.
4. Mix the flour, salt and baking-powder.
5. Sift into the mixture.
6. Turn into a prepared Swiss-roll tin.
7. Cook for about 12 minutes.   (Regulo 6.)
8. Turn on to a sugared paper and trim the edges.
9. Spread with hot jam and roll up quickly.
10. Keep the paper round it for a few minutes to keep it from cracking.

VICTORIA SANDWICH

Ingredients

2 eggs.   *Their weight in flour, butter and sugar.*
A pinch of salt.   1 *teaspoonful baking-powder.*

Method

1. Cream the butter and sugar together.
2. Add the eggs, beating each in separately.
3. Mix the flour, salt and baking-powder, and mix into the egg mixture.
4. Grease two sandwich tins and dust with a mixture of castor sugar and flour.
5. Turn in the mixture and cook for about 15 minutes. (Regulo 5.)
6. Cool on a tray.

Filling

½ gill of cream.   2 oz. chopped nuts.
2 oz. icing sugar.   A little orange juice.

Mix all together, whisking the cream first, and spread on one cake and cover with the second.

WALNUT CAKE

Ingredients

½ *lb. butter.*   ½ *lb. sugar.*   ¾ *lb. flour.*
1 *teaspoonful baking-powder.*   *A pinch of salt.*
2 *oz. chopped walnuts.*   3 *eggs.*

Method

1. Line a cake tin with greased paper.
2. Cream the butter and sugar.
3. Add eggs, one at a time. Beat well.
4. Mix flour, salt and baking-powder and sift into the mixture. Mix well.
5. Add the walnuts and turn into the prepared tin.
6. Bake for 1½ hours. (Regulo 4.) Cool on a tray.
7. The cake can be iced and decorated.

28. ICINGS

ALMOND ICING

Ingredients

½ *lb. ground almonds.*   *Orange-flower water.*
½ *lb. castor sugar.*   ½ *lb. icing sugar.*
Egg-whites, or yolks or whole eggs may be used.

Method

1. Sieve the icing sugar.
2. Mix with the castor sugar.
3. Add the ground almonds and orange-flower water.
4. Mix with egg to form a stiff dough.
5. Knead till quite smooth.
6. Use as required.

AMERICAN ICING

Ingredients

½ lb. sugar.   2 egg-whites.
Juice of a lemon.   2 tablespoonfuls water.

Method

1. Dissolve the sugar slowly in the water until the syrup forms a thread.
2. Add the strained lemon juice.
3. Beat the egg-whites till very stiff.
4. Add the syrup and beat well.
5. When quite white, thick and very smooth, pour over the cake and decorate as desired.

BUTTER ICING

Ingredients

¼ lb. icing sugar.   Any flavouring or colour.
3 oz. butter.

Method

1. Cream the butter and sugar together.
2. Add whatever colouring or flavour is desired.
3. Use as a filling or for decorating cakes.

CHOCOLATE BUTTER ICING

Ingredients

2 oz. Supex chocolate.   6 oz. icing sugar.   3 oz. butter.

Method

1. Melt the chocolate in a double pan.
2. Cream the butter and sugar and stir in the chocolate.

GLACÉ ICING

Ingredients

½ lb. icing sugar.   Some fruit juice.

Method

1. Sieve the sugar.
2. Beat in a little fruit juice at a time and work the icing gradually.

3. Beat well with a wooden spoon.
4. Icing should be smooth, glossy and thick enough to coat the back of a wooden spoon.
5. Add any colouring or flavouring desired.

ROYAL ICING

Ingredients

3 *egg-whites.*   1 *lb. icing sugar.*   *Orange-flower water.*

Method

1. Sift the icing sugar.
2. Whisk the whites till very stiff.
3. Gradually work in the sugar and flavouring.
4. Add colouring if desired.
5. The icing should be stiff enough to stand up in rough piles.

WATER ICING

Ingredients

Icing sugar.   *Boiling water.*   *Flavouring.*

Method

1. Sift the icing sugar.
2. Add sufficient boiling water to bind it.
3. Add any flavouring or colouring.

29. BREAD AND SCONES

BAKING-POWDER BREAD

Ingredients

½ *lb. flour.*   *A pinch of salt.*   1 *oz. lard.*
1 *teaspoonful baking-powder.*   *Milk to mix.*

Method

1. Measure the flour and add the salt.
2. Cut and then rub in the lard till fine.
3. Add baking-powder.
4. Mix to an elastic dough with milk.
5. Turn on to a floured board and cut off one-third of the dough.
6. Form the larger piece into a round.
7. Form the smaller piece into a round.
8. Moisten the top of the larger round and lay on the smaller.
9. Flour the finger and make a hole through the smaller to the larger.
10. Lay on a greased tin and bake till golden brown for about 30 minutes.   (Regulo 8.)

YEAST BREAD

Ingredients

3½ *lb. flour.*	1 *teaspoonful sugar.*	*Warm water.*
3 *teaspoonfuls salt.*	1 *oz. yeast.*	

Method

1. Carefully warm all the utensils to be used.
2. Prepare and grease bread tins.
3. Measure the flour and add the salt.
4. Cream the yeast and sugar.
5. Add about ¾ pint of warm water to the yeast.
6. Mix into the flour, adding more water if necessary to form an elastic dough.
7. Knead till smooth. Flour the bottom of the basin and cover with a cloth.
8. Leave to rise in a warm place till twice its size.
9. Turn on to a floured board and knead well.
10. Form into three loaves and place in the tins.
11. Set to prove in a warm place for ½ hour.
12. Bake for 1 hour. Have the oven very hot at first and then reduce to Regulo 6.
13. Cool on a tray.

BROWN BREAD

Ingredients

1 *lb. white flour.*	1 *oz. yeast.*	1 *teaspoonful sugar.*
2½ *lb. Allinson's flour.*	1 *oz. lard.*	*Warm water.*
3 *teaspoonfuls salt.*		

Method

1. Mix the brown and white flour together.
2. Add salt and rub in 1 oz. of lard.
3. Continue exactly as for Yeast Bread (see above).
4. Cool on a tray.
5. The oz. of butter or lard added keeps the bread moister. (This may be added to the white loaf.)

CHELSEA BUNS

Ingredients

½ *lb. flour.*	*A pinch of salt.*	½ *oz. yeast.*
1 *oz. sugar.*	2 *oz. currants.*	1 *oz. butter.*
½ *oz. sugar (extra).*	*Milk to mix.*	1 *egg.*

Method

1. Warm all the utensils.
2. Cream the yeast with ½ oz. of sugar.
3. Measure the flour and add salt and sugar.
4. Rub in the butter.

5. Warm the milk and pour over the beaten egg.

6. Mix yeast into egg-and-milk mixture.

7. Mix into the flour and knead well. Flour the bottom of the bowl and leave the dough to rise.

8. Knead after 1 hour on a floured board and roll out.

9. Sprinkle with cleaned currants and sugar and roll out.

10. Cut into slices 1 inch thick.

11. Lay on a tray cut side up and down and brush with egg.

12. Set to prove.

13. Bake in a hot oven for 15 minutes. (Regulo 6.)

CURRANT BREAD

Ingredients

1½ lb. flour.	1½ oz. butter.	2 teaspoonfuls sugar.
½ oz. yeast.	4 oz. currants.	A pinch of salt. Warm milk.

Method

1. Measure out the flour and add the salt.

2. Rub in the butter and add the sugar.

3. Cream the yeast with a little sugar.

4. Warm the milk and mix with the yeast.

5. Mix into the flour, knead and put to rise till twice its size.

6. Turn on to a floured board and knead again, working in the cleaned currants.

7. Form into two small loaves, put in greased tins and set to prove for 12–15 minutes.

8. Rub the top over with butter and bake for 35 minutes. (Regulo 6.)

9. Cool on a tray.

DINNER ROLLS

Ingredients

½ lb. flour.	½ teaspoonful salt.	½ oz. yeast.
1 oz. butter.	1 gill milk.	¼ oz. sugar.

Method

1. Measure the flour and add the salt. Rub in the butter.

2. Cream the yeast and sugar.

3. Add the warm milk.

4. Mix into the dough and leave to rise as usual.

5. Turn on to a floured board and knead.

6. Roll out to about ½ inch thick.

7. Cut into little round rolls and lay on a greased baking-sheet.

8. Set to prove.

9. Brush over with melted butter and bake for 10–15 minutes. (Regulo 6.)

10. Serve hot or cold.

DOUGH CAKE

Ingredients

1 *lb. flour.*	$\frac{3}{4}$ *lb. mixed fruit.*	$\frac{1}{4}$ *lb. sugar.*
$\frac{1}{4}$ *lb. butter.*	$\frac{1}{2}$ *teaspoonful salt.*	1 *egg.*
Warm milk to mix.	1 *oz. yeast.*	

Method

1. Make as for Currant Bread (see page 203).
2. Bake for $1\frac{1}{4}$ hours.

FRENCH BREAD

Use the same recipe as for Dinner Rolls (see page 203), but, instead of rolling out and cutting into rounds, cut in small pieces and twist and pleat into little fancy shapes.

GIRDLE SCONES

Ingredients

$\frac{1}{2}$ *lb. flour.*   1 *teaspoonful cream of tartar.*   *A pinch of salt.*
Milk to mix. $\frac{1}{2}$ *teaspoonful bicarbonate of soda.*
If using sour milk or butter-milk use only $\frac{1}{4}$ teaspoonful of bicarbonate of soda and $\frac{1}{2}$ teaspoonful of cream of tartar.

Method

1. Measure out the flour and add salt, baking soda and cream of tartar.
2. Mix to an elastic dough with milk.
3. Turn on to a greased board and roll out.
4. Cut into rounds.
5. Test the girdle before putting on the scones.
6. Place on the scones and cook for about 3 minutes, turn and cook on the second side.
7. Roll in a towel to steam.
8. Serve either hot and buttered; or cold with butter.

MILK SCONES

Ingredients

$\frac{1}{2}$ *lb. flour.*	*Milk to mix.*	*A pinch of salt.*
1 *teaspoonful cream of tartar.*		1 *oz. sugar.*
$\frac{1}{2}$ *teaspoonful bicarbonate of soda.*		1 *oz. butter.*

Method

1. Measure the flour and add the salt, cream of tartar and baking-soda.
2. Rub in the butter.
3. Add the sugar.
4. Mix to an elastic dough with milk.
5. Turn on to a floured board and cut in two.

6. Form each part into a round and cut in four.

7. Place on a baking-sheet and cook in the oven for 10 minutes. (Regulo 6.)

8. Cool on a tray.

OAT CAKES

Ingredients

1 *lb. fine oatmeal.*   1 *teaspoonful salt.*   *Boiling water.*
2 *tablespoonfuls melted dripping (bacon fat if possible).*

Method

1. Measure the oatmeal and add the salt.
2. Add the melted fat to the boiling water.
3. Mix into the oatmeal.
4. Shake some meal on to a board and roll out the mixture till very thin.
5. Keep in a round or cut in two and make into two rounds, which are easier to handle than one large one.
6. Lay on the girdle and cook both sides for about 3 minutes each side.
7. Curl in front of a good fire.
8. Store in an air-tight tin.

PLAIN FRUIT LOAF

Ingredients

1 *lb. flour.*   3 *oz. lard.*   4 *oz. sugar.*   *Milk to mix.*
1 *teaspoonful vinegar.*   3 *oz. margarine.*   8 *oz. mixed fruits.*
1 *teaspoonful bicarbonate of soda.*   *A pinch of salt.*

Method

1. Measure out the flour and add the salt.
2. Cut and then rub in the lard and margarine.
3. Add other ingredients and mix with milk to a rather soft dough.
4. Turn into a paper-lined tin and bake for 2 hours in a moderate oven (Regulo 5), and reduce to Regulo 4 after ½ hour.
5. Cool on a tray.

POTATO SCONES

Ingredients

½ *lb. sieved potatoes.*   ½ *oz. butter.*   *Flour to mix.*
A little warm milk.   *A pinch of salt.*

Method

1. Beat up the potatoes and salt.
2. Add the melted butter.
3. Add about 1 tablespoonful of warm milk.

4. Mix in sufficient flour to make the dough of a rolling consistency.

5. Turn on to a floured board and roll out as thinly as possible.

6. Cut in rounds and then cut each in four.

7. Place on a hot girdle. Prick over with a fork.

8. Cook about 3 minutes on each side.

9. Lay on a towel to cool.

Note.—This is a splendid method of using left-over potatoes.

SALLY LUNNS

Ingredients

1 *lb. flour.*	2 *oz. butter.*	1½ *oz. sugar.*
1 *egg.*	1 *oz. yeast.*	4 *oz. currants.*
¼ *teaspoonful salt.*	*Warm milk to mix.*	

Method

1. Measure the flour and add salt and sugar.

2. Cream the yeast and butter and add some warmed milk.

3. Whisk the egg and add to the milk.

4. Mix into the flour and knead. Put to rise.

5. After it has risen to twice its original size turn on to a floured board and knead in the currants.

6. Form into small rounds and lay on a greased tin.

7. Set to prove.

8. Bake for 10 minutes. (Regulo 6.) Brush over with egg and bake for 20 minutes longer. Cool on a tray.

SCOTCH PANCAKES
(DROPPED SCONES)

Ingredients

½ *lb. flour.*	1 *egg.*	2 *teaspoonfuls sugar.*
1 *teaspoonful cream of tartar.*		*A pinch of salt.*
½ *teaspoonful bicarbonate of soda.*		*Milk to mix.*

Method

1. Measure the flour and add the dry ingredients.

2. Beat the egg and add some milk to it.

3. Mix into the flour, adding sufficient milk to make a soft batter.

4. Heat the girdle and rub well over with suet.

5. Drop the batter on in spoonfuls.

6. Cook for 3 minutes and then turn.

7. Cool on a towel.

8. If crumpets are wanted, make the mixture thinner and put on in larger quantities.

9. A few currants may be added before turning.

SCOTCH MUFFINS

Ingredients

½ lb. flour.	1 teaspoonful cream of tartar.	1½ oz. sugar.
1½ oz. butter.	½ teaspoonful bicarbonate of	Milk to mix.
1 egg.	soda.	A pinch of salt.

Method

1. Measure the flour and add the salt, sugar, baking-soda, and cream of tartar.
2. Melt the butter.
3. Beat the egg and add a little milk.
4. Mix with the egg.
5. Pour into the flour and mix to a stiff dough.
6. Turn on to a floured board and roll out ½ inch thick.
7. Cut with a cutter.
8. Place on a greased sheet and cook for 10 minutes. (Regulo 6.)
9. Cool on a tray.

TEA CAKES

Ingredients

1 lb. flour.	1 oz. butter.	½ oz. yeast.
¼ oz. sugar.	Milk to mix.	A pinch of salt.

Method

1. Measure the flour and add the salt.
2. Cream yeast and sugar.
3. Add some warm milk to the yeast.
4. Mix into the flour.   Knead till smooth.
5. Leave to rise for about 1½ hours.
6. Turn on to a floured board and knead.
7. Divide into eight and form into rounds.
8. Put on a greased sheet and set to prove.
9. Put into a hot oven (Regulo 6) and cook for 10 minutes.
10. Brush with melted butter and cook for 10 minutes longer.
11. A little fruit may be added when kneading the second time.

TEA SCONES

Ingredients

½ lb. flour.	1 cupful milk.	2 egg-yolks.
1½ oz. butter.	1½ oz. castor sugar.	A pinch of salt.
1 teaspoonful baking-powder.		

Method

1. Cream the butter and sugar.
2. Add the egg-yolks.
3. Mix the flour, salt and baking-powder together.
4. Sift into the other mixture.

5. Add sufficient milk to mix into an elastic dough.
6. Turn on to a floured board and roll into a long, narrow strip.
7. Cut in fingers and lay on a greased sheet.
8. Brush with beaten egg and bake for 10 minutes. (Regulo 8.)

TREACLE SCONES

Ingredients

½ *lb. flour.* *A pinch of salt.*	2 *oz. lard.* *Milk to mix.*
½ *teaspoonful bicarbonate of soda.*	¼ *teaspoonful ground ginger.*
½ *teaspoonful cream of tartar.*	½ *teaspoonful ground spice.*
½ *teaspoonful cinnamon.*	2 *tablespoonfuls treacle.*

Method

1. Measure flour and add all dry ingredients.
2. Rub in the lard till fine.
3. Mix the treacle with a little milk and pour it into the mixture. Mix to an elastic dough.
4. Turn on to a floured board and knead till smooth.
5. Cut into scones and cook on a hot girdle, allowing about 3 minutes per side.
6. Cool on a towel.
7. The scones may be baked in the oven.

30. JAMS, JELLIES, AND MARMALADES

GENERAL RULES FOR JAM-MAKING

1. For jam-making choose fruit that is ripe and dry.
2. Jam can be made at almost any time of the year. Decide what fruits you want to make into jam and draw up your chart accordingly.
3. **January.** Grapefruit. Lemons. Tangerines. Oranges.
February. Grapefruit. Lemons. Tangerines. Seville oranges.
March. Apples. Young Rhubarb. African Plums.
April. Apples. Young Rhubarb. African Apricots.
May. Rhubarb. Figs. Grapefruit. Lemons.
June. Gooseberries. Rhubarb. Lemons.
July. Strawberries. Raspberries. Melons. Cherries.
August. Black Currants. Red Currants. Greengages. Loganberries.
September. Mulberries. Damsons. Plums. Cherry Plums.
October. Pears. Cranberries. Peaches. Bilberries.
November. Apples. Pears. Grapes. Grapefruit.
December. Apples. Pears. Grapes. Grapefruit. Lemons.
4. Do not use any berries that are decayed.
5. See that the jars have no cracks or chips and are clean and perfectly dry.

APRICOT JAM

Ingredients

    4 *lb. apricots.*   4 *lb. preserving-sugar.*   1 *gill water.*

Method

    1. Wash and stone the fruit.

    2. Rub a little glycerine round the preserving-pan and place in the fruit.

    3. Add water and heat slowly.

    4. Take about a dozen of the stones and remove the kernels. Blanch them and add them to the jam.

    5. Simmer until the fruit is tender.

    6. Add the sugar and stir until it has dissolved.

    7. Boil for about 20 minutes.

    8. Test a little on a plate, and if it sets remove the jam from the heat.

    9. When slightly cool, pour into the jars.

    10. When cold cover with gummed papers.

BLACK CURRANT JAM

Ingredients

    4 *lb. black currants.*   7 *lb. preserving-sugar.*
    3 *pints water.*   1 *oz. fresh butter.*

Method

    1. Rub the preserving-pan with salad oil or glycerine.

    2. Pick over the fruit and remove all the stalks.

    3. Place in the pan with the water and bring slowly to boiling point.

    4. Simmer gently for 1 hour.

    5. Allow to cool.

    6. Add the sugar and bring slowly to the boil.

    7. Cook until a little, when tested, sets easily.

    8. Just before it is ready add 1 oz. of fresh butter and stir till it melts.

    9. The butter helps to keep the currants from going hard after the jam has been kept.

    10. Pour into jars and cover.

DRIED APRICOT JAM

Ingredients

    3 *lb. sugar.*   3 *pints water.*
    1 *lb. dried apricots.*   A *few almonds.*

Method

    1. Wash the apricots and cut in quarters.

    2. Soak in the water for 1½ days.

3. Mix with the sugar and bring slowly to boiling point. Boil slowly for about 35 minutes.

4. Blanch the almonds and halve each.

5. Add to the jam.

6. Test on a plate to see if it sets well.

7. Pour into jars and cover as usual.

Note.—This jam can be made at any time of the year.

GOOSEBERRY JAM

Ingredients

4 lb. red gooseberries.   4 lb. sugar.   ½ gill water.

Method

1. Wash the berries, and top and tail each.

2. Heat the berries with the sugar and water, stirring constantly until the sugar has dissolved.

3. Stir till boiling.

4. Cook for 30 minutes.

5. Test for setting before pouring.

6. Pour and when cold cover.

GREENGAGE JAM

Ingredients

7 lb. greengages.   7 lb. sugar.   ½ gill water.

Method

1. Wipe the fruit and remove the stalks.

2. Stone and take the kernels from about one dozen.

3. Blanch the kernels and add to the stoned fruit.

4. Put on to cook with the sugar and water.

5. Stir till boiling.

6. Cook for about 20 minutes.

7. Test and when ready pour into jars.

8. Cover.

PLUM JAM

Ingredients

6 lb. plums.   6 lb. sugar.   ½ gill water.

Method

1. Wipe the plums and remove the stalks.

2. Remove the stones.

3. Put a layer of stoned plums in a basin and then a layer of sugar.

4. Continue until all the fruit and sugar are used.

5. Leave for 24 hours.

6. Put in a pan and heat slowly.

7. Stir till boiling.

8. Cook until a little tested jam sets: usually for about ½ hour.

9. Cover.

RASPBERRY JAM

Ingredients

4 *lb. raspberries.*　　　　　　4 *lb. sugar.*

Method

1. Pick over the berries and put in a large basin.
2. Pour over the sugar and leave for 24 hours.
3. Bring slowly to the boil.
4. Cook for about ½ hour or until a little tested jam sets.
5. Pour into jars and cover.

RHUBARB JAM

Ingredients

6 *lb. young rhubarb.*　　6 *lb. sugar.*　　¼ *lb. preserved ginger.*

Method

1. Wipe the rhubarb and cut up very small.
2. Put in a basin with the sugar and leave for 48 hours.
3. Bring slowly to the boil.
4. Boil until the rhubarb becomes clear: usually about 1 hour.
5. Cut up the ginger and add.　Test a little.
6. Pour into jars and cover.

STRAWBERRY JAM

Ingredients

6 *lb. firm small strawberries.*　　　　7 *lb. sugar.*
½ *pint of red currant or rhubarb juice.*

Method

1. Pick the berries.
2. Put in a preserving-pan with the sugar and juice.　Bring slowly to the boil.
3. Cook slowly until a little sets when tested—usually about 35 minutes.
4. Pour into jars and cover.

VEGETABLE-MARROW JAM

Ingredients

2 *lb. marrow (after removing skin and seeds).*　　6 *lb. sugar.*
2 *pints water.*　　　　　　　　　　　　　　　　4 *lb. quinces.*

Method

1. Cut the marrow in tiny cubes and steam.
2. When tender beat up thoroughly till smooth.

3. Peel the quinces and remove the cores.
4. Cut up and boil in 2 pints of water.
5. Cook until tender.
6. Beat up with a fork and mix with the marrow.
7. Add the sugar and stir till boiling.
8. Boil for 15–20 minutes.
9. Test and if quite ready pour into jars.
10. Cover.

JELLIES

APPLE JELLY

Ingredients

> 6 *lb. crab apples.*   *Enough water to cover.*
> *Sugar according to quantity of juice.*

Method

1. Wash the apples and cover with water.
2. Boil until quite soft.
3. Strain through a jelly bag.
4. Measure the juice and allow 1 lb. of sugar to each pint.
5. Boil slowly and test a little for setting.
6. Pour into jars and cover.

GOOSEBERRY JELLY

Ingredients

> 7 *lb. gooseberries (green).*   *Water.*   *Sugar.*

Method

1. Wash the berries, remove the stalks and cover with water.
2. Boil until the gooseberries are very soft and pulpy.
3. Strain through a jelly bag.
4. Measure the juice and allow 1 lb. of sugar to each pint.
5. Bring to the boil and simmer slowly until a little sets when tested.
6. Pour into jars and cover.

RED CURRANT JELLY

Ingredients

> 6 *lb. red currants.*   *Water.*   *Sugar.*

Method

1. Pick the currants and, if necessary, wash.   Drain in a strainer.
2. Put into a preserving-pan and cover with water.
3. Cook until the fruit is soft.
4. Strain through a bag.

5. Measure the juice and allow 1 lb. of sugar to 1 pint of juice.

6. Bring slowly to the boil and simmer until a little sets when tested.

7. Pour into jars and cover.

MARMALADES

MARMALADE

Ingredients

4 lb. Seville oranges.	Water to cover fruit.
Sugar.	2 lemons.

Method

1. Wash the oranges and lemons and pare off the skin. Cut this into fine shreds.

2. Cook these shreds in a little water until quite tender.

3. Take the pith off the fruit and cut the fruit in slices.

4. Put in a preserving-pan with sufficient water to cover.

5. Cook the pulp until tender.

6. Strain and measure the juice. Allow 1 lb. of sugar to 1 pint of juice.

7. Put on to boil and simmer slowly for 10 minutes. Add the chips and the water they were cooked in.

8. Boil until a little sets: usually 25–30 minutes.

9. Pour into jars and cover.

GRAPEFRUIT MARMALADE

Ingredients

2 grapefruit.	1 orange.	5 pints of water.
1 teaspoonful tartaric acid.	2 lemons.	5 lb. sugar.

Method

1. Wipe the fruit and quarter it. Take out the seeds.

2. Put all the juice into a large basin.

3. Add the water.

4. Put all the fruit through the mincer, using the fine cutter.

5. Add to the water and soak for 24 hours.

6. Put into a preserving-pan and boil.

7. Boil for 1 hour.

8. Pour into a basin and leave over-night.

9. Put into the pan and add the sugar.

10. Boil slowly and simmer for about 30 minutes. Just before pouring add 1 teaspoonful of tartaric acid.

11. Test and pour into pots.

12. Cover.

LEMON MARMALADE

Ingredients

4 lb. lemons.   4 pints water.   Sugar—about 8 lb.

Method

1. Wipe the fruit and cut in quarters.
2. Remove the seeds.
3. Put all the juice into a basin.
4. Mince all the remainder of fruit.
5. Soak in 4 pints of water over-night.
6. Boil up and simmer slowly for 1 hour, and cool.
7. Add the sugar and cook until a little sets when tested.
8. Pour into jars and cover.

MIXED MARMALADE

Ingredients

2 marmalade oranges.   2 grapefruit.   2 lemons.
2 apples.   8 pints water.   8 lb. sugar.

Method

1. Wash all the fruit and remove the seeds.
2. Put the juice into an earthenware basin.
3. Put the fruit through the mincer, and do not peel the apples.
4. Soak in the water for 24 hours.
5. Boil for 2 hours.
6. Cool and add the sugar.
7. Boil up and simmer slowly for 40 minutes.
8. Test and pour into jars.
9. Cover.

SCOTCH MARMALADE

Ingredients

5 Seville oranges.   2 lemons.   7 pints water.   7 lb. sugar.

Method

1. Wipe the fruit.   Quarter, and remove the pips.   Soak in water.
2. Take out the juice and put in a jar: add the water.
3. Mince the fruit and add to the water.
4. Soak over-night.   Add the water from the pips.
5. Boil next day and cook for 1½–2 hours.
6. Leave for 12 hours.
7. Add the sugar and stir till boiling.
8. Cook for about 35 minutes.   Test.
9. Pour into jars and cover.

31. FRUIT AND VEGETABLE BOTTLING

FRUIT BOTTLING

There are two chief methods of bottling fruit. These are:

    A. Sterilising under water.

    B. Sterilising in the oven, known as the Dry Method.

PREPARATIONS

The Jars: Types

There are many different types of jar, but the principle on which each works is the same. The jar containing the hot sterilised fruit is covered with a glass or metal lid which rests on a rubber ring, and it is this contact which makes the jar air-tight; a metal screw-band or clip holds the lid securely in place while the fruit cools. When the fruit is quite cold, the lid is secured by the vacuum formed and the jar is air-tight independently of the screw band or clip.

For sterilising under water the following jars give satisfactory results:

    (*a*) Screw-top Bottling Jars with rubber ring, glass top and screw-on metal collar.

    (*b*) Clip-top Bottling Jars with rubber ring and metal lid and clip.

For the Dry Method, these jars may be used:

    (*a*) Screw-top Bottling Jars.

    (*b*) Clip-top Bottling Jars.

    (*c*) Ordinary 1 lb. or 2 lb. jam jars used with mutton fat and paper or parchment covers.

It is most important before beginning the work of bottling to examine the jars to be used, to make sure they are without cracks, flaws or chips, and that lids and rubber bands are in good condition and fit accurately. Before use, wash the jars and rinse them out in cold water. Lids and bands must be quite clean and quite dry.

The Fruit

1. The fruit should be just ripe; it is better, however, that it is slightly under-ripe than over-ripe. If fruits of equal size are used, the packing is done more easily. Thus, when preparing gooseberries they should be sorted out into two piles—large and small berries. Then the small berries can be packed into jars by themselves and the larger ones into others. Fruit like plums should have the stones removed.

2. Wash and prepare the fruit according to its type, thus remove the stalks of strawberries, raspberries and similar fruit; top and tail gooseberries; cut rhubarb into equal-sized lengths.

Peaches and like fruits, which have somewhat tough skins, may have these removed by placing them gently in boiling water for a minute or two, after which the skins are easily removed by using a stainless steel knife. Apples should be peeled and cored and put into salt water (1 dessertspoonful of salt to 1 pint of water); then they are drained, rinsed and put into boiling water for 3 minutes to soften them. Pears are treated as apples, but stewed carefully until tender without their becoming broken.

The Syrup

Take ¾ lb. to 1 lb. of sugar and put it into a saucepan containing 1 quart of water, and bring slowly to the boil. Allow it to boil for 2 minutes, then strain it and allow to cool. It is then ready for use.

Cold water may be used instead of syrup if preferred, but the syrup improves the flavour of the fruit.

The Sterilising

Method A. Under Water

1. Prepare the fruit and pack it into jars, carefully, using the handles of two wooden spoons for this. Pack as closely as possible, but avoid bruising the fruit.

2. Pour in the prepared syrup or cold water and fill to the top.

3. Cover the jars according to type: (a) in the case of the Screw-top Bottling Jars, place the glass top and rubber ring evenly in position, put on the metal collar, and screw it tightly; then give the screw a half turn back to allow for expansion. (b) The rubber ring and metal lid of the Clip-top Bottling Jars should be secured with the clip.

4. Place the jars in a steriliser, a large steamer, or a fish-kettle, having at the bottom cardboard, a wad of folded newspapers or a folded piece of sacking, so that the jars do not touch the metal of the pan, otherwise they may crack. Care should be taken also to see that the jars do not touch the sides of the pan either. The water should cover the jars completely, or reach up to their shoulders.

5. Heat the water very slowly for about 1½ hours until the temperature given for the particular fruit in the Table on p. 217 is reached. This temperature should then be maintained for the time indicated.

6. After sterilisation is complete, take one jar at a time from the steamer and place it on a wooden board or table or on a surface covered with several layers of newspapers.

7. In the case of the Screw-top Jars, tighten the screw band immediately, and after a few minutes make sure that the band is quite tight.

The Clip-top Jars are already tight.

8. Next day unscrew the Screw-top Jars or remove the

Fruit.	Temperature in °F. to which fruit is to be raised in 1½ hours.	Time for which temperature is to be maintained.
Apples	165	10 mins.
Apricots . . .	165	10 ,,
Blackberries . . .	165	10 ,,
Damsons . . .	165	10 ,,
Gooseberries . . .	165	10 ,,
Loganberries . . .	165	10 ,,
Plums (whole) . .	165	10 ,,
Raspberries . . .	165	10 ,,
Rhubarb . . .	165	10 ,,
Greengages . . .	165	10 ,,
Strawberries . . .	165	10 ,,
Cherries . . .	190	10 ,,
Currants . . .	180	10 ,,
Pears	190	20 ,,

clips from the others and lift each jar by the lid. If this is possible, then the jar is air-tight and the sterilisation is complete. If not, repeat the sterilising process.

9. Label with the name of the fruit and the date of bottling.

Method B.   Sterilising in the Oven.

This method is unsuitable for apples and pears.

1. Prepare the fruit and pack it into the jars as for Method A, but do not add any syrup or water.

2. Cover each row of jars with lids or patty tins. This precaution is to prevent the fruit at the top from becoming scorched.

3. Place the jars on a sheet of thick cardboard in a slow oven (Regulo ½), and continue the heating until the fruit shrinks a little and the juice is seen to flow freely from it. (This should take about 1 hour.)

4. If at this stage any jars appear to be only partially filled, fill them up from other jars, and return them to the oven for 10 minutes to complete the sterilising process.

5. Remove one jar at a time, place it on a wooden surface. and fill up with fast-boiling syrup or water.

6. Cover each jar immediately. If ordinary jam jars are used, run on a little melted mutton fat and cover with a double cover of paper or parchment.

7. Next day test as for Method A, and label.

Storage of Bottled Fruit

1. Store in a cool, dry, dark place.

2. It is advisable to inspect the jars each week. If small bubbles are seen, or if the covers appear to have become loosened, the fruit must either be re-sterilised or used at once.

Tomatoes

Although regarded in the kitchen as a vegetable, botanically tomatoes are a fruit, and are therefore preserved in either of the ways applied to fruit. The tomatoes should be small, firm and ripe. A very little salt should be sprinkled among the tomatoes or a salt solution (1 oz. salt to 2 quarts of water may be poured into the jars in which they are packed). The temperature is raised to 190° F. during 1½ hours, and is then maintained at this level for 25 minutes.

BOTTLING OF VEGETABLES

The bottling of vegetables is a more difficult process than that of fruit. The only completely satisfactory method is that of sterilisation in a pressure cooker.

Method

1. Suitable vegetables for bottling are asparagus, beans, carrots, celery, peas, spinach. If possible, young vegetables should be selected and, in any case, they must be sound and quite fresh.

2. Prepare them according to kind and wash and rinse thoroughly. Cut up cauliflower, runner beans and other larger vegetables.

3. Tying loosely in muslin, dip them in boiling water for not more than 5 minutes; less time is required for very young vegetables. Then still in the muslin, dip them in and out of cold water.

4. Pack into the jars.

5. Fill up each jar with salt solution (1 oz. salt to 1 quart of water).

6. Put the rubber bands and other coverings into position as when bottling fruits.

7. Place the jars in the pressure cooker following the directions supplied by the makers of the type of cooker being used.

8. Test next day for perfect sterilisation.

9. Store as for fruit.

Note.—The time taken for sterilising is 25 minutes for asparagus, celery and mushrooms; 30 minutes for broad beans, French beans, beetroot, carrots; 35 minutes for peas and new potatoes; 45 minutes for spinach. During the time of sterilising the pressure is maintained at 10 lb.

PICKLING

APPLE CHUTNEY

Ingredients

4 *lb. Bramley apples.*   2 *onions.*   2 *lb. sugar.*   1 *lemon.*
2 *teaspoonfuls ground*   *A little mustard.*   1 *lb. seeded raisins.*
   ginger.   *Seasoning.*   2 *pints brown vinegar.*

Method

   1. Peel the onions.   Pare and core the apples.   Pass all through the mincer.
   2. Mince the raisins.
   3. Mix all together.
   4. Add all the other ingredients and the rind of half a lemon and all the juice.
   5. Bring to the boil, stirring all the time.
   6. Boil for 1 hour, or until all is tender.
   7. Pour into jars and cover when cold.
   8. Leave for 2 months before serving.

CHUTNEY

Ingredients

4 *lb. apples.*   2 *lb. sultanas.*   ¼ *oz. cayenne.*   4 *oz. garlic.*
2 *lb. brown sugar.*   ¼ *lb. green ginger.*   2 *pints vinegar.*

Method

   1. Pare and core the apples and cook in a little water until tender.
   2. Mince the raisins and garlic and add to the apples.   Add all the other ingredients.   Pour on the vinegar.
   3. Boil for 30 minutes.
   4. When cold pour into the jars.
   5. Cover and store for 6 weeks before using.

PICKLED ONIONS

Ingredients

Pickling onions.

Pickling Liquid

   1 *quart vinegar.*   2 *teaspoonfuls all-spice.*
   1 *dozen black peppercorns.*

Method

   1. Peel off the skins, using a silver knife.
   2. Put into clean jars.
   3. Mix the spices in the vinegar and pour over the onions.
   4. Cover the jars and leave for one month before using.

PICKLED RED CABBAGE

Ingredients

1 red cabbage.   Spiced vinegar.   Salt.

Method

1. Wash the cabbage and shred the leaves very finely.
2. Lay the shredded cabbage on a large dish or sieve, putting a layer of cabbage and then a layer of salt alternately.
3. Leave for 48 hours, mixing up the cabbage occasionally.
4. Put the mixed cabbage into clean jars and cover with the hot pickling liquid.
5. Seal down when cold.
6. Store in a cool dry cupboard.

PRESERVATION OF EGGS

PICKLED EGGS

Ingredients

180 new laid eggs.

For the Pickle

4 gallons water.   1 pint salt.
3 oz. cream of tartar.   1 pint slaked lime.

Method

1. Boil all the ingredients of the pickle together for about 20–30 minutes.
2. Set aside to cool.
3. Strain and pour the liquid over the eggs so that they are completely covered.

PRESERVED EGGS

Use waterglass and follow the directions given. This is a simple and easy method.

32. INVALID DISHES

APPLE WATER

Ingredients

1 lemon.   1 apple.   Sugar.   2 gills of water.

Method

1. Pare the apple, remove the core and cut up very fine.
2. Put in a jug and add grated lemon rind and juice.
3. Pour over the boiling water and lay aside till cold.
4. Strain and add sugar to taste.
5. Serve in small quantities.

APPLE PUDDING

Ingredients

1 *apple.*
Sponge fingers.

2 *tablespoonfuls cream.*
2 *teaspoonfuls sugar.*

Method

1. Wipe the apple and bake it till very soft.
2. Take out all the apple pulp, and beat with a fork till smooth.
3. Add the sugar.
4. Whisk the cream and fold it into the fruit mixture.
5. Serve in a small glass dish with sponge fingers.

ARROWROOT

Ingredients

2 *teaspoonfuls arrowroot.*
1 *teaspoonful sugar.*

1 *egg.*
½ *pint milk.*

Method

1. Blend the arrowroot with a little milk.
2. Boil the remainder and pour it over the blended arrowroot.
3. Cook for 1 minute.
4. Add the beaten egg-yolk and sugar.
5. Whisk the egg-white and fold in.
6. Pour into a buttered pie-dish and bake till nicely browned.
7. Serve at once.

Note.—Small puddings of this kind are best baked in Pyrex dishes and served in the dish they are cooked in.

BAKED SOLE

Ingredients

1 *gill milk.*
2 *small fillets of sole.*

Seasoning.
Lemon juice.

Method

1. Wash and dry the fillets.
2. Add seasoning and sprinkle on a little lemon juice.
3. Butter a deep plate and lay the fillets in it.
4. Pour over the milk and bake in a slow oven for 15 minutes. (Regulo 5.)
5. Thicken the milk with a little flour.
6. Serve hot.

BARLEY WATER

Ingredients

2 *pints water*   2 *oz. barley.*   *Lemon.*   *Sugar or salt.*

Method

1. Put the barley in a pointed strainer and wash thoroughly by running boiling water through.

2. Put in a pan with the water.
3. Add lemon rind.
4. Simmer very slowly for 2 hours.
5. Strain through muslin and add the lemon juice.
6. Add either sugar or salt according to taste.

BEEF TEA (1)

Ingredients

   ¼ *lb. round steak.*   *2 gills water.*   *Seasoning.*

Method

1. Remove any fat or gristle.
2. Scrape the meat till fine.
3. Put in a jar with the cold water, and a pinch of salt.
4. Leave for 1 hour.
5. Cover with a buttered paper and steam for 3 or 4 hours.
6. Decant the liquid and add seasoning.
7. Serve with fingers of dried toast.

BEEF TEA (2)

Ingredients

   ¼ *lb. round steak.*   *2 gills water.*   *Seasoning.*

Method

1. Remove fat or gristle.
2. Cut up the meat very fine or scrape it.
3. Put in a jar with water and a pinch of salt.   Soak for 1 hour.
4. Pour into a saucepan and cook for 1½ hours very slowly.
5. Decant and season.
6. Serve with fingers of toasted bread.

BREADBERRY

Ingredients

   1 *slice toast.*   *Water.*   ½ *teacupful milk.*   *Sugar.*

Method

1. Cut up the toast into small cubes.
2. Place in a basin and pour over boiling water, sufficient to cover.
3. Stand for ½ hour.
4. Pour off the water and press the bread with a fork to remove any moisture.
5. Add milk and a little sugar.
6. Reheat and serve.

CHICKEN BROTH

Ingredients

1 *small chicken.*	*Seasoning.*
2 *pints of water.*	*A little rice.*

Method

1. Joint the chicken and place in a stew-jar.
2. Add water and seasoning and about 1 tablespoonful of washed rice.
3. Cook very gently for 2 hours.
4. Season and serve the liquid after removing all grease.

Note.—The rice may be omitted, and the jelly from the chicken allowed to set. In this case serve cold with fingers of toast.

GRUEL

Ingredients

1 *tablespoonful oatmeal.*	*Sugar if liked.*	2 *gills milk.*
A small piece of fresh butter.	*A pinch of salt.*	

Method

1. Soak the meal in the milk for 1 hour.
2. Stir up and allow to settle.
3. Decant carefully, leaving the grains in the basin.
4. Stir over a gentle heat till boiling.
5. Add salt and a little sugar if liked.
6. Just before serving stir in a small piece of butter.
7. Serve hot.

LEMONADE

Ingredients

1 *pint water.*	2 *lemons.*	2–3 *oz. sugar.*

Method

1. Scrub the lemons and pare off the rind.
2. Remove the white pith and slice the lemons thinly.
3. Put the rind and slices in a jug with the sugar.
4. Boil the water and pour over the fruit.
5. Cover and lay aside till cold.

MUTTON BROTH

Ingredients

½ *lb. lean mutton.*	*Small piece of*	1½ *pints water.*	1 *oz. rice.*
½ *onion.*	*turnip.*	*Seasoning.*	1 *carrot.*

Method

1. Cut the meat into very small pieces, leaving out any fat.
2. Put in a pan with the cold water and a little salt.

3. Boil very slowly, and when the scum rises, take it off.
4. Prepare the vegetables and tie in a piece of muslin.
5. Add the washed rice to the soup and the vegetables, and simmer for 3 hours.
6. Take out the vegetables and strain the soup.
7. Reheat and season lightly.

PEPTONISED MILK

Ingredients

Peptonising powder.   1 gill water.   1 pint new milk.

Method

1. Into a clean 2-pint bottle put the peptonising powder from the tube.
2. Add 1 gill of water and 1 pint of new milk.
3. Mix together, but do not shake too much.
4. Place the bottle in hot water for 10 minutes.
5. Pour into a clean pan and boil.
6. Place on ice after it has cooled.

PEPTONISED GRUEL

Make with peptonised milk and follow the recipe for Gruel (see page 223).

RICE WATER

Ingredients

2 pints water.   Lemon rind.
3 oz. rice.   Either salt or sugar.

Method

1. Wash the rice and cook in the water until it is quite soft.
2. Strain and add a piece of lemon rind.
3. Reheat and add either sugar or salt to taste.

STEAMED CHOP

Ingredients

1 chop, not too thick.   Seasoning.   ½ oz. butter.

Method

1. Trim the chop carefully, taking off excess fat.
2. Butter a plate and place the chop on it.
3. Put a piece of butter on top and sprinkle on a little seasoning.
4. Cover with another plate and steam over boiling water.
5. Test with a fork before serving, to make sure it is quite tender.
6. Time varies according to the thickness of the chop.
7. Serve with a little pat of Maître d'Hôtel Butter (see page 123).

STEAMED FISH

Ingredients

2 *fillets of sole.*   *Seasoning.*   *Lemon juice.*   ½ *oz. butter.*

Method

1. Trim the fillets and season and sprinkle with lemon juice.
2. Lay on a buttered plate and put a piece of butter on top.
3. Cover with another plate and steam over boiling water for about 20 minutes.
4. Serve hot, garnished with parsley.

STEWED SWEETBREAD

Ingredients

1 *sweetbread.*   *Seasoning.*   ½ *pint milk.*
Some tiny pieces of vegetable.   *Cornflour.*

Method

1. Wash the sweetbread and soak for 1 hour.
2. Tie the vegetables in a muslin bag.
3. Place the sweetbread and vegetables in a pan and pour over the milk.
4. Simmer slowly till quite tender. The time varies, but about 1½ hours is generally required.
5. Lift out the vegetables.
6. Blend a little cornflour and stir into the milk. Add seasoning.
7. Serve hot, garnished with parsley and lemon.

33. BEVERAGES

CHOCOLATE

Ingredients

Chocolate.   *Cream.*
Milk (one breakfastcupful for each person).

Method

1. Allow about 1 teaspoonful of chocolate for each person.
2. Measure out the chocolate and blend it with a little cold milk.
3. Put it into a saucepan with the milk and stir till boiling. Boil for 5 minutes.
4. Add a teaspoonful of thick cream to each cupful.
5. Serve with sugar handed separately.

Note.—Milk and water may be used instead of milk alone.

H

COCOA

Ingredients

Cocoa.   Milk or milk and water.

Method

1. Measure out the cocoa, allowing one teaspoonful for each cupful.
2. Blend the cocoa with a little cold milk. Add the remainder of the milk, and put all in a saucepan.
3. Heat till boiling, stirring all the time. Whisk over the heat for a further 5 minutes.
4. Serve with sugar, handed separately.

Note.—A plainer cocoa may be made with water only; the milk and sugar being added to taste after it is served.

COFFEE

BLACK COFFEE

Ingredients

1 *tablespoonful coffee to each half-pint of water.*

Method

1. Coffee should be freshly roasted and ground just before being used. Therefore, since this is not possible in most homes, it must be bought in small quantities, and kept in a tin or glass jar fitted with a tightly-fitting lid.
2. If one of the many percolators on the market is used, full directions are given with the percolator; the amount of coffee is the same whatever the method.
3. If making it in a pan, bring the required amount of water to boiling point and add the coffee. Stir for a minute, and then strain. Heat up the strained coffee again, then strain again, and pour into the coffee-pot.
4. Serve with sugar crystals or demerara sugar and cream.

WHITE COFFEE

Ingredients

1 *tablespoonful coffee to each half-pint of water.* Milk.

Method

1. Make the coffee as for Black Coffee (see above).
2. Heat the milk, allowing an amount equal to that of the water, to boiling point, and strain to remove skin.
3. Serve with sugar crystals or demerara sugar. The best result is obtained if the coffee and hot milk are poured into each cup at the same time.

TEA

Ingredients

Tea, allow 1 teaspoonful to each person.   *Boiling water.*

Method

1. Have the water freshly boiling.
2. Rinse the teapot with some of the boiling water.
3. Put the tea in the pot and add the boiling water.
4. Let the tea infuse under a cosy for a few minutes.
5. Serve with sugar and cream or with lemon.

34. ODD DISHES AND PROCESSES

BOILED RICE

Ingredients

4 oz. Patna Rice.   *Salt.*   *Lemon juice.*   *Water.*

Method

1. Place the rice in a pointed strainer and run plenty of cold water through.
2. Put it on to boil in boiling salted water.
3. Add the juice of half a lemon.
4. Boil for 10 minutes.
5. Drain on to a sieve and rush cold water through. Shake well.
6. Butter a grease-proof paper and place the rice in it.
7. Put in a saucepan and steam slowly for 1 hour.
8. The rice should be soft and each grain separate.

BREAD RASPINGS

Ingredients

Scraps of bread and odd crusts.

Method

1. Keep a tin in the oven for odd pieces of crusts and bread that has got hard. If it is kept at the bottom of the oven, it can stay there for days without being in the way.
2. After several days' cooking the bread will be nicely browned and free from moisture.
3. Crush with a rolling-pin and then rub through a sieve.
4. Store in an air-tight tin, and use for fish-dressing, etc.

BROWNED CRUMBS

Ingredients

1 lb. bread-crumbs.   *¼ lb. butter.*   *Seasoning.*

Method

1. Put the crumbs in a large tin. Add seasoning and melted butter and stir well.

2. Cook in a warm oven till brown.
3. Stir up occasionally.
4. Use with fowls, game, etc.

CROÛTONS

Ingredients

Thin slices of bread.   *Fat to fry.*

Method

1. Cut the bread in very thin slices.
2. Remove crusts and cut the bread into tiny cubes.
3. Fry in fat till a golden brown.
4. Drain well.
5. Store in a tin.
6. Heat before serving.
7. Serve with soups, etc.

FORCEMEAT BALLS

Ingredients

1 *teacupful bread-crumbs.*	1 *oz. flour.*	1 *oz. butter.*
Chopped parsley.	*Mixed herbs.*	*Lemon juice.*
Egg and crumbs. 1 *egg.*	*Fat to fry.*	*Seasoning.*

Method

1. Mix all the ingredients except the flour.
2. Bind with beaten egg.
3. Form into balls and roll in the flour.
4. Egg and crumb each ball.
5. Fry in hot fat till a golden brown.

Note.—Forcemeat Balls may be fried, stewed or cooked in soup.

FRENCH DRESSING

Ingredients

3 *tablespoonfuls oil.*   *Seasoning.*   *A pinch of sugar.*
1 *tablespoonful lemon juice or wine vinegar.*

Method

1. Mix the ingredients together and shake well in a bottle.
2. Serve cold.

Note.—A very little chopped parsley or chopped mint may be added.

MAYONNAISE

Ingredients

5 *tablespoonfuls salad oil.*	2 *tablespoonfuls lemon juice.*
1 *hard-boiled egg-yolk.*	1 *tablespoonful vinegar.*
A little dry mustard.	1 *teaspoonful castor sugar.*
1 *raw egg-yolk.*	*Seasoning.*

Method

1. Beat the raw egg-yolk.
2. Gradually work in the hard-boiled yolk using a wooden spoon.
3. Add the oil very gradually, stirring constantly in the one direction.
4. Add lemon juice and vinegar, and lastly the seasonings.

PORRIDGE

Ingredients

2 oz. fine oatmeal.　　　1 pint water.　　　Salt.

Method

1. Boil the water and add a very little salt.
2. Blend the oatmeal with a little cold water and add to the boiling water.
3. Stir till boiling.
4. Boil with the lid on for 40 minutes.
5. Cook very slowly.
6. Add more salt to taste and serve with hot or cold milk or cream.

(Sufficient for 4 persons.)

POTATO PASTRY

Ingredients

¼ lb. flour.　　　1 teaspoonful baking-　　A pinch of salt.
3 oz. shortening.　　powder.　　　¼ lb. potatoes (sieved).

Method

1. Sieve the potatoes while they are hot.
2. Rub the fat into the flour and add the baking-powder and salt.
3. Add the potatoes and mix well.
4. Mix with cold water to a stiff dough.
5. Use as required.

SALAD DRESSING

Ingredients

2 egg-yolks.　　　1 oz. butter.　　　Seasoning.
A little dry mustard.　1 teaspoonful sugar.　½ pint milk.
1 teaspoonful cornflour.　1 tablespoonful vinegar.

Method

1. Beat up the egg-yolks.
2. Gradually add the milk.
3. Add the other ingredients.
4. Stir over a gentle heat until the mixture almost boils.
5. When cool pour into a bottle and store in a cool place.

SAVOURY BALLS

Ingredients

4 oz. flour.   A pinch of salt.   1 oz. chopped suet.
A pinch of chopped parsley.   Seasoning.
A pinch of baking-powder.   Water to mix.

Method

1. Measure the flour and add the salt and baking-powder.
2. Chop the suet.   Remove all strings and shreddy parts.
3. Mix into the flour.
4. Add parsley and seasoning.
5. Mix with cold water to an elastic consistency.
6. Form into balls, roll in dry flour, and add to the stew.
7. Cook till well risen and firm—about ¾ hour.

STUFFINGS FOR ROAST FOWL

1st Stuffing

Ingredients

5 oz. oatmeal.   3 oz. bacon.
1 small boiled onion.   1 oz. dripping.

Method

1. Chop the onion and bacon.
2. Melt the dripping and lightly fry the onion, bacon and oatmeal.
3. Fry for about 15 minutes.
4. Form into a ball and stuff the fowl with it.

2nd Stuffing

Ingredients

½ lb. sausage-meat.   2 tablespoonfuls bread-crumbs.
Chopped parsley.   Liver minced (from the fowl).   Seasoning.

Method

1. Mix all ingredients together and use as required.
2. If too dry add the yolk of one egg.

STUFFING FOR PORK

Ingredients

4 onions.   Sage leaves.   Seasoning.
1 oz. butter.   ½ lb. bread-crumbs.   A pinch of sugar.

Method

1. Peel the onions and cook till tender.
2. Chop very finely, and mix with the other ingredients and bind with the melted butter.
3. This stuffing is generally used with pork, but it is also good with goose or duck.

VEAL FORCEMEAT

Ingredients

6 *oz. bread-crumbs.*   1 *egg.*   *Chopped parsley.*
2 *oz. suet (finely chopped).*   *Seasoning.*

Method

1. Mix all the ingredients together.
2. Bind with beaten egg.

WHIPPED CREAM

Turn the cream into a basin and beat gently with a whisk till it becomes thick.   If wanted very thick, continue until the cream will stay piled up into a shape.

35. ADVENTURE IN COOKERY

It is surprising that little use is made in this country of the opportunity of adventuring into the realms of experimental cookery.   Yet a full realisation and appreciation of what can be done with available foodstuffs leads to two important results: an intriguing and appetising addition to the usual fare, and an increased enthusiasm on the part of the housewife for her oft-mundane task of cooking.

Successful adventure is generally fearless.   An explorer must be courageous, for he does not reach his objective unless he is bold enough to attempt the unknown.   Similarly, the housewife in her sphere must have this spirit of adventure, in order to produce new and exciting dishes: she must be alive to the possibilities of flavourings and ready to experiment with them.   Further, she must be eager to try new combinations of fruits, vegetables and cooking materials.   This does not necessarily involve much additional expenditure, but rather does it imply a healthy and thoughtful attitude to the manipulation of existing foodstuffs and a knowledge of seasonings. Indeed, a pleasing change to a dish may be brought about merely by the introduction of a new flavour.   Again, among the vegetables of our country there are several that are all too seldom made use of, such as kale, celeriac, endive, salsify and chicory.   Then there are the imported fruits, the increasing number of tinned foods, and the many spices.   All of these give scope for the provision of a wide range of varied dishes.

Undoubtedly, the housewife who would be an unusual cook must be prepared to depart from the traditional.   She will probably do this the more readily when she realises the strong interest which cookery will assume for her as soon as she begins to experiment.   Cooking is an art, and in this respect is worthy of taking its place with music, painting and literature.

British cookery is good when the materials to hand are intelligently used, but in the past we have lagged badly behind other countries where household cookery has been taken more seriously.

The housewife who wishes to provide for her family and guests dishes which are attractive, appetising, and at the same time nutritious, must exercise forethought and allow her imagination to operate freely. She must not condemn a new dish merely because it has not been experienced; she must try it. It is not sufficient to assume that roast chicken must always be served with sausages and watercress, or that day after day boiled potatoes must appear at lunch. There are many ways of preparing even the humble potato. Again, the housewife should be curious and anxious to try new methods when they come to her notice, and, further, she should think out new combinations for herself. Not only will this result in attractive meals, but the housewife will become possessed of an abiding interest.

Here are a few examples of adventuring in cookery:

Macaroni cheese to which a little finely chopped ham or other left-over meat is added to the sauce; a pear tart instead of the more usual apple pie; Brussels sprouts served with a white sauce to which a little grated nutmeg or grated cheese has been added; cheese pancakes made by using unsweetened batter to which grated cheese has been added and afterwards more grated cheese sprinkled on the pancake before rolling it and serving; fried plaice stuffed with a mixture of hard-boiled egg, pounded anchovies (or a little essence of anchovy) and a little butter; baked pears with chocolate sauce; veal cutlets with boiled cucumber; turkey stuffed with tomato purée and cooked haricot beans; herrings stuffed with the roe finely chopped, butter and hard-boiled eggs, and baked in the oven; a green salad to which is added sliced apples, chopped walnuts, or sliced oranges and bananas; tomatoes stuffed with mushrooms, egg and bread-crumbs; apple roll in which the apples have been sprinkled with a little cinnamon; fried bananas served on a bed of creamed spinach; lettuce and orange salad with a French dressing; an open rhubarb tart covered with red currant or apple jelly just before serving; pastry turn-over filled with a mixture of chopped ham and chicken or other left-over meat; potato and cauliflower croquettes; mayonnaise varied by adding tarragon, parsley, chives, cress, chervil and garlic; oysters fried with bread-crumbs in butter, served on slices of hot buttered toast and sprinkled with paprika; stews varied by the addition of left-over rice, a little macaroni or spaghetti and cooked in a casserole in the oven; fried eggs served surrounded by tomatoes halved and grilled or with tomatoes from which the insides have been scooped out and then filled with a mixture of chopped mushrooms fried with shallots, parsley and the removed tomato; ham minced, placed in a pie-dish, and then eggs broken on to the ham and cooked in the oven.

Now for some simple and interesting recipes. At the outset it should be understood that when stock is mentioned it should, of course, be used if the housewife has any—and a good meat or vegetable stock is an excellent standby—but otherwise one or other of the meat or vegetable extracts, such as Liebeg's, Bovril, Oxo or Marmite, should be used, making the quantity required according to the maker's directions.

HORS D'ŒUVRE

Among the easiest dishes with which to begin to experiment are those usually described as Hors D'œuvre and which, in addition to their formal use as appetisers for luncheon or dinner, may readily form a main course in themselves for either meal.

Due regard must be given to the arrangement of the various items in the preparation of such dishes. They may be served on individual plates, or on a large platter, or in the regulation hors d'œuvre dish with its several compartments.

Canapés—*i.e.*, bread toasted on both sides and buttered on one side or fried a delicate brown—are frequently used to hold the delicacies which form one or other of the hors d'œuvre. The variations which it is possible to make in hors d'œuvre are limited only by the materials to be obtained and the degree of imagination possessed.

Here are some suggestions:

FISH OR MEAT FINGERS

Ingredients

  2 slices of toast.   *Cucumber or tomato or hard-*
  Left-over meat or fish.   *boiled egg or anchovy.*

Method

1. Divide the toasted bread into fingers.

2. Mash left-over meat or chicken, shrimps or lobster with butter to a creamy paste and spread the mixture on the toasted bread.

3. Decorate each finger with a slice of either cucumber, tomato, hard-boiled egg or with an anchovy

Note.—This recipe can be varied by placing finely-chopped onion on a canapé and on it an anchovy, sardine, or part of a pilchard.

LUNCHEON DISH

Ingredients

Diced carrot and turnip.	*Peas.*	*Paprika.*
Mayonnaise (see page 228).	*Celery.*	*Cheese.*
A little cooked fish.	*4 eggs.*	*Butter.*
Lettuce or cress.	*8 olives.*	

Method

1. Dice the carrot and turnip and mix with the Mayonnaise.
2. Hard-boil the eggs, shell them, and cut each in two cross-ways. Remove the yolks and cream them with mayonnaise. Stuff each half-egg with the mixture and arrange all on a bed of lettuce or cress.
3. Remove the stones from the olives and stuff the spaces with cooked fish finely shredded and creamed with a little butter.
4. Prepare the celery and cut it in short lengths. Fill the crevice of each piece with creamed cheese sprinkled with paprika.
5. Arrange the vegetables, stuffed eggs, stuffed olives, and stuffed celery in separate compartments of a hors d'œuvre dish.

SALADS

For ease of preparation, salads naturally follow hors d'œuvre.

APPLE SALAD

Ingredients

4 large cooking apples.	*1 tablespoonful chopped carrot.*
1 tablespoonful chopped celery.	*1 tablespoonful chopped tomato.*
1 tablespoonful chopped cucumber.	*1 lettuce.*
Mayonnaise or French Dressing (see page 228).	*Sugar.*

Method

1. Prepare and core the apples. Remove a little of the apple pulp.
2. Stew the cored apples in a little water and sugar being careful they do not break.
3. Drain the apples and let them cool.
4. Mix together the finely chopped carrot, celery, tomato and cucumber. Add some Mayonnaise and mix again.
5. Fill each apple with the vegetable mixture.
6. Place the apples on a bed of lettuce.
7. Serve with Mayonnaise or French Dressing.

CREAM CHEESE AND PINEAPPLE SALAD

Ingredients

3 *heads of lettuce.*   4 *slices of tinned pineapple.*
1 *cream cheese.*   1 *orange.*

Method

1. Wash and prepare the lettuce and divide it into 4 portions.

2. Squeeze the juice from the orange and mix it with the cream cheese.   Then form this mixture into small balls.

3. .Place one slice of pineapple and some of the cheese balls on each portion of lettuce.

4. Serve with French Dressing (see page 228).

(Sufficient for 4 persons.)

MEAT SALAD

Ingredients

Potato Salad (see page 116 or page 236).
1 *bunch of radishes.*   4 *slices of brawn or*   1 *lettuce.*
2 *eggs (hard-boiled).*   *other cold meat.*   4 *gherkins.*

Method

1. Prepare a potato salad.

2. Arrange it in the middle of a large dish.

3. Round it place a layer of lettuce leaves.

4. On the lettuce put thin slices of the cold meat.

5. Garnish with sliced egg, gherkins and radishes.

(Sufficient for 4 persons.)

POTATO AND FENNEL SALAD

Ingredients

4 *large potatoes.*   *Fennel.*
½ *lb. French beans.*   *Mayonnaise* (see page 228).

Method

1. Prepare the potatoes as for Potato Salad (see page 116 or page 236).

2. Prepare the fennel.

3. Prepare the French beans.

4. Cook the fennel and French beans together.   Allow to cool.

5. Arrange the potatoes on the bottom of a glass dish, lay the fennel next, and cover with Mayonnaise.

6. Decorate with the French beans.

(Sufficient for 4 persons.)

POTATO, DATE AND BANANA SALAD

Ingredients

4 *large potatoes.*   4 *tomatoes.*   4 *bananas.*
Mayonnaise (see page 228).   ½ *lb. dates.*

Method

1. Prepare and cook the potatoes as for Potato Salad (see page 116 or below).
2. Peel the tomatoes and bananas.
3. Stone the dates.
4. Slice the bananas and cut up the dates and tomatoes. (Reserve a few slices of bananas and tomatoes.)
5. Put potatoes, dates, bananas and tomatoes in a glass dish.
6. Pour over Mayonnaise and mix well.
7. Decorate with slices of banana and tomato.

(Sufficient for 4 persons.)

POTATO SALAD

Ingredients

6 *potatoes.*   1 *small tin of pine-apple.*
French Dressing or Mayonnaise   1 *teaspoonful finely chopped*
(see page 228).   *parsley.*

Method

1. Boil the potatoes in their jackets until they are cooked but firm.
2. While they are still hot, peel them carefully and cut them into pieces.
3. Arrange these pieces in a glass dish and cover with either French Dressing or Mayonnaise making sure that each piece of potato is covered.
4. Sprinkle the chopped parsley over them.
5. Garnish by placing a slice of tinned pineapple on top and slices round the edge.

(Sufficient for 4 persons.)

RED CABBAGE AND POTATO SALAD

Ingredients

Potato Salad (see page 116 or above).   *Salt.*
French Dressing (see page 228).   *Vinegar.*
2 *hard-boiled eggs.*   ½ *red cabbage.*

Method

1. Prepare the red cabbage, chop it finely, put it in a pie dish, season with salt and vinegar, and place in a slow oven (Regulo 2) for 1 hour.
2. Drain the cabbage and cover with French Dressing.

3. Arrange the potato salad in a glass dish.
4. On it pile the chopped red cabbage.
5. On the red cabbage arrange the hard-boiled egg-whites cut in quarters.
6. Sprinkle the whole with the powdered egg-yolks.

(Sufficient for 4 persons.)

TOMATO SALAD

Ingredients

4 *tomatoes.*	2 *hard-boiled eggs.*	½ *cucumber.*
Paprika.	1 *bunch of radishes.*	*Shreds of onion.*
French Dressing (see page 228).		

Method

1. Peel the tomatoes and cut them in quarters.
2. Let them stand in French Dressing for about ½ hour.
3. Arrange them in a salad bowl and add thin slices of cucumber, shreds of onion and slices of hard-boiled egg.
4. Decorate with paprika and the radishes.

(Sufficient for 4 persons.)

WINTER SALAD

Ingredients

4 *potatoes.*	1 *pear.*	1 *banana.*
1 *apple.*	*Chicory leaves.*	*Juice of* 1 *lemon.*
French Dressing (see page 228).		

Method

1. Prepare and cook the potatoes as for Potato Salad (see page 116 or page 236).
2. Place them on the bottom of a salad bowl.
3. Clean the chicory and arrange it over the potato.
4. Prepare and slice the fruit and place it over the chicory.
5. Pour the lemon juice over all.
6. Cover with French Dressing.

(Sufficient for 4 persons.)

SOUPS

It is often stated that the English cook makes an insufficient use of soups. The difficulty of keeping a stock-pot going in a small kitchen is frequently instanced as a reason for this. There is no doubt that a constant supply of stock is enormously useful, but lack of it need not prevent the service of good soups. Instead of stock, meat or vegetable extract may be used, or left-over gravies, or milk, or even water. The two following soups are seldom served in the ordinary household in this country. Both are delicious.

CHEESE SOUP

Ingredients

2 oz. butter.	3 oz. cheese.	1 *pint milk.*	*Seasoning.*
2 oz. flour.	1 *pint stock.*	1 *egg-yolk.*	

Method

1. Melt the butter and add the flour, stirring till they are mixed.

2. Add the stock and milk and cook for about 15 minutes stirring constantly.

3. Grate the cheese finely and add it gradually but do not let it cook.

4. Just before serving stir in a little piece of butter and the yolk of an egg.

5. Serve with fingers of toast.

(Sufficient for 4 persons.)

ONION SOUP

Ingredients

2 *slices of bread.*	2 *oz. butter.*	*Salt.*	1 *quart stock.*
1½ *oz. grated cheese.*	3 *small onions.*		*Cayenne pepper.*

Method

1. Toast the slices of bread on both sides.

2. Fry them lightly in 1½ oz. of the butter and lay aside till needed.

3. Cut up the onions in small pieces and brown them in the remaining ½ oz. of butter, stirring them constantly so that they do not become too brown.

4. Add the fried bread broken into pieces and stir all together.

5. Add the stock which should be boiling, and season.

6. Cook all gently for about 20 minutes.

7. Just before serving sprinkle in the finely-grated cheese.

(Sufficient for 4 persons.)

FISH

FISH AND POACHED EGGS

Ingredients

1 *lb. cooked fish.*	1 *teaspoonful mixed herbs.*	4 *eggs.*
A little tomato ketchup.	*A little milk.*	*Seasoning.*

Method

1. Remove the skin and bone from the fish and flake it finely.

2. Heat it in a little milk.

3. Add the tomato ketchup and mixed herbs and mix.
4. Put all in a greased pie-dish.
5. Poach the eggs.
6. Place them on the fish, season and serve very hot.

(Sufficient for 4 persons.)

FLAKED FISH

Ingredients

1 lb. cooked fish.	2 oz. butter.	½ oz. capers (cut).
Bread-crumbs.	2 eggs.	Seasoning.
2 tablespoonfuls chopped onion.		1 oz. chopped parsley.
2 tablespoonfuls stock.		Juice of 1 lemon.

Method

1. Remove the skin and bones from the fish and flake it finely.
2. Put the butter in a pan and melt it.
3. Add the onion and the flaked fish.
4. Beat the eggs and add, and then add the capers, parsley, lemon juice, stock and seasoning.
5. Stir all together over a low heat and when they are thoroughly mixed, put into a pie-dish.
6. Sprinkle bread-crumbs over all and heat in the oven (Regulo 4) for 30 minutes.
7. Brown under the grill just before serving.

(Sufficient for 4 persons.)

SARDINES ON POTATOES

Ingredients

2 tins of sardines.	1 oz. chopped onion.
1 lb. mashed potatoes.	Juice of 1 lemon.
1 pint Béchamel Sauce (see page 118).	Seasoning.

Method

1. Put the mashed potato in a pie-dish.
2. Prepare the sardines and arrange them on the potato.
3. Make the Béchamel Sauce adding to it the finely chopped onion.
4. Pour the sauce over the sardines.
5. Sprinkle the lemon juice over all.   Add seasoning.
6. Heat in the oven (Regulo 4) for 10 minutes.

(Sufficient for 4 persons.)

SEASONED BAKED COD

Ingredients

4 small cod steaks.	Seasoning.	1 teaspoonful mixed herbs.
1 oz. butter.	1 egg.	1 breakfastcupful bread-crumbs.

Method

1. Place the cleaned and dried cod steaks in a greased pie-dish.
2. Mix the bread-crumbs, mixed herbs, and seasoning and bind with a well-beaten egg.
3. Put the bread-crumb mixture over the fish.
4. Add the butter in tiny pats and cook for about 20 minutes in a moderate oven. (Regulo 4.)

(Sufficient for 4 persons.)

WHITE FISH MORNAY

Ingredients

4 *fillets of white fish.*	2 *oz. grated cheese.*
1 *pint Mornay Sauce* (see page 124).	*Seasoning.*

Method

1. Prepare the fish.
2. Poach the fillets in water.
3. Prepare the Mornay Sauce and cover the bottom of a pie dish with some of it.
4. Lay the fish in the sauce. Add seasoning to taste.
5. Cover with the remainder of the sauce.
6. Grate cheese over the whole.
7. Brown under the grill.

(Sufficient for 4 persons.)

MEAT

FRICASSÉ OF CHICKEN

Ingredients

1 *lb. chicken.*	1 *large onion.*	4 *tomatoes.*
2 *pimentos.*	2 *oz. butter.*	*Seasoning.*
½ *pint stock or water.*	2 *oz. cooked rice.*	

Method

1. Prepare and slice the onion.
2. Brown the pieces of chicken and the chopped onion in the butter in a saucepan.
3. Add the rice and mix with the chicken and onion.
4. Add the stock or water.
5. Next peel and quarter the tomatoes and add.
6. Season with salt and pepper and add the chopped pimentos.
7. Cook slowly in the oven (Regulo 4) for 30 minutes.

(Sufficient for 4 persons.)

GOULASH

Ingredients

1 lb. lean beef.	8 potatoes.	4 tomatoes.
Seasoning.	4 onions.	½ pint water.
1 tablespoonful tomato juice.		2 oz. butter.

Method

1. Cut the beef into small pieces.
2. Peel and slice the onions and brown them in the butter in a saucepan.
3. Add the meat and the tomato juice.
4. Peel and slice the tomatoes and add them to the meat, etc.
5. Add seasoning.
6. Cover the pan and cook slowly for 1½ hours.
7. Prepare the potatoes, cut them into pieces and add, then cook slowly for ½ hour longer.
8. Water may be added if the goulash becomes dry.

(Sufficient for 4 persons.)

MEAT KEDGEREE

Ingredients

½ lb. chopped meat.	2 tablespoonfuls melted butter.	Nutmeg.
Salt and pepper.	2 eggs (hard-boiled).	½ lb. rice.

Method

1. Chop the whites of the eggs.
2. Boil and dry the rice.
3. Put the prepared rice in a pie-dish with the melted butter, the meat well minced, salt and pepper, grated nutmeg, and the chopped white of egg.   Heat in the oven for ½ hour.
4. Grate the egg-yolks and before serving sprinkle them over the kedgeree.

(Sufficient for 4 persons.)

PORK AND GREEN PEAS

Ingredients

A small fillet of pork.	½ lb. small onions.	½ lb. cooked peas.
Browned crumbs.	4 slices of bacon.	Seasoning.
½ pint Béchamel Sauce (see page 118).		1 lettuce.

Method

1. Prepare the pork.
2. Place it in a casserole with the slices of bacon over it and the onions round it.   Cover it and put it in the oven to cook. (Regulo 4.)
3. When cooked, slice the fillet.

4. Make a thick purée of the cooked peas. Spread this purée on one side of each piece of pork. Season.

5. Put the slices together again and cover all with the Béchamel Sauce.

6. Over the sauce sprinkle the browned crumbs and brown in the oven.

7. Serve with the bacon and onions.

(Sufficient for 4 persons.)

PRUNES AND BACON

Ingredients

8 *prunes*.	8 *rashers of bacon*.	2 *oz. bread-crumbs*.
4 *small rounds of bread*.		2 *oz. of grated cheese*.

Method

1. Soak the prunes overnight.

2. Stew them, remove the stones, and fill the spaces with a mixture of bread-crumbs and grated cheese.

3. Wrap each prune in a rasher of bacon, securing each rasher with a lightly-tied thread.

4. Fry the rashers until the bacon is cooked.

5. Fry the bread.

6. Put 2 rashers on each slice of bread and serve very hot.

(Sufficient for 4 persons.)

STUFFED SAUSAGES

Ingredients

4 *large sausages*.	1 *oz. bread-crumbs*.	4 *tomatoes*.
1 *egg-yolk*.	½ *lb. mashed potatoes*.	*Seasoning*.

Method

1. Boil the sausages for about 10 minutes. Dry each and make an incision in each lengthways to allow of filling being put in.

2. Skin the tomatoes, cut each into small pieces, add the bread-crumbs, seasoning and yolk of egg and mix well together.

3. Place a little of this mixture in the opening in each sausage.

4. Put the stuffed sausages in a greased tin, sprinkle with bread-crumbs, and bake for 10 minutes in the oven. (Regulo 4.)

5. Serve on a layer of mashed potatoes.

(Sufficient for 4 persons.)

CASSEROLE OF VEAL OR MUTTON CHOPS

Ingredients

4 *chops*.	2 *oz. butter*.	4 *onions*.	8 *potatoes*.
2 *carrots*.	¼ *lb. beans*.	¼ *lb. peas*.	*Seasoning*.

Method

1. Wash, trim and fry the chops lightly in a little of the butter.

2. Place them in a casserole.

3. Prepare and slice the onions and lightly fry them in butter.

4. To the chops, add the onions, sliced carrots, beans, peas, sliced potatoes, a little water and seasoning.

5. Cover and cook slowly in the oven until meat and vegetables are tender.   (Regulo 4.)

6. Serve on a meat dish with the vegetables arranged round the chops.   Hand Béchamel Sauce (see page 118).

(Sufficient for 4 persons.)

VEGETABLES

APPLES AND CHESTNUTS

Ingredients

    1 *lb. apples.*   2 *oz. butter.*   1 *lb. chestnuts.*

Method

1. Shell the chestnuts.

2. Put them in boiling water and let them simmer for 15 minutes.

3. Drain them and remove the skins.

4. Prepare and core the apples and cut them into pieces.

5. Put them into a casserole with the butter.

6. Add the chestnuts and a little water, cover, and let them cook (Regulo 4) until tender—about 1 hour.

(Sufficient for 4 persons.)

BAKED SALSIFY

Ingredients

    ½ *lb. salsify.*   2 *oz. bread-crumbs.*   1 *small onion.*
    1 *egg.*   1 *oz. butter.*   *Seasoning.*
    1 *dessertspoonful milk (if necessary).*

Method

1. Prepare the salsify and boil it until it is tender.

2. Drain it, add the bread-crumbs, the chopped onion and seasoning, and mash finely.

3. Beat the egg and add to the salsify mixture, adding the milk, if necessary.

4. Put all into a greased pie-dish, cover it with bread-crumbs and some small pieces of butter.

5. Bake in the oven (Regulo 6) until browned—about 10 minutes.

(Sufficient for 4 persons.)

BRAISED CABBAGE WITH ONIONS AND CHESTNUTS

Ingredients

> 1 *cabbage (medium size)*. 2 *onions*.
> 1 *lb. chestnuts*. 1 *oz. butter*.

Method

1. Prepare and boil the cabbage.
2. Peel and blanch the chestnuts and boil till cooked—about ½ hour.
3. Prepare, slice and fry the onions in the butter.
4. Chop up the cabbage finely and arrange in the middle of a dish. Put the fried onions over the cabbage and the chestnuts over and round it.

(Sufficient for 4 persons.)

CABBAGE MORNAY

Ingredients

> 1 *cabbage*. 1 *pint Mornay Sauce (see page* 124).

Method

1. Prepare the cabbage and divide it into quarters.
2. Boil it in salted water.
3. Chop the cooked cabbage finely.
4. Cover with Mornay Sauce.
5. Bake in the oven until brown.

(Sufficient for 4 persons.)

CREAMED ENDIVE

Ingredients

> 4 *heads of endive*. 2 *oz. butter*.
> *White Sauce (see page* 127). *Seasoning*.

Method

1. Wash the endive, taking off any coarse or discoloured leaves, and drain.
2. Blanch for 10 minutes in boiling water. Remove and place in cold water for a few minutes.
3. Drain, chop finely and cook till tender in the butter.
4. Season, add the White Sauce, and mix well together.
5. Serve very hot.

(Sufficient for 4 persons.)

HUNGARIAN POTATOES

Ingredients

> 2 *lb. potatoes*. 1 *oz. butter*. *Chopped parsley*.
> 1 *large onion*. 2 *tomatoes*. *Stock or water*.
> ½ *teaspoonful paprika*.

Method

1. Prepare and chop a large onion very finely.
2. Fry it in the butter to which the paprika has been added.
3. Slice the potatoes thickly, and add.
4. Peel and slice the tomatoes and add.
5. Cover the vegetables with water or stock and cook in the oven till the water has almost disappeared.
6. Before serving, sprinkle with chopped parsley.

(Sufficient for 4 persons.)

PURÉE OF BROAD BEANS AND GREEN PEAS

Ingredients

½ *lb. broad beans.*	2 *oz. watercress.*	½ *lb. peas.*
1 *sprig of mint.*	*Seasoning.*	½ *lettuce.*
1 *tablespoonful chopped onion.*	½ *oz. sugar.*	½ *oz. butter.*

Method

1. Prepare the beans, peas, watercress, lettuce, mint and onion.
2. Boil all together in a little water.
3. When the vegetables are soft, remove the mint, and put all the rest through a sieve.
4. Add seasoning, sugar and butter, stir all together, and reheat.

(Sufficient for 4 persons.)

SALSIFY AU GRATIN

Ingredients

1 *lb. salsify.*	2 *oz. butter.*	4 *oz. grated cheese.*
2 *oz. grated bread-crumbs.*	*Seasoning.*	

Method

1. Prepare the salsify and cut each piece in two.
2. Put it into cold water to which vinegar (1 tablespoonful to 1 pint) has been added to prevent discolouring, and let it soak for 20 minutes.
3. Remove and cook in boiling salted water till tender—about ½ hour.
4. Grease a fireproof dish and fill it with layers of salsify, grated cheese, seasoning and little pieces of butter. Proceed in this way until all the salsify is used.
5. Over the top, sprinkle finely grated bread-crumbs, grated cheese and a little butter.
6. Brown in the oven.

(Sufficient for 4 persons.)

SPINACH AU GRATIN

Ingredients

½ lb. spinach.   Bread raspings.   1 oz. butter.
1 pint Mornay Sauce (see page 124).   2 oz. grated cheese.

Method

1. Cut off the stock and wash the leaves of the spinach in several cold waters.
2. Blanch it for a few minutes in boiling water, then let cold water from the tap pass through it. Dry it.
3. Prepare the Mornay Sauce.
4. In a fireproof dish put a layer of spinach, then a layer of the sauce. Proceed in this way until all is used up.
5. Sprinkle the top with bread raspings, and over them the grated cheese and the butter (melted).
6. Cook till brown in a moderate oven. (Regulo 4.)

(Sufficient for 4 persons.)

STUFFED CUCUMBER

Ingredients

1 large cucumber.   2 tomatoes.   1 lettuce.   Seasoning.
¼ pint Mayonnaise (see page 228).   1 small tin of salmon.

Method

1. Peel the cucumber and cut it into 3-inch lengths.
2. Remove the pulp from the middle of each length.
3. Flake the salmon from which all skin and bone have been removed, and cream it with the removed cucumber, Mayonnaise and seasoning.
4. Stuff each piece of cucumber with the mixture.
5. Arrange the stuffed pieces on a bed of lettuce leaves and decorate with the sliced tomatoes.

(Sufficient for 4 persons.)

STUFFED POTATOES

Ingredients

4 large potatoes.   1 egg.   Salt.
1 oz. butter.   Paprika.   2 oz. grated cheese.

Method

1. Wash and dry the potatoes, and bake them in their jackets.
2. Cut each potato in half lengthwise.

3. Remove the pulp and mash it finely, add the butter, salt, paprika, grated cheese and a well-beaten egg, and mix thoroughly.

4. Fill the half-potato skins with this mixture.

5. Place on a greased baking sheet, sprinkle with melted butter and a little paprika, and bake in a moderate oven.

6. Before serving, brown under the grill.

(Sufficient for 4 persons.)

EGG DISHES

EGG AND MUSHROOM CROQUETTES

Ingredients

3 *hard-boiled eggs.*   *Seasoning.*   *Bread-crumbs.*
½ *pint Béchamel Sauce* (see page 118).   *Flour.*
¼ *lb. chopped mushrooms.*   *Fat for frying.*

Method

1. Shell the hard-boiled eggs and chop them finely.

2. Add the chopped mushrooms and seasoning.

3. Mix with a little of the Béchamel Sauce and shape into croquettes.

4. Roll each croquette in flour and then in bread-crumbs.

5. Fry in hot fat.

6. Serve with Béchamel Sauce.

(Sufficient for 4 persons.)

EGGS À LA PAPRIKA

Ingredients

4 *slices of buttered toast.*   ½ *pint White Sauce* (see page 127).
2 *oz. grated cheese.*   ½ *lemon.*   4 *eggs.*   *Paprika*

Method

1. Prepare four slices of buttered toast.

2. Make the White Sauce.

3. Boil the eggs, shell them and place one on each piece of toast.

4. Place a little of the White Sauce over each.

5. Sprinkle each with a little of the grated cheese, and over that sprinkle paprika.

6. Brown lightly under the grill.

7. Serve, garnished with slices of lemon.

(Sufficient for 4 persons.)

EGGS WITH GRATED CHEESE

Ingredients

½ lb. ham or bacon.

4 eggs.

Salt.

2 oz. grated cheese.

Method

1. Mince the ham or bacon and put it in the bottom of a pie-dish.

2. Break the eggs carefully and place them over the chopped ham.

3. Place the dish in a moderate oven for 2 minutes to make the whites of the eggs firm.

4. Remove the dish from the oven and sprinkle the eggs with salt.

5. Over the whole sprinkle the grated cheese.

(Sufficient for 4 persons.)

SWEETS

BREAD PUDDING

Ingredients

½ pint milk.

3 slices of bread.

Powdered cinnamon.

I egg.

½ oz. sugar.

I oz. butter.

A pinch of salt.

Flavouring.

Method

1. To the milk add ½ oz. sugar, salt and flavouring (orange, lemon or vanilla) to taste.

2. Cut the bread into fairly thick strips.

3. Let these soak in the milk mixture for a few minutes and then remove and drain.

4. Beat up the egg and pour into a pie-dish.

5. Put the bread strips into the egg mixture and let them soak for a few minutes.

6. Remove the slices and fry in the butter over a very low heat till golden brown.

7. Serve, sprinkled with cinnamon and fine sugar.

(Sufficient for 4 persons.)

CHOCOLATE APPLES

Ingredients

4 large cooking apples.

¼ lb. tablet of chocolate.

½ oz. powdered cinnamon.

I teaspoonful chocolate powder.

1½ oz. sugar.

2 egg-whites.

¾ pint water.

Method

1. Peel and core the cooking apples.

2. Cook them in a syrup made by adding the sugar to ¼ pint of water in an open pan and heating them until the syrup boils.

3. While they are cooking, prepare the chocolate filling. Break the tablet of chocolate into a pan containing ¼ pint of cold water and place the pan in a warm place until the chocolate melts.

4. Add ½ oz. powdered cinnamon and another ¼ pint of water.

5. Reduce this mixture over the fire, stirring all the time, until it is thick enough and then fill the cooked apples with it.

6. Beat the egg-whites with the sugar and 1 teaspoonful of Meunier's or other chocolate powder until they are stiff. Put this over the apples and brown in the oven.

(Sufficient for 4 persons.)

GROUND RICE AND APPLES

Ingredients

1 *pint milk.*   1½ oz. *brown sugar.*   1 *lb. apples.*
Nutmeg or cinnamon.   2½ oz. *ground rice.*

Method

1. Prepare and stew the apples and put them in a pie dish.
2. Place the brown sugar into ¾ pint of the milk, and warm.
3. Stir the ground rice into the ¼ pint of milk and add to the warm milk.
4. Boil all for 5 minutes, stirring all the time.
5. Pour the milk mixture over the apples.
6. Sprinkle cinnamon or grate nutmeg over the top.
7. Bake in the oven. (Regulo 1.)

(Sufficient for 4 persons.)

NEW YORK APPLE PIE

Ingredients

¾ *lb. apples.*   2 oz. *brown sugar.*
½ *lb. Short Pastry (see page* 139)   ½ oz. *butter.*

Method

1. Peel the apples, remove the cores and cut into quarters.
2. Prepare the pastry, roll it out thinly, and line a shallow, greased tin with it.
3. Arrange the apple pieces on the pastry in circles, beginning with the outside round first and working inwards.
4. Sprinkle the brown sugar over the apples and add the butter cut in tiny pieces.
5. Cover with a thin layer of pastry.
6. Bake in a fairly quick oven (Regulo 7) for half-an-hour.

(Sufficient for 4 persons.)

INDEX

PART I

PART II: RECIPES

GIVE INSTRUCTION
TO A WISE MAN...